THE COUNSEL OF ROGUES?

*In loving memory of
Lynette Grace Duxfield
1957–2004*

and

*with love to our wonderful daughters
Kelly and Max*

The Counsel of Rogues?
A Defence of the Standard Conception of the Lawyer's Role

TIM DARE
University of Auckland, New Zealand

ASHGATE

© Tim Dare 2009

All rights reserved. No part of this publication may be reproduced, stored in a retrieval system or transmitted in any form or by any means, electronic, mechanical, photocopying, recording or otherwise without the prior permission of the publisher.

Tim Dare has asserted his right under the Copyright, Designs and Patents Act, 1988, to be identified as the author of this work.

Published by
Ashgate Publishing Limited
Wey Court East
Union Road
Farnham
Surrey, GU9 7PT
England

Ashgate Publishing Company
Suite 420
101 Cherry Street
Burlington
VT 05401-4405
USA

www.ashgate.com

British Library Cataloguing in Publication Data
Dare, Tim
  The counsel of rogues? : a defence of the standard conception of the lawyer's role
  1. Practice of law 2. Legal ethics 3. Lawyers - Public opinion
  I. Title
  340.1'12

Library of Congress Cataloging-in-Publication Data
Dare, Tim, LLB.
  The counsel of rogues? : a defence of the standard conception of the lawyer's role / by Tim Dare.
      p. cm.
  Includes bibliographical references and index.
  ISBN 978-0-7546-4900-7
  1. Attorney and client. I. Title.
  K126.D37 2009
  347'.0504--dc22
                                                                2009000933

ISBN: 978-0-7546-4900-7 (hardback)
ISBN: 978-0-7546-9586-8 (e-book)

Printed and bound in Great Britain by
MPG Books Ltd, Bodmin, Cornwall.

Contents

Preface		ix
1	**The Standard Conception of the Lawyer's Role**	1
	What is it about lawyers?	1
	The standard conception of the lawyer's role	5
	The principle of partisanship	5
	The principle of neutrality	8
	The principle of non-accountability	10
	Summary of the standard conception	11
	Role-differentiated obligation	12
2	**The Critique of the Standard Conception**	15
	Introduction	15
	Criticism of the standard conception	15
	Morality and the standard conception	15
	Roles and responsibility	19
	Moral insensitivity	20
	Law's crisis of morale	24
3	**The Idea of Role-Obligation**	29
	Introduction	29
	What are roles and role-obligations?	30
	A prima facie case for role-obligations	31
	How roles generate obligations	33
	The direct route: role-obligations as obligations of ordinary morality	33
	A less direct route: role obligations as dependent rules	40
	A clean break: role-obligations as distinct from obligations of ordinary morality (the indirect route)	44
	Conclusion	57
4	**The Standard Conception and the Role of Law**	59
	Introduction	59
	The standard conception and the role of law	60
	Law and reasonable pluralism	60
	Legal ethics and legal positivism	63
	The role of law and the lawyer's role	74

	The principle of neutrality	74
	The principle of non-accountability	75
	The principle of partisanship	75
	A fictional application: The artists and the nasty landlord	86
5	**The Standard Conception and the Client-Professional Relationship**	**89**
	Introduction	89
	The relationship between clients and professionals	89
	The imbalance of expertise and power	89
	The importance of the matters about which clients consult professionals	90
	The opacity of professional diligence and expertise	91
	The limited nature of the relationship between clients and professionals	92
	Ethics and the client-professional relationship	93
	Significance for particular obligations	93
	Significance for the standard conception	94
	Charles Fried: The lawyer as the client's 'special purpose friend'	96
6	**Virtue Ethics, Legal Ethics and Harper Lee's *To Kill a Mockingbird***	**101**
	Introduction	101
	Character-based ethics and the nature of moral reasoning	103
	To Kill a Mockingbird: *an overview*	106
	Mockingbird *and legal ethics*	108
	Mockingbird's three great moments for legal ethics	108
	Mockingbird *and the return to virtue*	110
	An alternative reading of the three moments: Atticus as a tragic figure	113
	Challenges to Atticus as Phronemos: Boo's case	114
	Challenges to character-based approaches to legal ethics	117
	The role of law	117
	Anthony Kronman: The Lost Lawyer	118
	The client-professional relationship	119
	Virtue ethics and rules	120
7	**Detachment, Distance and Integrity**	**123**
	Introduction	123
	Integrity as autonomy	125
	Integrity as integration	132
	Integrity as identity	142
	Conclusion	145

8	**Conclusion: A Response to the Critique**	**147**
	The critique revisited	148
	Morality and the standard conception	148
	Roles and responsibility	150
	Moral insensitivity	153
	Law's crisis of morale	156
	Concluding remarks	158

Bibliography   *161*
Index   *167*

Preface

Too many people have contributed to this project over too long a period for me to be confident that I will here make all of the appropriate expressions of gratitude. Rick Bigwood, Stephen Davies, Rosalind Hursthouse and Christine Swanton, colleagues in law or philosophy at the University of Auckland, have all read all or a good deal of the manuscript at one time or another, and offered full and encouraging comments, even while disagreeing to greater and lesser degrees with my conclusions. From farther afield, Brad Wendel of Cornell University Law School, and Greg Cooper of Washington and Lee University have offered invaluable advice and collegial support and become good friends in the process. I have read various parts of the manuscript to conferences and departments in New Zealand, Australia and England and been challenged and encouraged, often by the same people at the same time.

Much of this material has been tried out on students in the University of Auckland Law School Legal Ethics course. One of the central ideas of this manuscript is that good lawyers must engage in sincere and critical reflection upon the justification and demands of their professional role, and those students have modeled this activity admirably. I hope they continue to do so in practice.

Sarah Anderson and James Edwards have been a tremendous help chasing up references in the final stages of the project and for the most part overcoming the considerable challenge posed by my haphazard record keeping.

My partner, Justine Kingsbury of the University of Waikato Philosophy Department, has given insightful comments on matters of substance. More importantly, Justine has provided wonderful support and encouragement. This expression of gratitude for her contribution to the completion of this book is but a tiny gesture toward acknowledging my debt to her.

I thank all of those who have contributed as I have worked my way through this project over the years. As ever, responsibility for remaining infelicities or down-right errors rest with the author.

I have dedicated this book to the memory of my wife and friend Lynette Duxfield, who died of breast cancer on October 9, 2004. I cannot overstate the importance of her love and support, not just to this project in its early stages, but in my life more generally. Caring for her during her illness – sharing her courage, resilience, humour and strength – was a life-changing experience. I also offer the book to our wonderful daughters, Kelly and Max, whose love I treasure.

Chapter 1
The Standard Conception of the Lawyer's Role

What is it about lawyers?

There is a widespread and ancient perception that lawyers are grasping, callous, self-serving, devious and indifferent to justice, truth and the public good. Ironically, the profession most obviously charged with the protection and defence of 'justice' is commonly regarded as being inimical to that very virtue. The perception is recorded in literature, in philosophy and in popular culture. One cannot pursue an inquiry into legal ethics far before being directed to the suggestion by Shakespeare's revolutionary that 'killing all the lawyers' would be an appropriate starting point for social reform. Even the philosopher Immanuel Kant, famed for his lugubriousness, was moved to quip that lawyers were apt to use the sword of justice not merely to protect the scales of right, but also to promote their client's interests more directly: 'Since if the scale does not sink the way he wishes, he … throws his sword in it …'[1] As for popular culture, the apparently universal genre of 'lawyer jokes' relies upon an equally universal association of lawyers with the vices listed above, coupled with an ironic appreciation of the tension between this association and the 'official' portrayal of law as an especially honourable and noble calling:

> Standing before a headstone inscribed 'Here lies a Lawyer and an Honest Man', a man turns to his companion and says, 'Look, they've buried them two to a plot.'

The graveside story works as a joke only because there is an almost universally accepted bit of folklore that one cannot be *both* a lawyer and an honest person.[2]

---

1 Immanuel Kant, *Project for a Perpetual Peace: A Philosophical Essay* (London, 1796) p. 44.

2 There is a considerable and engaging literature on jokes and humour. A common feature is the idea that jokes rely upon the audience's possession of shared knowledge or assumptions that allow them to recognise punchlines as surprising but also plausible conclusions to the joke narrative. Though the audience need not endorse these assumptions (for example, that lawyers are dishonest), they must at least see why one might end the joke that way, and why it is a departure from the dull and more obvious conclusion. See Ted Cohen, 'Jokes', *Encyclopedia of Aesthetics* (ed.) Michael Kelly (Oxford, 1998), vol.

The common perception that 'legal ethics' is an oxymoron is no doubt attributable in part to straightforward instances of misappropriation and dishonesty. Many people associate lawyers with the vices of dishonesty and deviousness because of well-publicised cases in which lawyers have made off with the contents of their trust accounts. But such cases do not really seem to explain, let alone justify, the particular content of the common feeling about lawyers. Accountants are not immune from the temptation of a well-stocked trust account. Jokes about them focus not upon their profession's intimate association with dishonesty, however, but upon the alleged dullness of the calling and its practitioners. This is the shared assumption which allows us to recognise the punchlines to 'accountant jokes' as surprising but plausible conclusions.[3] The difference between the lawyer jokes and accountant jokes is informative. Jokes about accountants do not trade upon dishonesty, even though there are plenty of spectacular cases of misappropriation by accountants, because there is no perception that the accountant's role is 'of its very nature' dishonest. The 'dishonest' punchline is not a sufficiently plausible conclusion to the narrative of the joke, because dishonest accountants are taken to act outside their professional roles. The difficulty for lawyers is that there is a widespread perception that even when lawyers are acting squarely within their roles – even when they act as good lawyers – they display the vices of dishonesty and deviousness. The widespread suspicion of lawyers' ethics – and hence the punchlines to lawyer-jokes – flows less from rare cases of misappropriation than from common perceptions of the day-to-day business of law.

At the heart of the difficulty is a conception of the lawyer's role – often called the standard conception – according to which lawyers owe special duties to their clients which render permissible, or even mandatory, acts that would otherwise count as morally impermissible. *Zabella* v *Pakel*[4] has become a classic illustration. The case raises the issue of a lawyer's use of legally available defences to allow a client to avoid a moral obligation. Joseph Zabella worked for John Pakel. Zabella was better off than his employer and from time to time loaned him money. Eventually Pakel owed Zabella $5,000. The two drafted and signed a simple contract, but Pakel declared bankruptcy before the debt was repaid. Some time later Zabella sued, claiming that, subsequent to the bankruptcy, Pakel had made a new promise to repay the debt. The new promise would have blocked the bankruptcy defence, but because it was not in writing Pakel was able to plead a statute of limitations to prevent legal enforcement. The defence was successful, though the court was quite explicit that the statute did not extinguish Pakel's moral obligation to repay Zabella. The immorality of Pakel's reliance upon the statute was made all the more striking since by the time of the suit Pakel had become the

---

3, pp. 9–12, and Noël Carroll, 'On Jokes', *Midwest Studies in Philosophy*, vol. 16 (1991) pp. 280–301.

   3   Did you hear about the accountant who became a rock star? His idea of trashing his hotel room was to refuse to fill out the guest comment card.

   4   *Zabella* v *Pakel* 42 F2d 452 (7th Cir. 1957).

well-paid Chief Executive Officer of the Chicago Savings and Loan Association, and could have repaid the money without hardship. Though they felt obliged to allow the defence, the court made clear they thought Pakel was a scoundrel, who, being 'in a position of some affluence ... should feel obliged to pay an honest debt to his old friend, employee and countryman'.[5]

Surely the court is right about Pakel. Somebody who relies upon a technical rule of law to avoid paying an honest debt to an old friend who helped the debtor when the debtor was in need, when the old friend is now in need, and when payment would not significantly reduce the debtor's own welfare, acts immorally. What, though, of Pakel's lawyer? Normally one who knowingly helps another obtain an immoral end acts immorally. But the standard conception gives lawyers a different and straightforward answer. According to the standard conception, not only did Pakel's lawyer do no wrong in helping Pakel secure his rights under the statute of limitations, he had a positive professional duty to do so. Being a good lawyer required conduct which would have been condemned as morally improper had it been performed by a layperson. It is the conception of the lawyer's role which has this result that prompted Macaulay to ask how 'it be right that a man should, with a wig on his head and a band around his neck, do for a guinea what, without these appendages, he would think it wicked and infamous to do for an empire?'[6] and it is this conception that creates in the minds of many an enduring and intimate connection between the practice of law and the vices of deviousness and dishonesty.

This analysis may seem to have an obvious implication. If it is this conception of the lawyer's role that explains the common association of lawyers with the vices of dishonesty and deviousness shouldn't we abandon the conception? Indeed we will see that the difficulty may be rather more onerous than has so far been suggested. The standard conception has been subject to a diverse and sustained critique. According to this critique, set out in more detail in Chapter 2, lawyers acting under the standard conception are alienated from ordinary morality; are invited to deny responsibility for the things they do (and thus to deny their status as moral agents, capable of choosing to do otherwise); are rendered morally insensitive in ways which impair their ability both to live a satisfactory life outside of their professional roles and to perform their professional roles adequately; and are likely to find their work deeply unsatisfying because of the striking discord between the apparently obvious and public concern of law and lawyers with justice and morality, and the reality of practice under a conception which separates the moral obligations of the lawyer from those of the rest.

Again then, isn't the implication of all of this that we should abandon the standard conception? Certainly this is an implication drawn often enough to make

---

5   Ibid., p. 455.
6   Lord Macaulay, 'Lord Bacon' (1837), in Thomas Babington, Lord Macaulay, *Critical and Historical Essays Contributed to the Edinburgh Review,* 5th edn in 3 vols. (London, 1848) vol. 2, pp. 280–429, p. 318.

the 'standard conception' an ironic epithet. If numbers count, the standard view is now that the conception cannot be right. It has passed from orthodoxy to fair game, replaced by a new orthodoxy that it 'must be abandoned, to be replaced by a conception that better allows the lawyer to bring his full moral sensibilities to play in his professional role'.[7] But I do not believe that the standard conception should be abandoned. I shall argue that a slightly modified version of it is essentially the right way of conceiving of the ethical obligations of lawyers. Those concerned with the ethics of the profession – whether these assessors are themselves lawyers or not – should regard lawyers as subject to distinct obligations and permissions when acting in their professional capacities. And yet the long line of criticisms of the conception cannot be ignored. I hope to show why we should hold onto the standard conception, and how we can do so while acknowledging the most significant aspects of the critique.

The overall strategy is straightforward. I argue that lawyers have *moral* grounds for regarding themselves as having duties to their clients which may allow or require them to act in ways which would be immoral were they acting outside of their professional roles. The fact that lawyers act within professional roles, I claim, makes a moral difference. If the moral justifications of the lawyer's role can be defended and are sufficiently weighty many of the criticisms of the standard conception fall away. Most generally, if there are moral reasons for taking the standard conception seriously then we should not too readily accept the claim that the conception alienates lawyers from morality. This is to say that we should not overdraw the conception's break between 'personal' or 'ordinary' morality on the one hand and professional morality on the other. If the moral defence of the standard conception is successful an adequate personal or ordinary morality will entail a proper respect for the moral demands and permissions of professional roles. The moral argument also suggests a solution to the crisis of morale. It suggests that contemporary liberal communities rely to a considerable extent upon the practice of law as conceived by the standard conception. Law so practised allows people who are committed to a range of diverse but reasonable views about how we should live, to form stable and just communities. The lawyer's role so conceived is one in which lawyers should take a good deal of satisfaction. The crisis of morale that troubles so many commentators is attributable, I will suggest, to a failure to appreciate the moral justification for the role rather than to any general licensing of immoral professional conduct.

Indeed, once the moral arguments for the standard conception are made explicit, those arguments themselves suggest limits to the things lawyers may justifiably do within their professional roles. The moral implications of the standard conception are often mischaracterised. Commentators suggest that the conception requires lawyers to secure any advantage the law can be made to give. But I shall argue that the standard conception, understood in light of its proper

---

7 Gerald Postema, 'Moral Responsibility in Professional Ethics', *New York University Law Review,* vol. 55 (1980) pp. 63–89, p. 64.

moral justification, requires no such thing. It justifies a more limited and moderate sphere of professional conduct. Clearly more needs to be said on all of these issues and aspects of the critique remain unaddressed. This will do, however, to indicate the direction of the argument advanced in this book.

The standard conception of the lawyer's role

I begin by setting out the principles that comprise the standard conception of the lawyer's role. According to that conception, the relationship between the lawyer and the client is mediated by three principles.

The principle of partisanship

First, the *principle of partisanship* specifies that the lawyer's sole allegiance is to the client. Within, but all the way up to, the limits of the law, the lawyer is committed to the aggressive and single-minded pursuit of the client's objectives. Lord Brougham's defence of Queen Caroline is often regarded as the classic statement of the principle. Caroline and the Prince of Wales entered into an arranged marriage in 1795. The Prince's main motivation was not romance, but a pressing need for financial support from a parliament insisting he abandon a spendthrift bachelorhood. The couple met only shortly before the wedding, and seem to have instantly fallen into a deep, mutual and enduring loathing.[8] They separated almost immediately. Caroline did not retire into a demure solitude. Rather, she led a merry life in London[9] before returning to Europe in 1814, where she toured and eventually settled with an Italian cavalry officer who was plainly more than a mere travelling companion. When George came to the throne in 1820 Caroline was offered a gratuity to renounce the title of Queen. She refused. At George's insistence, a reluctant government introduced what was in effect a 'divorce bill' to the House of Lords. Lord Brougham defended Caroline against what were essentially charges of adultery. He had an ace up his sleeve. He knew that in 1785 George had secretly married Maria Fitzherbert, a Catholic widow. The marriage was almost certainly invalid – the Act of Succession prohibited heirs to

---

8   At their first meeting the Prince stood incognito among other gentlemen. At Caroline's appearance, he is reported to have turned to his friend James Harris saying, 'I am unwell, Harris. Get me a glass of brandy', before going off to complain to his mother, the Queen. 'Was that the prince of Wales?' Caroline asked as he left, adding, 'He's not half as beautiful as his picture and twice as fat.' (Joseph Nightingale, *Memoirs of the Public and Private Life of Queen Caroline* (1820–21), (ed.) C. Hibbert (London, 1978) pp. 15–16).

9   An inquiry into her conduct during this period, known as 'The Delicate Investigation', was informed bluntly by a footman, Samuel Roberts, that, 'The Princess is very fond of fucking.' Quoted by Christopher Hibbert in his introduction to Nightingale, *Memoirs*, p. 19.

the throne marrying Catholics – but Brougham believed that he could bring down the unpopular King by publicising George's marriage to Mrs Fitzherbert, and insisted that he was duty bound to use that power if he could advance his client's cause by doing so. An advocate, in the discharge of his duty, he said,

> knows but one person in all the world, and that person is his client. To save that client by all means and expedients, and at all hazards and costs to other persons, and among them, to himself, is his first and only duty; and in performing this duty he must not regard the alarm, the torments, the destruction which he may bring others. Separating the duty of a patriot from that of an advocate, he must go on reckless of consequences, though it should be his unhappy fate to involve his country in confusion.[10]

In the face of Brougham's defence the Bill sneaked through the House by a mere nine votes. Given the level of public and political opposition, the Government quietly dropped the Bill.[11]

The principle of partisanship, often referred to simply as the 'duty of zeal', appears in one form or another in the professional codes of the lawyers of many jurisdictions. The American Bar Association states that a 'lawyer should represent a client zealously within the bounds of the law'.[12] An earlier version, from a less succinct age, proclaimed that the 'lawyer owes entire devotion to the interests of the client, warm zeal in the maintenance and defence of his rights and the exertion of his utmost learning and ability…'.[13] The International Code of Ethics specifies that a 'lawyer shall without fear defend the interests of his client and without regard to any unpleasant consequences to himself or to any other person'.[14] The

---

10 Joseph Nightingale (ed.), *The Trial of Queen Caroline* (1820–1821), vol. 2, p. 8.

11 The place of Queen Caroline's trial in the legal ethics debate is marvelously ironic. Driven largely by political self-interest, Brougham was determined to avoid settlement, and to that end simply failed to tell Caroline of compromises that may have served her interests: 'Brougham had his game,' wrote the Prime Minister George Canning, 'he dreaded compromise. He thought he saw how it might be effected. He barred that course by offering his own mediation. He thus got the thing into his own hands; and having got it there, he let it languish till success was hopeless.' (Augustus Granville, *George Canning and his Times* (London, 1859) pp. 299–300). The strategy before the House of Lords is itself remarkable in the context of a discussion of 'partisanship' and representation. Instead of moving a normal Act of Parliament, which would have allowed Caroline to raise George's own notorious infidelities, the Government bought a 'Bill of Pains and Penalties', which allowed Caroline – or Brougham – to put a defence, but not to raise counter-charges against the King. All in all, then, a peculiar source for one of the great strands of a debate on legal ethics and the obligation to give priority to the interests of the client.

12 American Bar Association, *Code of Professional Responsibility*, 1969, Canon 7.

13 American Bar Association, *Canons of Professional Ethics*, 1908, Canon 15.

14 *International Code of Ethics,* adopted Oslo, July 1956, amended Mexico, 1964, Clause 6.6.

New Zealand Rules provide that lawyers shall, subject again to a duty to the court, 'fearlessly uphold the client's interests, without regard for personal interests or concerns'.[15]

The principle is standardly portrayed as flowing directly from the adversarial system, which is said to structure legal proceedings as contests – jousts even – between the parties. A lawyer acts as their client's champion. They are to do all they possibly can, within the rules of the game, to see that their client's interests prevail. Judges act as impartial umpires, seeing to it that the parties follow specified procedural rules and deciding which side makes the best case in light of the relevant substantive and procedural law. The very presence of such umpires may provoke especially zealous advocacy. In an umpired contest, it is the umpire's job to spot fouls, to interpret and apply rules, and to decide who has won. 'Players' may abrogate responsibility for ensuring compliance with the rules to the umpire, pursuing any advantage the umpire will allow. The game can continue with little self-restraint from the players, deviations being limited by the umpire. In an informal or non-umpired game, by contrast, if each side insists on doing whatever they can get away with, the game will stall: 'Teams and coaches must, therefore, exercise more restraint in the pick-up game than in the refereed contest.'[16]

We will examine the justification of the principle of partisanship in greater detail below. Before moving on, however, I wish to introduce two alternative ways of understanding the principle. The difference between the two turns upon the ends toward which the lawyer's zeal must be directed. According to one, the principle calls upon lawyers to exercise what I shall call 'mere-zeal'. Merely zealous lawyers are concerned solely with their clients' legal rights. They pursue those rights 'without fear...and without regard to any unpleasant consequences to [themselves] or to any other person'. According to an alternative understanding, the principle requires lawyers to exercise what we can call 'hyper-zeal'.[17] Hyper-zealous lawyers are concerned not merely to secure their clients' legal rights, but instead to pursue any advantage obtainable for the clients through the law. Indeed, they are not really attempting to defend legal rights at all: they are attempting to win. The difference between the merely- and the hyper-zealous lawyer turns upon the distinction between a person's legal rights, and 'all that the law can be made to give them'. David Luban writes:

---

15 New Zealand Law Society, *Rules of Professional Conduct for Barristers and Solicitors*, 7th edn (1990) commentary on rule 8.01.

16 Murray L. Schwartz, 'The Professionalism and Accountability of Lawyers', *California Law Review*, vol. 66 (1978) pp. 669–697, p. 678.

17 Since the difference between the two types of zeal is the *end* towards which zealous advocacy is directed – rights or mere advantages – rather than the degree of zeal with which that end is pursued, the mere-zeal/ hyper-zeal tags are not quite right. But I have already gone public with the mere-zeal/hyper-zeal option (Tim Dare, 'Mere-Zeal, Hyper-Zeal and the Ethical obligations of Lawyers', *Legal Ethics*, vol. 7 (2004) pp. 24–38), and rights-zeal/advantage-zeal doesn't have the same ring.

> My legal rights are everything I am in fact legally entitled to, not everything the law can be made to give. For obviously a good lawyer may be able to get me things to which I am not entitled. Every lawyer knows tricks of the trade that can be used to do opponents out of their legal deserts – using delaying tactics for example, to make it too costly for an opponent without much money to prosecute a lengthy suit even though the law is on her side, or filing a nuisance claim carefully calculated to be cheaper to settle than defend.[18]

Put in terms of the distinction between mere- and hyper-zeal, Luban takes the standard conception to call upon lawyers to secure the goals of mere-zeal (the defence of clients' rights) by adopting the tactics of hyper-zeal (by trying to get everything the law can be made to give): 'The no-holds-barred zealous advocate,' he writes, 'tries to get everything the law can give, and thereby does a better job of defending the client's legal rights than a less committed lawyer would do.'[19] He concludes, then, that the standard conception requires lawyers to act hyper-zealously and hence improperly. But I will argue that the distinction between mere- and hyper-zeal can be maintained, and that with the distinction in place, the demands of the standard conception are quite proper.[20]

The principle of neutrality

The second principle of the standard conception states that the lawyer must remain professionally neutral with respect to the moral merits of the client or the client's objectives. According to the *principle of neutrality*, the lawyer must not allow their own view of the moral status of the client's objectives or character to affect the diligence or zealousness with which they pursue the client's lawful objectives. The rationale for the second principle is clear enough. It guards against the possibility that someone might be denied rights allocated by a legal system because its lawyers find those rights or their allocation to that person morally objectionable. In the extreme case, if we assume that legal representation is at least sometimes necessary to secure legal rights, the lawyer or community of lawyers could render the person's claim to their lawful rights worthless by refusing to represent them at all, or by making a less than zealous effort on their behalf. Richard Wasserstrom makes the point in a classic article,

> If lawyers were to substitute their own private views of what ought to be legally permissible and impermissible for those of the legislature, this would

---

18   David Luban, *Lawyers and Justice* (Princeton, 1988) p. 75.
19   Ibid.
20   See Chapter 4.

constitute a surreptitious and dangerous shift from a democracy to an oligarchy of lawyers.[21]

Put this way, the principle seems designed to protect clients from the chicanery of lawyers. It is easy to imagine circumstances in which a lawyer troubled by legislation or judicial interpretation might quietly steer clients toward the lawyer's preferred outcome, but one need not imagine such cases to see a need for the principle of neutrality. The complexity of contemporary legal systems will do the job. Given that complexity, individuals will often require expert assistance to avail themselves of the rights and autonomy allowed them by law. Without such an adviser, the law would impose constraints on individuals that it was neither entitled nor intended to impose.[22] Even a legal system, and a body of legal professionals intent upon securing for their client's legal rights, would require a principle of neutrality, since such a system would not serve those goals unless clients could claim a neutral expert's assistance in realising the rights and autonomy granted to them by law. Here the principle recognises that the allocation of rights which is to guide the lawyer is that which is protected by law, not that which even a diligent and well-meaning lawyer may prefer.

The principle is often discussed as though there is an important difference between the situation in which lawyers are deciding whether or not to take on clients and the situation in which they are deciding upon the degree of zeal with which to pursue the interests of an existing client. No doubt the two situations raise different issues. It is likely to be more difficult for clients to change lawyers mid-stream than to select a different lawyer at the outset, and lawyers will owe contractual and fiduciary duties to existing clients that they do not owe to potential clients. But if the rationale sketched in the last paragraph is correct then it would seem to apply to both situations. If what makes it wrong for a lawyer to calibrate their pursuit of an existing client's interests according to their own moral view is that by doing so they may thwart a lawful allocation of rights, it appears to be equally objectionable to achieve that same end by declining to take a case at the outset.

Understood this way, the principle of neutrality finds expression in some jurisdictions in the 'cab-rank' rule, which requires a lawyer to take on any case within their area of competence as though they were the next cab or taxi at the rank – provided only that the lawyer has time to take the case, has sufficient experience and expertise, a reasonable fare (or fee) is agreed, and that the lawyer has no prior

---

21 Richard Wasserstrom, 'Lawyers as Professionals: Some Moral Issues', *Human Rights*, vol. 5 (1975) pp. 1–24, p. 6. Wasserstrom was concerned to question the scope of the standard conception.

22 Charles Fried, 'The Lawyer as Friend: The Moral Foundations of the Lawyer-Client Relation', *Yale Law Journal*, vol. 85 (1976) pp. 1060–1089, p. 1073.

inconsistent interest or engagement.[23] The classic illustration of the rule allows us a serendipitous economy of villains, albeit at the cost of remaining in the eighteenth century. In 1792 Thomas Paine was charged with treason following the publication of *The Rights of Man*, in which he supported the French Revolution and advocated the overthrow of the British Monarchy. Thomas Erskine was Attorney-General to the very Prince of Wales who would marry Caroline three years later. Erskine was sacked to popular acclaim when he took on Paine's defence. But, said Erskine:

> From the moment that any advocate can be permitted to say that he will or will not stand between the Crown and the subject arraigned in the court where he daily sits to practise, from that moment the liberties of England are at an end. If the advocate refuses to defend, from what he may think of the charge or the defence, he assumes the character of the judge; nay, he assumes it before the hour of judgement.[24]

The principle of non-accountability

The third and final principle of the standard conception is the *principle of non-accountability*. Of the three principles, this is the one that most clearly expresses the core idea of the standard conception: the idea that the 'role-obligations' of lawyers are distinct from those of ordinary morality. The principle of neutrality purports to exempt lawyers from the normal moral practice of judging someone to have acted immorally if they have knowingly and deliberately helped another to act immorally. According to the principle, a lawyer is not to be judged by the moral status of their client's projects, even though without the lawyer's assistance the client would not have been able to pursue those projects. Since the lawyer 'lends his exertions to all; himself to none',[25] we cannot identify the moral character of the lawyer by reference to the causes they have advocated.

So understood, the principle follows naturally from the first two principles, though it is importantly different from them. It follows from them in acknowledging that, given the standard conception, we cannot properly assume that lawyers identify or sympathise with their client's goals. The lawyer might have strong moral objections to a client's projects, but be forbidden from relying upon those objections by the principle of neutrality and obliged to assist the client zealously by the principle of partisanship. The principle of non-accountability differs from the first two principles, however, in focusing not upon how lawyers should conduct themselves in professional practice, but upon the grounds on which lawyers might legitimately be judged from a moral point of view.

---

23 Of course, even in jurisdictions in which the rule is in place, the exceptions allow lawyers who are not moved by the moral arguments for the rule to ignore it more or less at will. Still, it matters that they act against the point of the rule when they do so.
24 *R v Paine* (1792) 22 *State Trials* 357, 412.
25 *Ex Parte Lloyd*, 1822, note.

Thus the principle is primarily an invitation to those who would evaluate lawyers (including lawyers themselves), rather than a piece of professional advice. This is an invitation often declined. Without doubt, a good deal of the widespread public dissatisfaction with the ethical standards of the law profession flows precisely from the tendency of observers to do what the principle says they should not do – assume that lawyers endorse or sympathise with their client's causes. The vice was dramatically illustrated when the American Nazi Party proposed holding public meetings in Skokie, Illinois. When no private lawyers were prepared to represent the Nazi Party at hearings to consider the granting of an injunction to stop the meetings, the American Civil Liberties Union took on the Party's case. John Basten writes, 'The sad story of vituperation and abuse, tacitly supported by the silence of the Chicago Bar, illustrates the difficulty lawyers still face in representing unpopular causes. Efforts to protest that the ACLU attorneys concerned did not agree with what the Nazis wanted to say, nor even necessarily with their right to say it, were largely ignored.'[26]

Of course, the principle of non-accountability does have implications for professional practice. It reinforces the principle of neutrality by telling lawyers that they should regard themselves as free to act for clients whose moral views and legal goals do not accord with their own. I suggested that the cab-rank rule flowed from the principle of neutrality. The rule is significantly connected with the principle of non-accountability as well. When viewed in light of the principle of neutrality, a principle concerned to tell lawyers how to act, it appears as a positive duty to take on cases. When viewed in light of the principle of non-accountability, a principle concerned with the appropriate assessment of lawyers, the rule is a defence for those who do take on unpopular cases. They may plead the rule in response to the mistaken assumption that they would not have taken on the case if they did not endorse the goals of the client. Hence the cab-rank rule contributes to the effectiveness of the principle of non-accountability. Lord Reid wields the rule in this guise when he writes of the duty to act 'for any person however unpopular or even offensive he or his opinions may be' that, 'If counsel is bound to act for such a person, no reasonable man could think the less of any counsel because of his association with such a client, but if counsel could pick and choose, his reputation might suffer if he chose to act for such a client, and the client might have great difficult in obtaining proper legal assistance.'[27]

Summary of the standard conception

The standard conception of the lawyer's role, then, consists of these three principles: the principle of partisanship, the principle of neutrality and the principle of non-

---

26 John Basten, 'Control and the Lawyer-Client Relationship' *Journal of the Legal Profession*, vol. 6 (1981) pp. 7–38, p. 35.

27 *Rondel* v *Worsley* [1969] 1 AC 191, 227.

accountability. The effect of these three principles is supposed to be this: lawyers have a positive duty to promote the lawful interests of their clients zealously. A lawyer may not allow their own judgment of the moral status of the client, of the client's lawful ends or of the lawful means to those ends, to effect the discharge of this duty. If a lawyer knows of a legal means to attain a client's ends, they must use it though they think both the means and the ends are immoral. Furthermore a lawyer is not to be judged by the immorality of either the means or the ends. The standard conception, then, portrays lawyers as having a duty to further the interests of clients, even where the lawyer judges those interests to be wicked or immoral, and further, as being insulated from the moral censure that the pursuit of those interests might properly attract were it carried out by a non-lawyer.

So, for instance, Pakel's lawyer can escape blame for helping his client act immorally. Not only did he do no wrong in advising Pakel to plead the statute of limitations, and in representing him with all of his professional zeal in the conduct of the defence, he had a positive professional duty to do so: so says the principle of partisanship. It was not for the lawyer to judge the moral merits of his client's objectives: So says the principle of neutrality. And whatever the moral status of the client's goals and the means used to attain them, that status does not reflect upon the character of the lawyer: So says the principle of non-accountability.

Role-differentiated obligation

This conception of the lawyer's role relies upon a broader picture of the structure of ethical obligation, according to which such obligation may be 'role-differentiated'. Ethical obligations, the idea goes, attach primarily to social roles. There are numerous roles within communities, and individuals inevitably occupy more than one: I am a friend, a son, a parent, a university lecturer, a sometime lawyer. As I move from role to role, the role-differentiation thesis has it, the obligations and permissions to which I am subject alter, and, as *Zabella* v *Pakel* demonstrates, those which apply to me in one role may conflict with and take priority over those to which I am subject in another. The conduct of Pakel's lawyer seems to violate a plausible maxim of 'ordinary' or general morality, but, the claim goes, his conduct is not properly judged from that perspective alone. The fact that he was acting within his professional role provides him with a defence against those who question the ethical propriety of his conduct.

It has seemed to some that the idea of role-differentiation provides an adequate answer to Macaulay's question: how can it be right that a person wearing lawyer's garb should do for a guinea what they would think it wicked to do for a fortune if in civilian dress? Well, the two roles are quite literally subject to different moral standards. There are things one is permitted and perhaps even required to do as a lawyer which it is wicked to do as a civilian. Michel Montaigne appears to have had this confidence in the force of role-differentiation when he remarked that there is no reason for lawyers to deny 'the knavery' of their calling.[28] They could quite properly be indifferent to such knavery, Montaigne thought, provided they kept their personal and professional personalities distinct from each other. For his own part, he said, 'I have been able to concern myself with public affairs without moving the length of my fingernail from myself. The Mayor [of Bordeaux] and Montaigne have always been two people, clearly separated.'[29] Only a little more recently Charles Curtis has recommended that lawyers follow Montaigne's example. In speaking of the ethics of advocacy, he writes that, '[W]e are talking about the special moral code which governs a man who is acting for another. Lawyers in their practice...put off more and more of our common morals the farther they go in [the] profession.'[30]

Earlier, I gave a brief overview of the argument offered in this book. My aim is to defend a moderate version of the standard conception, one which allows us to acknowledge significant criticisms while holding on to the important core of the conception. I will argue that lawyers have moral grounds for regarding themselves as having duties to their clients which may allow or require them to act in ways which would be immoral were they acting outside of their professional roles. If this argument can be made out we will have an answer to many of the common criticisms of the standard conception. The moral argument allows a response to claims that the conception alienates lawyers from morality, suggests a solution to the alleged crisis of morale which rests to a large extent upon that alienation, and allows us to specify limits to legitimate advocacy.

We can recast this summary in the language of role-differentiated moral obligation, and understand this book as concerned to defend a role-differentiated conception of the lawyer's professional ethical obligations. I will argue, then, that there are moral reasons to treat those obligations as attaching to the lawyer's role largely independently of the personal moral views and character of role-occupants. To become a lawyer, I will claim, is to take on a role already richly bedecked with distinct obligations and permissions. Of course I must hope that my professional takes their role-differentiated obligations seriously. Convincing them to do so is perhaps the central task of an adequate legal ethic. An adequate defence of professional ethics should give lawyers (and other professionals) knowledge of the distinct, role-differentiated, permissions and obligations that attach to professional roles, and respect for the justifications of those permissions and obligations. If we can do this, remedying a current failure, we will not need to teach lawyers a new

---

28   Michel de Montaigne, 'Of Husbanding Your Will' (1580) in *The Complete Works of Montaigne: Essays, Travel Journal, Letters*, (ed.) Donald M. Frame (London, 1958) pp. 766–784, p. 774.

29   Ibid, 770.

30   Charles P. Curtis, 'The Ethics of Advocacy', *Stanford Law Review*, vol. 4 (1951) pp. 3–23, p. 16.

conception of their role, the old one will do, and will provide protection for clients, guidance for lawyers and reason to regard law as a respectable and important profession whose practitioners may take pride in their calling.

Chapter 2
The Critique of the Standard Conception

Introduction

The conception of the lawyer's role we have just sketched will serve as a stalking-horse for much of the discussion in this book. We began by noting a widespread dissatisfaction with the ethical standards of the legal profession. Expressions of that dissatisfaction often amount to calls for lawyers to abandon the standard conception and to reject the idea that their roles allow them to appeal to distinct, role-differentiated, ethical justifications and excuses. Though there are various strands to the critique, it will do for the moment to portray them as sharing an ambition to weaken the distinction that the conception seeks to draw between professional and general morality. It will be useful to sketch the principal strands of the critique at the outset. I do not attempt at this point to answer these objections. The issues are difficult and reflect widely different starting points and concerns. Instead, I set out to provide a fair survey of the critique of the standard conception to which we will return, armed with the approach to legal ethics defended in the next few chapters. The success of the approach might be to at least some degree measured by its capacity to provide a response – if not a refutation – to the various strands of the critique. Hence, the conclusion of the book, Chapter 8, is a review of the critique in light of the intervening discussion.

Criticism of the standard conception

Morality and the standard conception

Perhaps the most obvious objection is simply that the standard conception leads lawyers to act in ways that are immoral. The objection is manifest in the common tendency to describe the standard conception as providing an 'institutional excuse'.[1] The description is significant. Excuses are particular sorts of exculpatory considerations. If successful they show we should not hold someone responsible for a wrong that has occurred. Justifications, by contrast, show that no wrong has been done: if successful, they show that the conduct complained of was, in the circumstances, not wrong at all. Hence characterisations that portray the standard conception as providing lawyers with an excuse accept that lawyers are involved in wrongs – albeit ones for which they should (perhaps) be excused.

---

1 Luban, *Lawyers and Justice*, p. 56.

Consider responses to Daniel Kornstein's praise of Max Steuer's cross examination in the Triangle Shirtwaist Fire Case. One hundred and forty six sweatshop workers, most young immigrant women, died in the Triangle Shirtwaist Factory fire in New York City on 25 March 1911. Workers' advocates marked the 75th anniversary of the tragedy, celebrating the workplace safety reforms it prompted.[2] 'But,' wrote Daniel Kornstein, 'as important as those reforms are… they are not the only reason for lawyers to remember the Triangle Shirtwaist Fire…Lawyers should remember it because it was the subject of one of the all-time great cross-examinations in American courtroom history.'[3] Legislation required that factory doors 'shall not be locked, bolted or fastened during working hours'. The owners were charged with manslaughter in the face of the 'undisputed facts – locked doors forcing scores of women, clothes and hair ablaze, to leap from windows to their deaths'. The final prosecution witness was a young woman, Kate Alterman, who had escaped the fire. She was called to testify that one of the victims, burned beyond recognition, was indeed the Rose Schwartz named in the indictment. Her evidence was heartrending. She told how she had turned, just before leaping from a window, to see Rose Schwartz 'with both hands on the knob of the door desperately turning and pushing, but the door would not give'. She saw Rose rise and fall twice, enveloped by flames, as she wrestled with the door. As the flames approached Kate, she saw Rose on her knees, screaming and praying, turning the door handle back and forth, pulling and pushing the door, before falling to the floor, completely engulfed by flames. Kate Alterman's testimony had some of the jury in tears.

Max D. Steuer defended the owners. After 30 minutes of gentle preliminary cross-examination he asked Kate to tell him what she had seen. Kate did not merely 're-present' the account of Rose Schwartz's death she had given in response to prosecutor's question; she repeated it word for word. Steuer shifted focus for a while and then asked Kate to describe what she had seen again. Once more Kate repeated her story exactly – almost. Steuer noticed that she had missed a word. He asked her about the omission. She began repeating her story quietly, to herself, until she came to the missing word and then said, 'Yes, I made a mistake. I left that word out.' 'But otherwise your story was correct?' asked Steuer. Again Kate began to recite her story to herself and then replied, 'Yes, otherwise my answer is correct.' When Steuer asked the same question a third time, the prosecutor objected, but was

---

2 See for instance William Serrin, 'Labor marks 75th Anniversary of Triangle Shirtwaist Fire', *The New York Times* March 25, 1986; Laurie Goldstein, '1911 N.Y. Factory Fire bought wave of reform', *The Washington Post* Sept 5, 1991; and Elaine Woo, 'Last survivor of 1911 Sweatshop fire dies: Rose Freedman was a link to New York's Triangle Shirtwaist blaze, a turning point for U.S. labor' (Obituary), *Los Angeles Times* Feb 17, 2001.

3 Daniel J. Kornstein, 'A Tragic Fire – A Great Cross-Examination', *New York Law Journal*, 28 Mar. 1986, p. 2; reprinted in Stephen Gillers, *Regulation of Lawyers: Problems of Law and Ethics*, 6th edn (New York, 2002) pp. 466–469.

overruled. Again Kate repeated her account verbatim. After 20 minutes addressing other matters, Steuer asked for the fourth time, 'Will you please tell the jury what you saw and what you did after you first observed any sign of the flames?' Again Kate repeated her story, but this time omitted a different word. Steuer asked about this omission and again Kate repeated her story quietly to herself until she reached the omission and said she had missed the word. Steuer's cross-examination had completely destroyed Kate's credibility. The constant repetition of her story suggested to the jury they were witnessing a carefully prepared recital, rather than a reliable recollection of what had happened. Her carefully prepared story made the jury suspicious of the entire prosecution case. The owners were acquitted.

Daniel Kornstein accepts that the owners had locked the factory doors and that Rose Schwartz and 145 others died in the fire at least in part because of that breach of safety regulations. He accepts that the acquittal was the 'wrong result': justice was not done. A clever advocate – a good lawyer – had destroyed the credibility of a truth-telling witness. Yet Kornstein describes Steuer as a 'courtroom legend' and his cross-examination as brilliant. In the face of overwhelming evidence of his client's guilt, he writes, 'Steuer had to bring to bear all of his considerable skills.' Called to task for his assessment,[4] Kornstein conceded that he should have distinguished between 'outright perjury and overly rehearsed, overly memorized, but essentially true testimony', but still he insists,

> It may be that, in some cosmic sense, the wrong side prevailed in the Triangle Shirtwaist factory case; but it was not because Steuer did anything inappropriate. He did precisely what he should have done – and what any good lawyer should have done.[5]

Kornstein's praise of Steuer is an endorsement of the standard conception. Though Steuer helped to defeat justice 'in some cosmic sense' he did not act inappropriately. He is to be praised for being a good lawyer, not condemned for acting immorally, and yet, as the Rubens' response illustrates, if one does not

---

4   Ann Ruben and Emily Ruben, 'Letter to the Editor' *New York Law Journal*, April 14, 1986 p. 2, reprinted in Gillers, pp. 469–470. The Rubens write: 'Mr Kornstein exhibits all the narrow mindedness of the men (judge, jury, and lawyers) who exonerated those responsible for…this tragic fire. He fails even to consider the very obvious and likely possibility that the testimony was not perjured. To equate Kate Alterman's possibly rehearsed testimony with premeditated dishonesty represents an enormous leap of faith and completely ignores the socio-economic and historic context of that testimony. The women who testified … spoke little English. Approximately half of them spoke no English at all, and many of those who did were illiterate. They had barely survived a traumatic fire in which many of their friends and colleagues had burned to death. The notorious conditions under which they had worked … provided no basis for them to believe that their own words would sway the power structure the legal system represented.'

5   Daniel J. Kornstein, letter to Stephen Gillers, reprinted in Gillers, *Regulation of Lawyers*, p. 470.

accept the efficacy of the standard conception's institutional excuse, it is easy to think Steuer simply acted immorally. The Triangle Shirtwaist case, then, raises the same issues as *Pakel* v *Zabella*. Pakel's lawyer deliberately and knowingly helped his client act immorally. Qua lay-person he seems open to moral criticism. Qua lawyer, however, he was not only allowed but required to act as he did.

David Luban gives other, more general, examples in support of the objection that the standard conception calls upon lawyers to act immorally. He writes:

> The rules of discovery, initiated to enable one side to find out crucial facts from the other, are used nowadays to delay trial or to impose added expenses on the other side; conversely one might respond to an interrogatory by delivering to the discoverer tons of miscellaneous documents to run up their legal bills or to conceal a needle in a haystack. Similarly, rules involving conflicts of interest are now regularly used by adversaries to drive up the other side's costs by having their counsel disqualified.[6]

The objection claims that these tactics are used to determine cases by, for instance, making it too expensive for one side to continue. And of course it may well be in the interests of a client – especially one with a weak case – to do so. But now, if a client has a lawful right to extend proceedings, and it is in the client's interest to do so, the standard conception seems actually to require lawyers to help them to that end. But sometimes this will be plainly immoral, and surely lawyers should not be encouraged, let alone required, to prevent meritorious claims from being properly considered. If this *is* what it recommends so much the worse for the standard conception. According to the objection, furthermore, these examples are only aspects of a more general problem. The standard conception requires lawyers to do much that is morally questionable; indeed, it requires them to be morally questionable people. Andreas Esthete writes,

> Effective adversarial advocacy demands measures that are unacceptable from a moral point of view. A firm and settled disposition to truthfulness, fairness, goodwill, and the like would thwart the lawyer's capacity to do his tasks well. To excel as a lawyer, it would be beneficial to possess combative character traits such as cunning.[7]

More generally the conception is portrayed as claiming that 'standards of ordinary morality have no place in the evaluation of [the lawyer's] professional conduct.'[8]

---

6 Luban, *Lawyers and Justice*, p. 51.
7 Andreas Esthete, 'Does a Lawyer's Conscience Matter?' in David Luban (ed.), *The Good Lawyer: Lawyers' Roles and Lawyers' Ethics* (Totowa, NJ., 1983) pp. 270–285, p. 74.
8 Dean Cocking and Justin Oakley, 'Doing justice to the lawyer's role', *Proceedings of the Fourth Annual Conference of the Australasian Association for Professional and*

But, the objection insists, whether or not one acts morally is to be determined by a common moral standard. Lawyers acting in ways that would be judged immoral from the perspective of general morality are acting immorally *simpliciter*. They cannot properly avoid moral censure by appeal to a distinct institutional morality. According to David Luban, '[T]he lawyer's role carries no moral privileges and immunities. If a lawyer is permitted to puff, bluff, or threaten on certain occasions, this is not because of the [standard conception] but because in such circumstances, anyone would be permitted to do these things.'9 We will examine Luban's view in more detail below and will see that there are important nuances to be added. Nevertheless, the basic idea is as stated: no significant role-differentiated permissions or obligations attach to the lawyer's role. If Pakel's lawyer acted immorally by the lights of general morality, then he acted immorally and that assessment is not altered by the fact that he acted within a professional role.

Roles and responsibility

Gerald Postema's important article 'Moral responsibility in professional ethics' raises a number of concerns about role-differentiation.10 One of the principal strands of Postema's critique is derived from Sartre's existentialism. The essential feature of humans, according to Sartre, is their capacity to define themselves through choice and action. As Sartre puts it, 'existence precedes essence' – humans first exist and then make themselves the people they are by choosing what they will do, what they will value, how they will be. One of the worst things humans can do, on this account, is to deny this freedom – to pretend that they cannot act other than as they do. A particularly tempting form of 'bad faith' is to identify with a role – to say that we act as we do because we occupy a role of some sort, as a lawyer or a waiter perhaps, and because the occupants of such roles must act as we act. Simply to identify with a role is to ignore the fact that as humans we can choose to act in another way. The demands of roles are determined by others, by those who design the roles or by less explicit social pressure. When we act as we do merely because we occupy a role, we deny our freedom, and hence our humanity, and pass responsibility to those others. The only way to recognise obligations while respecting our freedom, it seems, is to reassert those obligations constantly for ourselves. We cannot simply accept them as given to us by others, by our positions or by our roles. In Postema's words,

> [Role] identification is a strategy for evading one's freedom and, consequently, one's responsibility for who one is and what one does. By taking shelter in the

---

Applied Ethics (Melbourne, 1998) pp. 77–86, p. 84.

9 Luban, *Lawyers and Justice*, p. 154–155.

10 Gerald Postema, 'Moral Responsibility in Professional Ethics', *New York University Law Review*, vol. 55 (1980) pp. 63–89.

role, the individual places the responsibility for all his acts at the door of the institutional author of the role.[11]

Moral insensitivity

It is objected that role-differentiation and the standard conception undermine the moral sensitivity of lawyers. The objection suggests that the conception requires lawyers to develop a certain degree of moral callousness or indifference to the situations they confront, or that it undermines their ability to respond appropriately by simply prohibiting appeal to the sorts of moral resources and experience necessary to moral competence. These concerns are sometimes directed at the significance of this moral insensitivity for lawyers acting outside their professional roles and sometimes at its significance for lawyers acting within those roles.

Moral insensitivity: Significance outside the professional role   Even if we accept that lawyers should not be blamed for the wrongdoings of their clients, nevertheless the standard conception portrays them as playing a central role in projects in which wrongs are done. Occupying this role continually, even with the benefit of the institutional excuse, seems to require lawyers to develop a hardness – literally an insensitivity – to wrongs in which they are involved.

Concern for the moral sensitivity of lawyers might be motivated by concern for the communities they serve. For better or worse, lawyers fill many socially significant roles in our communities. Most obviously, the profession is disproportionately represented in public and political office, but lawyers also hold many significant posts in the commercial world. From such positions lawyers have considerable influence whether through the administration of significant corporations or through input into the development and implementation of social policy. It seems reasonable to hope that the occupants of such roles would be particularly sensitive to the claims and needs of those who rely upon them. It might seem especially undesirable, then, that the standard conception of their professional role should dispose lawyers toward moral insensitivity. Communities that rely upon the judgment of lawyers should be concerned about a demise in the moral sensitivity which informs and directs those judgements.

Other reasons to worry about the effect of the standard conception on the moral sensitivity of lawyers flow from concern for the wellbeing of lawyers as individuals. Notwithstanding Montaigne's insistence that his professional and lay personalities were 'two different people, clearly separated', it seems likely that the long hours immersed in professional roles and the degree of engagement with professional duties typically required of professionals will tend to shape the 'at-home' moral personalities of role-occupants. It may not be easy for lawyers to cast off the 'moral calluses' – developed to allow them to remain indifferent to wrongs

---

11   Ibid., p. 74.

in which they are involved at work – when they step outside their professional roles. Richard Wasserstrom makes the point when he writes that,

> To become and be a professional, such as a lawyer, is to incorporate within oneself ways of behaving and ways of thinking that shape the whole person. It is especially hard, if not impossible, because of the nature of the professions, for one's professional way of thinking not to dominate one's entire adult life.[12]

Kazuo Ishiguro's Booker Prize winning novel, *The Remains of the Day*, is a striking treatment of these issues. The lead character, Mr Stevens, is a butler who aspires to professional excellence, and to understand 'what it is that separates a "great" butler from a merely competent one'.[13] The great butler, he concludes, is marked by a 'dignity in keeping with his position', and Stevens continues, in a passage which resonates powerfully with the themes we have been discussing:

> [L]et me now posit this: 'dignity' has to do crucially with a butler's ability not to abandon the professional being he inhabits. Lesser butlers will abandon the professional being for the private one at the least provocation. For such persons, being a butler is like playing a pantomime role; a small push, a slight stumble, and the facade will drop off to reveal the actor underneath. The great butlers are great by virtue of their ability to inhabit their professional role and inhabit it to the utmost. They wear their professionalism as a decent gentleman will wear his suit: he will not let ruffians or circumstances tear it off him.[14]

Mr Stevens *never* allows the butler's facade to slip. Indeed, he takes the butler's virtue to excess. *The Remains of the Day* tells of his inability to step from the role under *any* circumstances and of the personal costs of this failure. On Stevens' interpretation, the butler's role precludes close personal relations: '[T]here is one situation and one situation only in which a butler who cares about his dignity may feel free to unburden himself of his role; that is to say, when he is entirely alone.'[15] Even when his father dies he cannot respond as a person, let alone a son. The butler's role comes first. He goes to his father's deathbed too late, and only after house guests have been seen to. Yet he regards his response with a 'sense of triumph', as suggesting that he might possess 'at least in some modest degree, a dignity worthy of the great butler'.[16] And though Miss Kenton, the housekeeper, hints at her love for him, Stevens cannot respond or recognise his own affection for her. He deals with her strictly as butler and senior servant, until it is too late for

---

12 Richard Wasserstrom, 'Lawyers as Professionals: Some Moral Issues', *Human Rights*, vol. 5 (1975) pp. 1–24, p. 14.
13 Kazuo Ishiguro, *The Remains of the Day* (London, 1989) p. 42.
14 Ibid., pp. 42–43.
15 Ibid., p. 43.
16 Ibid., p. 110.

that as well. *The Remains of the Day* is the story of a man so steeped in his role that he cannot respond other than through the norms of the role – norms which on Stevens' reading demand crippling dignity and distance.

Moral insensitivity: Significance inside the professional role   The concerns about moral sensitivity raised so far focus upon the effects on lawyers acting outside their professional roles. Other forms of the concern focus upon the need for moral sensitivity within the lawyer's role. In these forms the objection asserts a striking irony. The standard conception gives priority to the professional obligation to promote the legal interests of clients. The principles of partisanship, neutrality and non-accountability, and the model of role-differentiation are all intended to serve this priority. But, the suggestion is, effective promotion of the interests of clients requires precisely that lawyers have access to the full resources of ordinary morality and personal moral experience – just the things put aside under the standard conception. Hence the very structure the standard conception erects to give priority to the interests of clients reduces the ability of lawyers to promote those interests. There are a number of ways in which the moral insensitivity threatened by the conception seems to undercut the professional competence of lawyers.

Most straightforwardly, clients often want more than merely technical advice from their lawyers. When clients consult a lawyer about estate planning, for instance, finding out what they are required or allowed to do with their estates may only be a small part of their goal. Their main concern may be to obtain advice on which of various possible courses of action is *fair*. They may want advice, for instance, as to whether it is fair to take the relative wealth of surviving children into account in allocating shares of the estate, or as to whether it is fair to exclude one child, or to give different shares to male and female children. Such questions of fairness may tax a client even after they have been fully apprised of the requirements of family protection legislation and the like. In these sorts of cases, clients seek what is essentially moral advice. If it is true that lawyers are rendered morally insensitive by the standard conception, or that the quality of their moral judgement is reduced because they cannot legitimately appeal to the full resources of ordinary morality and their personal moral experience, then the standard conception and role-differentiation seem actually to reduce the ability of lawyers to promote the interests of their clients. Such clients are not well-served by lawyers whose moral sensitivity and moral competence is diminished, nor by lawyers who simply repeat the client's own moral judgments back to them. Adequate performance of these sorts of professional tasks seems to require moral sensitivity and access to general morality, apparently excluded by the standard conception and the idea of role differentiation.

We can follow a less direct strand of this criticism to the very centre of Western philosophy of law, and to the ancient question to be found there: Is there a necessary connection between law and morality? We will see as we go on that there are many connections between this question and the debate about legal ethics. The relevant connection for the moment concerns the role of morality in identifying and interpreting law. According to broadly natural law approaches, identifying legal obligations necessarily involves working out whether putative laws are consistent with morality. In the words of Augustine, made famous by Aquinas: '*lex injusta non est lex*': an unjust law is not a law at all.[17] If we accept that consistency with morality is a necessary condition for status as law, and hence for the generation of legal obligation, it seems that lawyers – those who identify law professionally – must have recourse to morality in order to perform their roles. This characterisation of natural law is terribly crude. No natural lawyers, including Aquinas, have endorsed the *lex injusta* principle in its crudest form.[18] Nevertheless, many (perhaps most) contemporary philosophers of law accept *some* version of the claim that moral arguments have a central role in identifying law and its proper interpretations. Ronald Dworkin has argued that the law is not just a model of rules. It contains moral and political principles as well, and judges must appeal to those principles in identifying, interpreting and applying law.[19] Even the most influential contemporary positivist, HLA Hart, insists that there are universally recognised principles of conduct which comprise a minimum content of natural law, and which all legal systems must acknowledge.[20] More recently, 'inclusive legal positivists' have developed the idea that there is nothing in the positivist idea that law *need not* be subject to moral tests to prevent particular jurisdictions in fact making it so subject. The constitutions of many countries, they argue, do stipulate moral tests for status as law.[21]

These jurisprudential accounts of the nature of law and interpretation, and the relation between law and morality, have tended to focus upon the role of judges. But it is easy enough to see implications for lawyers. If judges must identify the best moral interpretation of law, or work out whether a claim or a statute is consistent with a moral conception of equality, for instance, then it seems that the lawyers who seek to convince judges to adopt particular views of these matters must themselves be able to construct moral arguments in favour of their submissions. And now the concern is that by denying lawyers access to the full resources of ordinary morality and their own moral experience, the standard conception and the idea of role morality undermine the capacity of lawyers to adequately fulfil their professional roles: 'The lawyer who must detach professional judgement

---

17   St Thomas Aquinas, 'Treatise on Law' (1265–1272) in *Basic Writings of St Thomas Aquinas*, edited and annotated by Anton C. Pegis (New York, 1944).

18   See John Finnis, *Natural Law and Natural Rights* (Oxford, 1979).

19   Though the presentation of Dworkin's views has changed over the years, these central themes have remained constant, and they are perhaps most clearly stated in his early and classic book, *Taking Rights Seriously* (Cambridge, Mass., 1978).

20   H.L.A. Hart, *The Concept of Law* (Oxford, 1961); 2nd edn, (eds) Penelope Bullock and Joseph Raz (Oxford, 1994), Chapter 9.

21   See for example W.J. Waluchow, *Inclusive Legal Positivism* (Oxford, 1994). Hart endorsed inclusive positivism in the posthumously published 'Postscript' in the 2nd edn of the *Concept of Law* at pp. 237, 247–48.

from his own moral judgement is deprived of the resources from which arguments regarding his client's legal rights and duties can be fashioned.'[22]

A related reason that has been advanced for thinking that the role-differentiated model reduces professional effectiveness maintains that systems of rules always require the support of the background moral principles. No matter how carefully we construct our systems of rules and principles, this is to say, cases inevitably arise in which we are unsure which rule applies, in which we want to make an exception to an applicable rule, or in which we think an apparently inapplicable rule should after all be applied in a particular case. In such cases, judgement or practical wisdom – what Aristotle called *phronesis* – is required if we are to obtain the benefit of general rules and principles, without paying the considerable costs threatened by their mindless application. The practically wise person must know, not merely what the rules are, but why they were chosen in the first place, what background values are at issue, what trade-offs are acceptable in light of those values, what the likely consequences of granting exceptions or extending rules in particular cases will be, and so on. These judgements require access to the full range of a person's experience and moral knowledge. Again, in limiting the resources to which lawyers may appeal, the standard conception undercuts their ability to make them adequately.[23]

I said at the outset that well-publicised cases of dishonesty – straightforward instances of misappropriation and embezzlement – did not adequately explain the widespread concern about the ethics of lawyers. I suggested that the interesting issues flowed from the standard conception and the related idea of role-differentiated obligation. It may be, however, that the discussion in this section provides a link to those more straightforward instances of dishonesty. One might speculate that the standard conception makes it more likely that lawyers will commit such acts of dishonesty, perhaps because their sense of responsibility to the clients whose funds they embezzle or interests they harm is weakened by the desensitising effects of the standard conception. If so, the tendency to condemn the ethics of the legal profession in response to such cases may not, after all, be so far off the mark. This sort of connection would suggest that such cases were indeed attributable, in part at least, to the ethical structure of the professional role.

Law's crisis of morale

A further cluster of criticisms blames the standard conception and role differentiation for a significant crisis of morale in the legal profession, a crisis, according to Anthony Kronman, which though '[d]isguised by the material well-being of lawyers ... strikes at the heart of their professional pride' and threatens

---

22 Postema, 'Moral Responsibility', p. 79.
23 See for instance Postema, 'Moral Responsibility', and Anthony Kronman, *The Lost Lawyer:Failing Ideals of the Legal Profession* (Cambridge, Mass., 1993).

the very soul of the profession.[24] The conception may contribute to such a crisis in a number of ways.

First, it may be demoralising simply because it calls upon lawyers to act in ways which, as individuals, they regard as immoral, distasteful or unsatisfying. Having chosen to become lawyers in part at least to fight for truth and justice, lawyers find themselves under positive professional obligations to zealously promote the venal interests of the likes of Pakel, whose projects they find personally objectionable. Given the standard conception, lawyers cannot be confident that they will typically leave their offices knowing that their hard day's work has advanced worthy and deserving causes, and yet many began their careers, if not their work day, hoping to do just that. 'No social role,' writes William Simon, in the opening words of his sustained critique of the standard conception, 'encourages such ambitious moral aspirations as the lawyer's, and no social role so consistently disappoints the aspirations it encourages.'[25]

Second, the role-differentiated model may be morally unsettling since it seems to require lawyers to divide themselves morally, to live by two sometimes inconsistent sets of moral constraints. The standard conception seems to threaten the lawyer's moral integrity in a most literal sense. No matter how committed they are to a particular moral view 'at home', they must be prepared to put aside their own moral beliefs when at work and zealously commit themselves to the attainment of goals which they find morally objectionable. Their choice of a profession threatens their ability to live a coherent moral life. The costs of this 'moral dualism' may be exacerbated by the lawyer's role as advocate. Many of us tolerate conduct that we regard as improper. Toleration may have its costs. Standing by as others act in ways we find offensive may be stressful and frustrating. How much worse is the position of the lawyer who must actually *assert* the interest of the client, and try to convince others that the cause of which they personally disapprove should prevail? Lawyers are not just passive witnesses to the wrongs of their clients. Not only must they tolerate projects of which they disapprove, but they must actually lend their professional efforts to those projects. Once again, in practice it is likely to be difficult to maintain Montaigne's confidence that professional and lay personalities are 'two different people, clearly separated'. Both the attempt to maintain this separation and its probable failure tax the morale of professionals.

Third, the standard conception may contribute to a crisis of morale indirectly, by lowering the public esteem in which lawyers are held. From the lay-person's perspective, the law allows many immoral schemes and projects, and the standard conception limits the right of lawyers to avoid them when allocating their professional expertise. Lawyers are implicated as they make their words, thoughts and zealous efforts available to any client who can pay their fee, whatever the merit of their claim. To the extent that the moral satisfaction to be had from one's

---

24 Kronman, *The Lost Lawyer*, pp. 1–2.
25 William H. Simon, *The Practice of Justice: A Theory of Lawyers' Ethics* (Cambridge, Mass., 1998) p. 1.

profession depends upon how that profession is regarded by one's fellow citizens, the standard conception undercuts a ground upon which lawyers might draw moral satisfaction from their occupation.

Anthony Kronman, with whom this section began, suggests another way in which the standard conception threatens the morale of lawyers. Kronman attributes the current crisis to the demise of a professional ideal that emphasised the lawyer's need for practical wisdom. Under this ideal, lawyers were not merely skilled technicians, able to advise clients on how to use the law to achieve preset goals. Rather, they exercised genuine wisdom and judgement in guiding clients and entire communities toward defining choices when there were no 'mechanically deducible' answers to be given. The performance of these sorts of tasks required lawyers to have certain kinds of laudable character traits associated with practical wisdom. 'In these traits,' he maintains, 'we may hope to find a foundation that to be a lawyer is to be a person of a particular kind, a person one may take pride in being, rather than an expert with no particular character at all.'[26]

William Simon offers a similar diagnosis.[27] As we have seen, he begins with the idea that no social role promises so much morally, and delivers so little, as that of the lawyer.[28] This conflict, between the aspirations the lawyer's role encourages and those it actually allows, gives rise to a profound alienation among lawyers, who are constantly confronted with the disparity between the justice-orientated ends of law and the demands of their roles.[29] On Simon's account, this alienation springs in large part from the 'categorical' norms which govern legal practice and leave no place for discretionary judgement on the part of practitioners, and which as a matter of substance or content, pay no regard to ideals of justice.

The standard conception seems to be inconsistent with these models of good legal practice in at least a couple of ways. First, when acting under the conception lawyers do seem to perform essentially instrumental and technical tasks: clients arrive at the lawyer's office, their goal already settled, wanting only technical expertise from the lawyer, rather than genuine judgment or wisdom about appropriate ends. Second, when acting under the standard conception, the lawyer's own character seems largely irrelevant, its role minimised by the separation of personal and professional selves under the idea of role-differentiation and by the transformation of the role into one of technical expert rather than one requiring individual judgement and engagement.

---

26 Anthony Kronman, 'Practical Wisdom and Professional Character' *Social Philosophy and Policy*, vol. 4 (1986) pp. 203–234, p. 208.

27 William Simon, *The Practice of Justice*. Though Simon takes pains to distinguish his view from Kronman, whose focus on the lawyer-statesman, he argues, suggests that Kronman 'finds the tasks of ordinary lawyering empty of moral and intellectual challenge' (Simon, p. 24).

28 Ibid., p. 1.

29 Ibid., p. 7.

Thus Kronman attempts to revise the essentially Aristotelian ideal of the lawyer-statesman, with its recognition of the importance of the character of professionals, hoping to show that to be a good lawyer one must possess certain desirable and more or less peculiarly legal character traits, and so to address the crisis of morale which he believes poses a serious threat to the profession. More generally, the Aristotelian ideal stands opposed to the standard conception that, according to critics, seeks to diminish the importance of the lawyer's character or personal moral views relative to the moral norms that come with the roles they occupy.

Chapter 3
The Idea of Role-Obligation

Introduction

The previous chapter attempted to gather and sketch the principal strands of the critique of the standard conception. If nothing else, the discussion will surely have shown that the 'standard' conception is hardly standard: it is widely thought to be mistaken. Critics have sought to establish a new approach – one which will weaken the distinction the standard conception seeks to draw between ordinary and professional morality. But I do not think the goal of this search is desirable. The standard conception is, I believe, basically the right way of conceiving of the ethical obligations of lawyers. We should regard lawyers as subject to distinct, role-differentiated, obligations when acting in their professional capacities. And yet the long line of criticisms set out in the previous chapter obviously cannot be ignored.

I hope to show why we should hold on to the standard conception, and how we can do so while acknowledging the most significant aspects of the critique. Doing so will involve a number of steps. I begin in this chapter with an explication and defence of the idea of role-obligation. Having given an account of roles and role-obligations, I will suggest that there are at least prima facie reasons to think that role-obligations do indeed exist. At best, however, the prima facie case suggests that there *are* role-differentiated obligations. It remains to be shown just how roles could establish such obligations. I examine three possible explanations or routes to this stronger conclusion: The 'direct route' attempts to derive role-obligations directly from ordinary morality; the 'less direct route' grounds roles in institutional rules which are derived from and answerable to ordinary morality; and the 'indirect route' suggests that, though institutional rules might be grounded in ordinary morality, obligations under those rules are distinct from ordinary morality. Only the indirect route appears to preserve distinct role-differentiated obligations. If we understand role-obligations in terms of either of the other two routes, they will be completely absorbed by ordinary morality. If we wish to preserve the possibility of distinct, role-differentiated obligations, we must understand them in terms of the indirect route. I present the indirect route, and defend it against an objection by Arthur Applbaum. In subsequent chapters I go on to suggest that there are independent reasons to think that we should indeed preserve role-obligations; that we can establish a better-than-prima facie case in their favour.

What are roles and role-obligations?

It may be useful to say briefly at the outset what I mean by 'role' and 'role-obligation'. To avoid begging questions, I begin with a broad view of what might count as a role. At one extreme, we can regard a role as 'a nameable position within a social network; those who hold the position are expected to act, and perhaps feel in certain ways. Deviations generate surprise, uneasiness, disappointment, or disapproval'.[1] At the other extreme, roles are 'constellations of institutionally specified rights and duties organised around an institutionally specified social function. ... [A] role obligation is a moral requirement, which attaches to an institutional role ... To say that a role obligation "attaches to an institutional role" is to say that it applies to an individual in her capacity as an occupant of that role'.[2]

Clearly, there are potentially important differences between these two views. Perhaps most obviously, the second suggests that roles are the product of something akin to deliberate institutional design, where the first portrays roles as generated by the simple fact that people have come to expect certain things of those who call themselves 'lawyers' or 'parents' or 'university lecturers', or what-have-you, and are disappointed when those expectations are not met. We should not make too much of the distinction. Probably few if any roles fall purely at one or the other extreme. Professional roles may be the product of deliberate institutional design, prompted by a view about the proper function of the role, but the announcement that one is a lawyer (or a teacher, or an accountant, or ...) also triggers expectations about how one should behave and feel, deviation from which generates surprise, uneasiness, disappointment and disapproval. And, despite the potentially important differences between the two extremes, they also share significant common ground. According to both views the moral obligations which attach to roles – whether understood explicitly and directly as clusters of rights and duties or less directly as 'grounds for expectation, disappointment and disapproval' – are there, ready and waiting, for any individual who takes on the role. The expectations arise because of the nature of the role rather than because of anything about the role-occupant as an individual. The clusters of rights and duties define and adhere to the role which is then donned by an individual, like a suit of clothes already tailored and sewn.[3]

For our purposes, the similarities will matter more than the differences. Thus when we speak of roles, we will mean positions in social networks that bring with them specific sets of moral obligations that attach to those who come to occupy

---

1 Judith Andre, 'Role Morality as a Complex Instance of Ordinary Morality', *American Philosophical Quarterly*, vol. 28 (1991) pp. 73–79, p. 78.

2 Michael Hardimon, 'Role Obligations', *Journal of Philosophy*, vol. 91 (1994) pp. 333–363, pp. 334–335.

3 'The great butlers are great by virtue of their ability to inhabit their professional role and inhabit it to the utmost. They wear their professionalism as a decent gentleman will wear his suit.' Ishiguro, *The Remains of the Day*, pp. 42–43.

the positions. To say that a role-obligation 'attaches to a role-occupant' is to say that it applies to an individual in their capacity as, and by virtue of, their status as an occupant of that role. Given this, questions about the obligations which rest upon role-occupants – about, for instance, what they are and about what weight they should be given in moral deliberation – are settled by reference to the role, and in practice will depend upon the function and moral significance of the role itself: '[A] role obligation is a moral requirement ... whose content is fixed by the function of the role, and whose normative force flows from the role.'[4]

A prima facie case for role-obligations

Are there in fact obligations which attach specifically to roles and which may require or allow role-occupants to act in ways which are inconsistent with ordinary morality?

Given the discussion in the previous section, we might begin to answer this question by simply pointing out the extent to which our understanding and definitions of roles incorporate moral terms. Roles are standardly defined as 'clusters of rights and duties'; as placing 'normative demands' on role-occupants; as being 'complex instances of ordinary morality'. Departures from roles are portrayed as warranting 'disapproval'. These understandings of what roles *are* suggest that role-obligations may simply be part of the 'role-package', such that one cannot acknowledge the existence of distinct social roles without also acknowledging role-differentiated obligations. Roles just are clusters of rights, duties, powers and permissions.

Note as well the ubiquity of roles and, apparently at least, of role-differentiated obligations. Like everyone else, I occupy many different roles. I am a parent, a son, a brother, a friend, a university lecturer, a lawyer of sorts, chair of my local research ethics committee, and so on. Moving between these roles certainly seems to do *something* to the obligations and permissions to which I am subject. Contrast my obligations and permissions as parent with those to which I am subject as university lecturer. It is a moral commonplace that as a parent I am entitled to prefer the interests of my children over those of other children. I am entitled to allocate energy and goods to my children, even though the more pressing needs of other children would be met by a different allocation.[5] One of my children has also been a student in a large undergraduate ethics course I taught. I then occupied a different role in her regard, that of university lecturer. The obligations and permissions I had to her in that capacity were very different from those I

---

4   Hardimon, 'Role Obligations', p. 334.

5   For other commentators who appeal to the example of the family to illustrate the idea of role differentiation, see Wasserstrom, 'Lawyers as Professionals', p. 2; Hardimon, 'Role Obligations', p. 342; and Alan Goldman, *The Moral Foundations of Professional Ethics* (Totowa, NJ, 1980) p. 4.

had to her as parent. In particular, I would have acted wrongly had I preferred her interests in the allocation of my professional efforts. Just as the parental role allows and requires me to do things that I would not be permitted to do outside that role, so the role of university lecturer brings a set of role-specific obligations and permissions. One of the latter obligations is to allocate professional effort and assess academic performance without regard to considerations such as familial ties. The contrast between the obligations and permissions which attach to the role of parent on the one hand, and those which attach to the role of university lecturer on the other, seem to be at least prima facie evidence that role-differentiated obligations do indeed exist. Some commentators have drawn considerably bolder conclusions. Michael Hardimon, for instance, writes that, '[A]bandoning the idea that we have...role obligations would .. require a radical transformation in the way in which we live our lives, for relating to family members and citizens as family members and citizens, something that is central to our lives, essentially involves acting in accordance with a conception of ourselves as occupants of these roles.'[6]

Or imagine the following case, borrowed from Brad Wendel.[7] We overhear a conversation between strangers at a nearby table. After a preliminary exchange, the man begins a series of very direct questions about the woman's sex life: 'How many sexual partners have you had in the past three years?' 'How much did you know of their sexual history before you had sex with them?' The questioning is obviously making the woman uncomfortable, but the man carries on: 'Did you use protection?' 'Were the last three years typical of your sexual history?' What should we think of the man? To make a judgment, we need more information. If the table is in a restaurant, and the pair is on a first dinner date, he's probably a creep. Suppose, however, that the table is in the private interview room of the local family planning clinic, and the man is a gynecologist. Or that he is a researcher updating the *Hite Report*, having carefully explained the sorts of questions he will ask and obtained written consent to the interview. Or that the woman is the plaintiff in an action against the manufacturer of an inter-uterine contraceptive device alleged to have caused pelvic inflammatory disease, a disease that has a variety of causes, some associated with a history of multiple sexual partners. The man is the woman's lawyer, preparing her response to the manufacturer's defence. I said we needed more information to make a judgement about the man. One of the things we need more information about, these alternatives suggest, is what role he occupies. Conduct that would show him to be a creep qua date, shows him to be thorough qua researcher, or diligent qua gynecologist, or professional qua lawyer.[8]

---

6   Hardimon, 'Role Obligations', p. 346.

7   W. Bradley Wendel, 'Professional Roles and Moral Agency', A review of *Ethics for Adversaries: The Morality of Roles in Public and Professional Life* by Arthur Isak Applbaum, *Georgetown Law Journal* (2001) 89 pp. 667–718, p. 681.

8   Of course one needn't agree that such questions would be appropriate for these role-occupants either, but this doubt itself supposes that roles make a difference and that may be

The contrasts between the role of the parent and the role of the university lecturer, or the role of the creepy first date and the roles of the researcher, the gynecologist and the lawyer, suggest that moving between roles does *something* to our moral duties. But it does not yet tell us what it is that it does. One can imagine Macaulay complaining that the prima facie case is really only a re-description of the phenomenon that troubled him. Pointing out that we do seem to encounter role-differentiated obligations does not settle whether we should do so, or just how entering a professional role can transform the immoral into the moral, the prohibited into the required, the 'wicked and infamous' into the right. Thus we cannot just assert the existence of role-differentiated moral obligation. We also need to provide an account of how roles generate distinct obligations– an account of how occupying a role has the normative significance claimed for it by champions of the standard conception.

How roles generate obligations

The key issue raised by the idea of role-differentiated obligation, as that idea has featured in this discussion, concerns the relation between role-morality and ordinary morality. In the form targeted by the critique sketched in the previous chapter, role-morality is portrayed as proposing distinct, role-specific obligations and permissions. Ultimately I shall defend just such a picture of role-differentiated obligation. But it is not the only picture which has been advanced. Significant contributors to the legal ethics debate have attempted to derive role-obligations more directly from ordinary morality than this picture allows. In the next two sections I examine these more direct derivations of role-morality, and applications of them, before turning to the account which proposes distinct, role-specific obligations and permissions. I begin with the most direct route: the attempt to secure role-morality by direct appeal to ordinary morality.

The direct route: role-obligations as obligations of ordinary morality

The idea here is that role-morality is generated by applying ordinary morality to the circumstances that confront particular role-occupants. If roles generate obligations, the claim goes, it is only because 'one has reasons – reasons of ordinary morality – to act as one's role requires.'[9] The idea is an old one, even if its application to roles as we have used that term is more recent, and it receives its most eloquent statement from the early utilitarians. They proposed one fundamental principle of morality: we should act so as to achieve the greatest happiness for the greatest number. On the face of it, utilitarianism does not preserve the moral commonplace that allows parents to prefer the interests of their own children over the children of others.

---

all we need for the prima facie case.
   9   Andre, 'Role Morality', p. 75.

Bluntly, it seems unlikely that the uneven distribution of benefits and burdens allowed by that commonplace would normally create the greatest happiness for the greatest number. Classical utilitarians, such as John Stuart Mill and Henry Sidgwick, responded not by abandoning the commonplace, but by arguing that it was indeed supported by utilitarianism, since considerations such as proximity and the greater knowledge we have of those closest to us mean that efforts to benefit those people are more likely to be successful than efforts to benefit strangers or the collectivity as a whole, and hence are endorsed by the principle of utility.[10]

Notice what this argument is meant to achieve. If successful, it derives role-differentiated obligations directly from ordinary morality (where, in this illustration, ordinary morality is utilitarian). There are, on this account, no special role-differentiated principles that attach to the parent's role. It is simply that principles of ordinary utilitarian morality, correctly applied to the particular circumstances that mark familial relationships, recommend something which at least looks normatively equivalent to the role-differentiated commonplace.

The upshot is that different roles generate different obligations, according to this account, simply by putting their occupants in different circumstances. The obligations of the lawyer differ from those of the parent only because the same principles applied with sensitivity to the different problems encountered by the lawyer and the parent require different responses. In each case the relevant obligations and permissions are properly identified by working out what a common set of moral principles requires in the face of the facts confronted by the occupants of the two roles. The 'particular facts' will no doubt differ, and roles might create new reasons relevant to ethical deliberation, such as the particular expectations and reliance of clients or children, but there will be no point in someone pointing to their role as, in and of itself, a morally determinative factor.

On this account, role-occupants are entitled, indeed required, to appeal back to principles of ordinary morality in determining the obligations to which they are subject within their roles. The 'moral work' is done by principles of ordinary morality. Any 'differentiation' that arises, does so because the facts of the professional's circumstances are more or less peculiar to the particular professional context. The appeal will generate role-specific obligations, the claim goes, since (and only to the extent) that the role-occupant's position is unique. If lawyers are required and entitled to 'defend the interests of their clients...without regard to any unpleasant consequences to himself or to any other person', it is only because they are more likely to promote the greatest happiness for the greatest number by doing so.

We ended the previous section with the prima facie conclusion that there were indeed role-differentiated obligations. It seems unlikely that the direct route can secure that conclusion. There are at least two related difficulties. First, one might continue to doubt that direct appeal to utilitarianism at least really would preserve

---

10   John Stuart Mill, *Utilitarianism* (1863) (Indianapolis, 1979) p. 59; Henry Sidgwick, *The Methods of Ethics* (1874) (Indianapolis, 1962) pp. 241ff.

the moral commonplace that allows me to prefer the interests of my own children over the interests of strangers. It might be true that I am more familiar with my children's interests than I am with the interests of strangers, but often that familiarity will be irrelevant, or make too little difference to carry the day. I do not need any special knowledge to know that the satisfaction of many of my children's fairly typical middle class preferences would do less to promote the greatest happiness of the greatest number than satisfying the more fundamental and unmet interests of strangers. Contrary to the intuition that drives the prima facie case, then, it might turn out according to the moral arithmetic I should *not* normally prefer the interests of my own to children to those of others. Second, one might think that the intuition behind the prima facie case could not be satisfied, by utilitarianism at least, since part of the intuition is precisely that we are not required to make the sort of cost–benefit analysis utilitarianism requires. So no matter how the moral arithmetic turned out, it would not be true that direct appeal to the principles of ordinary (utilitarian) morality recommended something normatively equivalent to the role-differentiated commonplace. The utilitarian version of the parental permission is not the *same* as the role-differentiated commonplace, since it is part of the role-differentiated commonplace that parental entitlement is not dependent upon the outcome of calculations of utility. '[I]t is just my point,' writes Charles Fried, 'that *this* is an inquiry we are not required, indeed sometimes not even authorised, to make. When we decide to care for our children ... we do not do so as a result of a cost-benefit inquiry.'[11]

And all of this seems likely to hold, *mutatis mutandis*, of the role-differentiated obligations and permissions of the lawyer-client relationship. Often, the moral arithmetic would not allow lawyers to prefer the interests of their clients over the interests of others, and, no matter whether it did or not, the idea that lawyers were entitled to make the calculation – to determine case by case by direct appeal to ordinary moral theory whether they were entitled to maintain confidentiality or to 'defend the interests of their clients ... without regard to any unpleasant consequences to himself or to any other person' – would already be to give up the prima facie conclusion.

Of course, we may simply think 'so much the worse for the prima facie case' or 'so much the worse for this rather crude version of utilitarianism'.[12] For the moment however, I want to leave aside the possibility that we should abandon the role-differentiated model altogether or that a different 'ordinary moral theory' might fare better. As signalled earlier, we will look at arguments in favour of the

---

11 Charles Fried, 'The Lawyer as Friend: The Moral Foundations of the Lawyer-Client Relation', *Yale Law Journal*, vol. 85 (1976) pp. 1060–1089, p. 1067.

12 For defenders of consequentialism (the genus of which utilitarianism is a species) who have taken roughly these routes, see Tim Mulgan, *The Demands of Consequentialism* (Oxford, 2001) and Shelly Kagan, *The Limits of Morality* (Oxford, 1989). Kagan argues that although consequentialism 'strikes us as outrageously extreme in its demands ... it is nonetheless true' (Kagan, 1989, p. 2).

model and discuss alternative moral theories in subsequent chapters. For now I am concerned with the possibility of role-differentiated obligation and with just how such obligations might arise. My conclusion thus far is that it will not be supported by the direct route, at least as we have so far understood that route. None of this is surprising. We characterised roles as positions which 'bring with them' specific sets of moral obligations which attach to those who come to occupy the positions. Role-obligations, we said, are moral requirements whose content is fixed by the function of the role, whose normative force flows from the role, and that apply to an individual by virtue of their status as a role-occupant. The direct route does not preserve these aspects of role-obligation, since, according to it, no independent obligations attach to roles. The obligations which we encounter in roles are obligations of ordinary morality. They apply to the role-occupant not because of their capacity as a role-occupant, but because they are subject to ordinary moral obligation and find themselves in a particular set of circumstances. The normative force of the obligations flow not from the role, but directly from ordinary morality. As I said, this conclusion should not be surprising given the way we have understood roles. Nonetheless, it may be useful to reinforce it, at the same time taking the opportunity to consider an important contribution to the legal ethics literature, by seeing how the direct approach has been applied (and come to grief) in David Luban's influential book, *Lawyers and Justice*[13]

The direct route applied: David Luban's Lawyers and Justice   David Luban's important and sustained criticism of the standard conception provides both an application, and an illustration, of the danger of the direct approach. Luban's primary target is the principle of partisanship – the principle, recall, which commits the lawyer to the aggressive and single-minded pursuit of the client's objectives – though he directs his critique more broadly at the adversary system which spawns the principle. Luban argues that none of the normal justifications for the adversary system in fact succeeds: the system does not maximise the discovery of truth or the protection of rights; it is not an intrinsic good or a condition of human dignity; it is not essential to maintain the social fabric.[14] But Luban does not think the system is completely unjustified. While the normal list of stately and ambitious justifications fail, there is a more mundane alternative available. The system is justified because, even given its imperfections, it is not demonstrably worse than alternatives such as the civil law system, because we need some adjudicatory system, and because it is the way we have always done things.[15] The adversary system and the principle of partisanship it spawns, this is to say, are justified on merely pragmatic grounds

---

13   Luban, *Lawyers and Justice*. Luban's argument also provides some warrant for our focus on utilitarianism, since he relies on that 'ordinary moral theory'.
14   Luban, *Lawyers and Justice*, pp. 68–92.
15   Ibid., p. 92.

– we are not prepared to bear the costs of replacing them given that they do as good a job as any alternative of a job that needs doing.

From here, Luban argues that the strength of an institutional excuse is dependent upon the strength of the justification of the institution: 'The institution creating the role passes along its moral cachet to the requirements of the role ... [T]he weaker the justification of the institution, the slighter the moral significance of special institutional duties.'[16] And now we see the significance of Luban's argument that the adversary system can only be weakly justified. Since the adversarial system is only weakly – or pragmatically – justified, it passes only a weak justification to acts performed by the occupants of the roles within the system. Where an adversary system role – say that of the lawyer – calls upon the occupant to do something which conflicts with the demands of ordinary morality, the fact the lawyer acts in a role is not itself a very weighty consideration. Hence the institutional excuse provided by the weakly justified adversarial system cannot justify very dramatic departures from non-role morality, and will certainly not provide the wholesale justification of partisan conduct contemplated by the standard conception.[17]

Notice how this connects to the 'direct route' discussed in the previous section. Although Luban concludes that the standard conception gives too much weight to role-obligations, he does not wish to discard the idea of role-obligations altogether. Rather, he writes, 'we want to give considerations of role morality their proper weight without permitting them to simply override common morality.'[18] He does so by requiring role-occupants to 'balance the moral reasons incorporated in [a] role...against the moral reasons for breaking the role expressed in common morality.'[19] In doing so he is quite explicit that ordinary morality determines the moral obligations of role-occupants. '[T]he appeal to a role in moral justification,' he writes, 'is simply a shorthand method of appealing to the moral reasons incorporated in that role.'[20]

Translated from the 'shorthand method', the process of reasoning Luban suggests looks complicated. Lawyers are to balance ordinary and role-obligation by working through a four-step derivation.[21] The first step is to justify the institution to which the role belongs 'by demonstrating its moral goodness'; the second step shows that the role is required if the good of the institution is to be achieved; the

---

16   Ibid., p. 129.

17   One could question Luban's argument by examining the claim that his pragmatic justification is weak. If we really do need the job done by the adversary system to be done, and if no alternative is any better, then the 'collateral costs' of replacing the system may be crucial and legitimate considerations, but I will not pursue this criticism here.

18   Luban, *Lawyers and Justice*, p. 128.

19   Ibid., p. 125.

20   Ibid.

21   By way of a small philosophical bon mot Luban calls this four-step argument 'the four-fold root of sufficient reasoning' after Arthur Schopenhauer's completely unrelated *Fourfold Root of the Principle of Sufficient Reasoning*.

third step justifies the role-obligation by showing that it is essential to the role; and the fourth and final step justifies a particular action by showing that it is required by the role-obligation. The role-act will be justified, according to Luban, if the combined force of these justifications for the role-act, outweigh the moral reasons for acting according to ordinary morality. But this complex derivation should not disguise the fact that it is primarily a device for transmitting the justification of the institution – a justification to be carried out by direct appeal to ordinary morality – through the role and role-obligation to the particular act.

We can see the dangers of the approach in the two cases Luban offers by way of illustration. The first, a fictional and rather fantastic hypothetical, concerns a logistics officer for an aid organisation, the institution, whose sole function is to distribute food to famine stricken people in impoverished areas of the world. The logistics officer's role within the institution imposes the role-obligation of procuring the means of transporting food, which in turn requires the performance of various particular actions, or role-acts. Luban presents a scenario in which one of these role-acts requires maintaining silence about an impending murder. A local henchman, P, has control of the only available transport. The logistics officer overhears P planning to have a man murdered. P, discovering that the officer has heard the plan, tells her that no transport will be provided if the man is warned. Luban maintains that the four step argument shows that the officer is justified in keeping silent: the role-act of complying with P is required by her role-obligation to procure transport, which is in turn necessary to perform the role's institutional task of getting food to the starving, which is ultimately justified by the positive moral good of the institution: the saving of many innocent lives. 'Taken together,' writes Luban, 'these justifications for the role act outweigh the obligation to P's unfortunate victim.'[22]

Although Luban maintains that his model preserves a significant function for role morality, it seems in fact to render role-obligation otiose. For if it is true that the logistics officer is justified in keeping quiet about the impending murder, it is not *because* of the institution and the role-obligations it imposes. It is rather because she finds herself able to save many lives by failing to save one, and because the ordinary morality Luban makes relevant requires her to choose the many over the one, and because her role puts her in the position to make that choice. But now Luban's claim that his model preserves an important function for role-obligation seems to be false. The institution is not doing the justificatory job at all. It is merely a conduit for the sanction of ordinary morality. The institution and the role are eliminable.[23] As Luban himself says, 'If a lawyer is permitted to puff, bluff or threaten on certain occasions this is...because in such circumstances anyone would be permitted to do these things.'[24]

---

22 Ibid., p. 130.
23 See Daniel Wueste, 'Taking Role Moralities Seriously' *Southern Journal of Philosophy*, vol. 24 (1991) pp. 407–417 for a discussion of Luban in just these terms.
24 Luban, *Lawyers and Justice*, pp. 154–155.

Luban's second case is real, though scarcely less fantastic. Robert Garrow, was charged with the murder of teenage camper at the inaptly named Lake Pleasant. He told his lawyers, Frank Belge and Frank Armani, of two other murders he had committed. The lawyers verified Garrow's confession, following his instructions to locate and photograph the bodies, but kept their knowledge to themselves. They maintained confidentiality even when the father of one of the new victims asked whether they knew anything about his missing daughter. It seems clear enough what ordinary morality would require in these circumstances: surely, by the lights of ordinary morality, the lawyers should have told the distraught father what they knew.

In this case, however, Luban maintains that role-obligation carries the day.[25] Though the justification for the adversary system in general is much weaker than is supposed as standard, and so justifies few departures from ordinary morality, Garrow's case is among a small class of exceptions. When lawyers represent the poor, the oppressed, or otherwise vulnerable clients such as criminal defendants against powerful state-like institutions, the single-minded zeal of the lawyer helps to maintain the balance of an otherwise lopsided contest by 'over protecting' the rights of the weaker party.[26] And now, writes Luban:

> The lawyers' role acts (preserving the defendant's confidences, photographing the bodies but telling nobody) were required by the general duty of confidentiality – the role-obligation. This is justified by arguments that confidentiality is required in order to guarantee an adequate criminal defence – the institutional task.. The next step is to show that zealous criminal defence is required by the adversary system, and this in turn ...serves the positive moral good of over-protecting individual rights against the encroachments of the state.[27]

But Luban has since acknowledged that the Lake Pleasant Bodies case does not do the job he hoped.[28] It does not seem to be a case in which Luban's model would support role-obligation over ordinary morality after all. Still its failure is instructive. Luban's general idea is that we are to determine whether a role-obligation should be overridden in a particular case by asking whether the good

---

25 As it did in fact. Although a grand jury indicted Belge for health law violations pertaining to a speedy burial – he had found one of the bodies on his own – charges never proceeded. The same jury exonerated Armani at the outset. The New York State Bar Association later found there had been no violation.

26 Luban, *Lawyers and Justice*, pp. 58–66.

27 Ibid., p. 149. Notice Luban's sanguine inclusion of 'photographing the bodies' among the lawyers' role obligations!

28 David Luban, 'Freedom and Constraint in Legal Ethics: Some Mid-Course Corrections to *Lawyers and Justice*', *Maryland Law Review*, vol. 49 (1990) pp. 424–459, pp. 430–435. 'Freedom and Constraint' is a response to David Wasserman, 'Should a Good Lawyer Do the Right Thing? David Luban on the Morality of Adversary Representation', *Maryland Law Review*, vol. 49 (1990) pp. 392–423.

achieved by the default outweighs the harm that is done to the institution's justified function. In the logistics officer's case, the answer is 'no': the good (saving the individual) that would be achieved by defaulting from the role-obligation does not outweigh the harm (sacrificing the many) done to the mission of the institution. But this result is likely to be quite rare. It comes about in the logistics officer's case only because the case is structured so that the default is *sufficient* to thwart the good of the institution. Failing to maintain silence is enough on its own, on the facts of the case, to prevent the institution doing its job. But that is almost certainly not so in the Lake Pleasant Bodies case, or in most other actual cases. The damage to the institution of criminal defence itself, which would have resulted had Belge and Armani violated Garrow's confidence, would surely have been very slight: 'indeed far too slight to outweigh the good that violating confidentiality in this one case would accomplish'.[29] In the real world, single breaches are rarely sufficient to thwart institutional goals: '[T]he marginal harms to the system that result from violating one's professional duty typically are slight in a single case. On the other side of the ledger, the marginal benefits of following common morality rather than professional duty may be great. Thus when common morality clashes with role morality ... role morality usually loses.'[30] Hence, the direct route – the application of ordinary (utilitarian) morality to particular cases, even via the transmission device of Luban's ostensibly complex four-step derivation – threatens to do away with role-differentiated moral obligation altogether. As Luban concedes, if the 'consequentialist reading of the four-fold root argument is correct, the argument would virtually abolish the attorney–client relationship as we know it'.[31] Luban sets out to give 'considerations of role morality their proper weight without permitting them simply to override common morality'.[32] The direct route certainly prevents role morality from swamping common morality, but it does so by given it no weight at all.

A less direct route: role obligations as dependent rules

Again, then, it does not seem that the direct route can secure the prima facie conclusion that there are indeed role-differentiated obligations. There seem to be both conceptual grounds, flowing from the way we have understood roles, and lessons from Luban's attempt to apply the direct route, to think that we need another way if we are to hold on to that conclusion.

We can remain with David Luban to present and assess one possible alternative. Luban attributes the failure of the approach in *Lawyers and Justice* to the fact that it is really a 'sophisticated act-utilitarianism'.[33] It is no surprise, given this, that it

---

29   Luban, 'Freedom and Constraint', p. 430.
30   Ibid., 431.
31   Ibid.
32   Luban, *Lawyers and Justice*, p. 128.
33   Wassersman, 'Should a Good Lawyer Do the Right Thing?', p. 395.

does not preserve role-obligations. It has long been appreciated that utilitarianism does not preserve 'practices' if applied to particular cases. Consider promises. In essence, utilitarians say that promise is justified because it has good consequences. But if a promisor really is a utilitarian, and it becomes clear on a particular occasion that better consequences would be secured by breaking a promise than by keeping it, breaking the promise may not only be permitted but actually required. After all, the utilitarian promisor is required to do that thing which will achieve the best consequences. This objection has led critics to conclude bluntly that utilitarianism cannot give an account of the practice of promise at all. Promises that mean only 'I shall do as I say unless it would be better for me to do otherwise' do not seem to be promises at all.

As remarked, this is all very familiar and utilitarians have an equally familiar response. 'Rule-utilitarians' apply the utilitarian calculus not to particular acts but to general rules. Hence the rule-utilitarian promisor is to ask not, 'Would it be best on utilitarian grounds to keep or break this promise?', but rather, 'Is a general rule requiring people to keep promises justified on utilitarian grounds?' The answer to this latter question is almost certainly 'yes': cooperation has high utility-value and promising facilitates cooperation by allowing potential cooperators to know which of a person's statements of intention can be relied upon. Thus the rule requiring people to keep promises has high utility-value, and rule-utilitarian promisors should comply with it, even where more utility would be generated by not doing so on a particular occasion.[34]

And now Luban proposes to avoid the criticisms of the approach in *Lawyers and Justice* by recasting it in rule-utilitarian terms. Lawyers considering whether to maintain a client's confidence are to ask themselves not, 'Does ordinary (utilitarian) morality require me to maintain or break confidence in this very case?' (where, for reasons set out in the discussion of the Lake Pleasant Bodies case above, the answer will often – even typically – be 'no'), but rather: 'Is the rule requiring me to maintain client confidence justified by ordinary (utilitarian) morality?' And, just as in the case of promising, the answer to this general question about the rule is quite probably 'yes'. If so, lawyers should follow this rule, rather than the recommendations of a direct act-by-act appeal to the principle of utility.

In the terms in which we have approached role-differentiation, the move to rule-utilitarianism is an attempt to follow 'a less direct route'. Rule-utilitarianism establishes rules by appeal to the underlying moral theory, but the obligations of those subject to the rules are specified by the rules and not by the underlying moral theory. If role-obligations could be specified by rule-utilitarian rules, then, it seems genuine role-differentiated obligations could be secured. Such, at least, is Luban's

---

34 Philosophers will realise that this is a crude sketch of what has become a subtle and complex discussion. Rule-utilitarianism has long given way to more sophisticated versions of 'indirect consequentialism'. See Mulgan *The Demands of Consequentialism* for a contemporary treatment.

hope. He appeals to rule-utilitarianism in order to accord role-obligations their proper weight, while preventing them from swamping ordinary morality.

Unfortunately, however, rule-utilitarianism is widely thought to have delivered less than it promised. The most general problem is this: rule-utilitarians regard rules as authoritative because they promote utility. But if this is their ground for regarding rules as authoritative, it seems that they must be sensitive to whether or not a rule *does* promote utility on a particular occasion. And if it transpires that it does not do so, then they seem forced to the conclusion that it would be wrong to follow the rule on that occasion. As Bernard Williams puts the point:

> Whatever the general utility of having a certain rule, if one has actually reached the point of seeing that the utility of breaking it on a certain occasion is greater than that of following it [and one is a utilitarian], then surely it would be pure irrationality not to break it?[35]

This difficulty appears to generate a dilemma for rule-utilitarians: they must either eschew sensitivity to utility and stick with their rules no matter what the consequences, or they must assess the utility value of compliance with a rule on each occasion. If they take the first option, they abandon utilitarianism altogether. If they take the second, they are act-utilitarians after all, and all the reservations about the capacity of act-utilitarianism to sustain practices arise anew.

In the context of a general discussion this might be sufficient consideration of rule-utilitarianism. Since we have cast Luban as a protagonist, however, some further comment is in order. Luban's appeal to rule-utilitarianism seems especially curious, since the central argument in *Lawyers and Justice* – the idea that the strength of an institutional excuse depends upon the strength of the justification of the institution – appears to *be* a version of the standard criticism of rule-utilitarianism. The criticism depends upon the idea that utilitarians cannot really eschew case-by-case appeal to utility. The strength of the utilitarian's rules in a particular case, the idea goes, must depend upon the strength of the utilitarian justification for applying the rule in that case. But if that is right, say critics like Williams, then rule-utilitarianism collapses into act-utilitarianism. Luban's general criticism of role-differentiation has the same structure: roles cannot really establish obligations which are independent of ordinary morality, it claims, since the strength of a role-obligation depends upon the strength of the justification of the institution which generates it. Indeed Luban says just this in *Lawyers and Justice*. Characterising the general argument, he writes, 'I shall argue...that the weaker the justification of the institution, the slighter the moral significance of special institutional duties,' before continuing,

> the same is true, I believe, for utilitarianism. Rule-utilitarianism tells us that if a rule is justified (no matter how marginally) we must perform the acts it requires.

---

35 Bernard Williams, *Morality* (New York, 1972), p. 102.

On my view, this cannot be right: the question of whether the rule is strongly or weakly justified must affect its ability to require acts.[36]

Luban tells us that only a 'moral prig' or a 'moral monster' could really be prepared to follow rules where it was clear on a particular occasion that from the perspective of the very moral theory which generated the rules it would be better not to do so. At least at this point, then, he does not regard rule-utilitarianism as a plausible option.

Hence, Luban's subsequent endorsement of rule-utilitarianism seems inconsistent both with his explicit remarks and with the general structure of his position. Luban claims, however, that 'the contradiction...is merely apparent'. He offers two grounds for thinking so. First, he maintains that rule-utilitarianism establishes merely prima facie duties. Such duties may always 'be overridden in exigent circumstances, and thus we must always be ready to scrutinise particular acts to determine if the circumstances are exigent'. Second, he claims that his criticism of rule-utilitarianism in *Lawyers and Justice* was motivated by the idea that the approach ignores 'the fact that duties differ in their strength'.[37] The problem with rule-utilitarianism, according to this criticism, is that once a rule is found to be justified on utilitarian grounds, it settles what ought to be done. Luban thinks that the rules which specify role-obligations should not be 'on or off' in this fashion. Rather they should reflect the fact that some rules are strongly justified while others only just make the required utility threshold. And again, claims Luban, the version of rule-utilitarianism he endorses in response to David Wasserman is sensitive to variations in the strength of the justifications of rules in the required fashion: '[T]he whole purpose of the four-fold root,' he writes, 'is to help us understand the different strengths of legitimate duties, and thus the four-fold root yields a version of rule-consequentialism that escapes this criticism as well.'[38]

But I do not think either of these arguments work. Indeed, they both turn upon the very considerations that led critics to claim that rule-utilitarianism collapsed into act-utilitarianism: if the utilitarian must always check for 'exigencies warranting an exception', or always determine the strength of the justification for applying a rule in a particular case, then they are act- and not rule-utilitarians. If Luban's rule-utilitarian role-occupant must 'always be ready to scrutinise particular acts to determine if the circumstances are exigent', then they are appealing to utility on a case-by-case basis: they are act- and not rule-utilitarians. This is just to say that Luban chooses to impale himself on the second horn of the dilemma sketched above: he avoids the rule-worship threatened by the first horn, but at the cost of defending once again a 'sophisticated act-utilitarianism', with the result that he is vulnerable to all the criticisms of that position.

---

36 Luban, *Lawyers and Justice*, p. 129.
37 Luban, 'Freedom and constraint', p. 442.
38 Ibid.

Luban's manoeuvrings over this issue are explained by a more general difficulty. By the time he endorses rule-utilitarianism, Luban appreciates that the direct, act-utilitarian model defended in *Lawyers and Justice* will not preserve any significant role-obligation after all. As he writes, '[I]f the consequentialist reading of the four-fold root argument is correct, the argument would virtually abolish the attorney-client relationship as we know it.'[39] The move to rule-utilitarianism is an attempt to find a middle ground between ordinary and role-morality. But Luban does not want to abandon his central idea that institutional rules 'transmit' the justifications of ordinary morality on to role-occupants and role-acts. Luban's problem is that holding on to that idea prevents him proposing a very sharp break between the justification of institutions and the justification of role-acts. The idea requires that ordinary morality has a direct influence on the assessment of role-acts. Luban, then, creates his own version of the rule-utilitarian's dilemma: he can either abandon the key idea of his critique of role-differentiation and the standard conception, and deny that ordinary morality has a direct say in determining the strength and content of role-obligations, or he can hold on to that idea, but leave himself vulnerable to the sorts of criticisms of act-utilitarianism set out in the previous section and which re-emerge against this 'collapsed form' of rule-utilitarianism. As we have seen, Luban chooses the second horn of this dilemma. In doing so he defends a model which, once again, cannot effectively secure role-differentiated obligation. For that, we need another, less direct route.

A clean break: role-obligations as distinct from obligations of ordinary morality (the indirect route)

This brings us to an alternative account, according to which role-occupants are not entitled to appeal to ordinary morality from within their roles. Rather, they are limited to moral principles and resources 'internal' to the role. It is some such account which Postema and others have in mind when they say that under the standard conception the 'lawyer's moral experience is sharply constrained by the boundaries of the moral universe of the role',[40] and which is the target of many of the criticisms sketched in the last chapter.

This alternative account depends upon an idea which sounds odd when first encountered, but which has become part of the furniture of contemporary normative theory. It is the idea that the justifications we give for institutions or practices may differ from – and perhaps even conflict with – the justifications we give for conduct within those institutions or practices. John Rawls provides the classic statement of this distinction between levels of justification in a paper which addresses the very problems we have been discussing: act-utilitarianism cannot preserve practices, rule-utilitarianism is unstable, hence '[i]t seems to follow that a utilitarian account of [for example] promise cannot be successfully carried

---

39 Ibid.
40 Postema, 'Moral Responsibility in Professional Ethics', p. 78.

out'.[41] Rawls proposes a solution. We can cast his discussion in our terms this way: Critics of utilitarian accounts of promising portray promisors deciding whether to keep promises as entitled to appeal directly back to the same sorts of moral considerations which justify the practice of promise. They assume, that is, that if the practice of promise is justified on utilitarian grounds, then whether or not particular promises should be kept is also to be settled by appeal to utility. Rawls's solution turns upon the claim that this assumption is not warranted. The critics 'fail to make the distinction between the justification of a practice and the justification of a particular action falling under it'.[42] Before promises are made, promisors are free to weigh up the merits and do whatever seems best on the balance of reasons. Once a promise is made, however, others have grounds to believe that that sort of deliberation is over. Now, they are entitled to think, promisors have a duty to act as they have promised to act and promisees have a correlative right that they do so. Indeed, the function of promise, on this account, is precisely to establish rights and duties and so rule out certain kinds of deliberation. As Rawls puts it, 'The point of the practice is to abdicate one's title to act in accordance with utilitarian and prudential considerations in order that the future might be tied down and plans coordinated in advance.'[43] If this model of promise is correct, then the appropriate justifications for conduct within the practice of promising differ dramatically from the justifications of the practice itself. We may be utilitarians when designing the institution, but build into the design a set of hard and fast rules – what philosophers call 'deonotological' constraints – which exclude appeal to utilitarian considerations from within the institution.

I hope it is clear how this is meant to be relevant to the assessment and understanding of the standard conception and the idea of role-differentiated obligation. The Rawlsian approach is intended to show that institutions may be justified by appeal to ordinary or general morality, but that the conduct of those within those institutions is to be governed not by the original moral considerations but by the rules of the institution. This is just the way the standard conception portrays the lawyer's role. According to that conception, occupants of the lawyer's role are subject to a distinct set of role-differentiated obligations and permissions. When they act within their professional roles they may not appeal to the considerations of ordinary morality that justify the roles themselves. There are variations on this basic distinction. In one form or another, however, the distinction allows us to see how there might be role-differentiated obligations that are distinct from the obligations of ordinary morality.

We can employ a version of Luban's four-fold root to set out the process more explicitly: we are to first, justify the institution to which the role belongs 'by demonstrating its moral goodness'; second, show that the role is required if the

---

41   John Rawls, 'Two Concepts of Rules' *Philosophical Review*, vol. 64 (1955) pp. 3–32, p. 16.
42   Ibid.
43   Ibid.

good of the institution is to be achieved; third, justify the role-obligation by showing that it is essential to the role; and, finally, justify a particular action by showing that it is required by the role-obligation. According to Luban, recall, the role-act will be justified if 'taken together these justifications for the role-act outweigh' the moral reasons for acting according to ordinary morality. Armed with Rawls's distinction, we can see how this last balancing step may be resisted. For Luban the normative force of the role-obligation depends upon the transmission on to the role-act of the normative force of ordinary morality. But Rawls has shown that there need be no direct transmission. The roles and role-obligations established by justified institutions function as independent sources of moral obligation for those acting within them.

Luban set out to give role-morality its proper weight without allowing it to swamp ordinary morality. He did not succeed. But the Rawlsian approach does seem to secure the desired balance between ordinary and role-morality. On the one hand, the distinction between the justification of practices and the justification of actions within practices allows us to see how roles might function as independent sources of obligation for role-occupants, and so avoids the collapse of role- into ordinary-morality. On the other hand, the approach preserves the significance of ordinary morality. We are to construct roles, building our 'constellations of institutionally specified rights and duties … around … institutionally specified social functions', with all the resources of 'ordinary' morality at our disposal. And the perspective of ordinary morality always remains available to us. Although what counts as a promise will be determined by the rules of the institution (by what Rawls calls the practice rules) we can always judge the institution from the perspective of ordinary morality, perhaps lobbying for a change in the practice (for a change in what Rawls calls the constitutive rules) when the practice seems to have come apart from the concerns of ordinary morality which drove its construction.[44] This straightforward but important point allows us an immediate response to a common criticism of the standard conception.

Some writers have claimed that the standard conception makes ordinary morality irrelevant to the assessment of the conduct of lawyers. According to Dean Cocking and Justin Oakley, for instance: 'Various writers have wanted to defend a conception of the lawyer's role where the lawyer's advocacy of her client's legal rights is not constrained by broad-based moral concerns with which this advocacy might conflict,' and have claimed that, 'standards of ordinary morality have no place in the evaluation of professional conduct.'[45] But while these characterisations allow a striking contrast between the standard conception and its opponents, they are unhelpful and inaccurate. It is simply not true on this reading of the

---

44 See the related discussion below, p. 53ff, where I argue lawyers have a positive duty to engage in this sort of external assessment of their roles.

45 Cocking and Oakley, 'Doing Justice to the Lawyer's Role', pp. 77 and 84. Cocking and Oakley give a more sympathetic account of the model in their subsequent book *Virtue Ethics and Professional Roles* (Cambridge, 2001).

standard conception, or any plausible alternative, that 'the lawyer's advocacy... is not constrained by broad-based moral concerns' or that 'standards of ordinary morality have no place in the evaluation of professional conduct' under the standard conception, or that, more broadly, the approach does not allow us to distinguish between morally justified and morally unjustified roles.[46] Even on the indirect approach, let alone on the Rawlsian model, role-obligation flows from institutions structured with reference to ordinary morality. It is true that the approach does not allow direct appeal to ordinary morality, but this is not equivalent to saying that role-occupants are not answerable to ordinary morality at all. Under the standard conception, ordinary morality bears upon the justification of the institutions that generate professional roles. The debate, this is to say, is about the role ordinary morality should have in determining the obligations of professionals, not about whether it should have any role at all.

Arthur Applbaum and the argument from redescription But there may be a more troubling objection to the Rawlsian model. I have suggested that Rawls' distinction between constitutive and practice rules allows us to defend the possibility of role-differentiated obligation while resisting the claim that 'standards of ordinary morality have no place in the evaluation of professional conduct'.[47] Arthur Applbaum has come to a very different conclusion about the significance of this same distinction. According to Applbaum, if we conceive of lawyers' obligations in terms of the Rawlsian model then '[m]oral criticism of...particular action from outside the practice is logically precluded'.[48] Where I have argued that the Rawlsian model preserves the possibility of effective moral evaluation, then, Applbaum argues that the model rules it out. Applbaum does not conclude that we should eschew moral evaluation or that lawyers should act in ways that seem immoral. If the Rawlsian model rules out effective moral evaluation of lawyers' conduct, he concludes, so much the worse for the model. We should abandon it in favour of the alternative he goes on to offer. But I do not think Applbaum is right about the implications of the Rawlsian model.

Constitutive rules create practices or institutions. They make it possible to perform actions that would otherwise be impossible. Actions such as hitting a home run, striking out or hitting a four are possible only because of the constitutive rules of baseball and cricket. Actions such as making a will and incorporating a company are possible only because of the constitutive rules of equity or company law. Although we might in some sense 'do the same thing' – hit a ball a certain

---

46   So their observation that there 'may be features distinguishing what it is to be a good torturer but this would hardly suffice to show the role to be a morally good one', ('Doing Justice to the Lawyer's Role', p. 78), is plainly correct, but is not a criticism of the standard conception.

47   Cocking and Oakley, 'Doing Justice to the Lawyer's Role', p. 77.

48   Arthur Applbaum, *Ethics for Adversaries: The Morality of Roles in Public and Professional Life* (Princeton, 1999), p. 85.

distance, record our testamentary wishes in a certain form – we would not perform the same action:

> No matter what a person did, what they did would not be described as stealing a base or striking out or drawing a walk unless they could also be described as playing baseball, and for them to be doing this presupposes the rule like practice which constitutes the game.[49]

The possibility of some actions, then, is literally created by constitutive rules. Equally, to the extent a practice is exhaustively defined by its constitutive rules, *only* conduct recognised by the rules counts as an action within that practice. If a baseball batter, having swung and missed three times, turns to the umpire and seriously suggests they be allowed an extra strike, they would show that they did not understand what it was to play baseball. It is not just that they would be suggesting that the umpire give them a break. Their proposal would amount to the suggestion that they be allowed to stop playing baseball and begin to participate in some other, new, practice: one which recognised a new action – the fourth strike. And so it is, Applbaum argues, with the lawyer. The advocate who acts in ways unrecognised by the constitutive rules of legal practice is on a par with the revisionist baseball batter.

> A lawyer advocating on behalf of a client who wishes to avoid paying an acknowledged debt cannot refuse to plead the statute of limitations and still call themselves an advocate, for unless the defining rules of lawyering are changed, a lawyer who is not a diligent advocate for the legal interests of their client is not engaged in the proper practice of advocacy.[50]

According to Applbaum, then, far from facilitating 'ethical lawyering' Rawls's model severely curtails it. 'Moral criticism of…particular action from outside the practice is logically precluded' and many of the acts evaluation might recommend, such as curtailing excessively zealous advocacy, may not be available to practitioners given the constitutive rules of the practice. If we embrace the model, then one cannot *be* a lawyer, given the way the practice is constituted, and act in ways that are inconsistent with the practice as it stands.

It is useful to identify two aspects to Applbaum's criticism, one internal and the other external. The internal aspect is the claim that since the constitutive rules of a practice settle what will count as an action within that practice, it is not possible for practitioners to act other than as the practice licenses. If the constitutive rules of the practice required Pakel's lawyer to plead a statute of limitations, then it makes no sense to suggest that a better practitioner would have resisted Pakel's

---

49 Rawls, 'Two Concepts of Rules', p. 25.
50 Applbaum, *Ethics for Adversaries*, p. 85. The facts will be familiar. They are broadly those of *Zabella* v *Pakel*.

instructions to plead the statute, since resistance would have amounted to a refusal to *be* a practitioner.

But I do not think the internal aspect of the critique is compelling. The practice of law, in the Rawlsian sense of practice, is significantly different from the practice of baseball, and not just in the obvious points of detail. The rules that constitute different practices do not specify those practices with equal precision. Quite simply, the constitutive rules of some practices allow greater latitude in what will count as activity within the practice than others. Some of this latitude is unavoidable. As Hart writes, if: 'The world in which we live were characterized only by a finite number of features, and these together with all the modes in which they combine could be known to us,' perhaps, 'we could make rules, the application of which to particular cases never called for further choice.' But our relative 'ignorance of fact' and 'indeterminacy of aim' mean that ours is not a 'world fit for mechanical jurisprudence'.[51] No matter how carefully we create the practice of advocacy there will always be a degree of imprecision. Some of this latitude is a matter of deliberate institutional design. Just how precisely we define practices is likely to depend upon a number of factors, including the relative costs of precision and latitude. In the sports arena we place high value on clear rules and speedy decisions. We recognise that this carries a cost: every sports fan can think of an important game influenced by a controversial umpiring decision. We are prepared to bear these costs of precision, however, given the relative triviality of sporting contests and the countervailing preferences for, among other things, predictability, speed and finality. So institutional design in baseball is driven in part by the high value we place on clear rules and speedy decisions. Institutional design in law, by contrast, is driven in part by recognition that the stakes are often high, that there will not be another game tomorrow, that the parties are more interested in particular victories and decisions than in winning percentages across a long season, and that there is, at least often, opportunity to consider opposing views of how the practice should be understood – to consider disagreements over what will count as zealous advocacy, disagreements over whether a defence lawyer should inform the court of some information harmful to their client, disagreements over whether a representative must plead every available defence, and so on. The upshot is that it is just not as clear that an advocate who turns to a judge or a client and asks about these issues 'stops playing the game', as it is that a batter who asks for a fourth strike mid-game has an odd view of the game of baseball. So while we may agree with Applbaum about the lawyer in a case such as *Pakel* v *Zabella*,[52] we should not

---

51   Hart, *The Concept of Law*, pp. 120–130.
52   And of course one might be suspicious of just how straightforward such cases seem to the participants: 'clients ... do not present unambiguous stories of injustice, corruption, or unconscionability. ... I do not know what really happened in the *Zabella* v. *Pakel* case...but I will bet that when those types of cases come to a lawyer, the creditor does not say, 'I owe the money. I can afford to pay it. I have not lost any papers and my memory is clear. The guy's a good guy, and he is poor, and he needs the money. But let us

assume too restricted a view about what actions will count as actions within legal practice. If this is right, then much of the force of Applbaum's objection seems to be deflected. The constitutive rules of law, unlike those of baseball, permit lawyers to question clients and judges about their decisions, to appeal decisions, to run arguments challenging orthodox interpretations, to seek equitable intervention in extraordinary cases, and the like.

A more general point about the Rawlsian model lies behind these remarks. The idea that the constitutive rules of a practice settle what will count as an action under that practice tells us nothing about the constitutive rules of any particular practice. We cannot draw conclusions from the model itself about what a practitioner can and cannot do within a practice. That will depend upon the particular practice rules. Whether or not 'a lawyer advocating on behalf of a client who wishes to avoid paying an acknowledged debt' can 'refuse to plead the statute of limitations and still call herself an advocate', for instance, will depend upon what the constitutive rules of the relevant practice do and do not allow.

Brad Wendel has also offered a 'law is not baseball' response to Applbaum, focussing on the differing degrees of precision to be found in practices of law and baseball. Legal practice, Wendel argues, incorporates 'a plurality of visions of morally acceptable practice'[53] and so is less amenable to precise definition than baseball. Applbaum, he remarks, relies upon a model of legal practice constituted by 'relatively clear and unambiguous' rules. It is this precision and clarity which allows Applbaum to say that Pakel's lawyers would have stepped outside the clearly defined lines of legal practice had he declined to plead the statute of limitations. But, Wendel continues:

> ... law is not baseball, where it is easy to spot departures from the rules. [R]unning from home plate to third base is plainly excluded as a move within baseball, but aggressively cross examining a truthful witness or taking an extremely tendentious position in response to discovery requests are moves that may be acceptable in some professional communities but ruled out in others.[54]

I have a good deal of sympathy with Wendel's analysis. I agree that law incorporates 'a plurality of visions of morally acceptable practice', and will make

---

screw him. Can we find some technicality?' The rich guy has excuses; he has accusations about the poor guy; he has a history that makes his case far more complicated. Justice is on my side, he says. The lawyer may suspect that all of this is just twaddle, but for him to betray his client he must be sure – ever so sure – that it is indeed twaddle. I suspect that lawyers are very seldom so sure': Paul Tremblay, 'Client-Centered Counseling and Moral Activism' contribution to Robert F. Cochrane, Jnr, Deborah L. Rhode, Paul R. Tremblay, Thomas L. Shaffer 'Symposium: Client Counseling and Moral Responsibility' *Pepperdine Law Review*, vol. 30 (2002–2003) pp. 591–639, pp. 621–622.

53   Wendel, 'Professional Roles and Moral Agency', p. 60.
54   Ibid.

something of that plurality in the next chapter. For the moment I would emphasise only that if it is easier to spot departures from the rules of baseball than departures from the rules of legal practice, it is not simply because the subject matter of the former is more amenable to precise regulation than that of the latter. Perhaps Hart's twin handicaps of the 'human predicament' – 'our relative ignorance of fact' and 'our relative indeterminacy of aim' – are less disabling in the sports world, whose topography is more straightforward than that encountered outside the ballpark. But we should not overdraw the ontological differences between the worlds. On the one hand, there are many clear cases in legal practice (we are all just as sure an advocate may not physically attack a witness as we are that you may not round the bases in reverse). On the other hand, many of the boundaries between acting within and outside sporting practices could be just as blurry as those in law: we could, for instance, allow more sustained inquiry into whether a called strike *was* a strike. To the extent boundaries are clearer in sport, then, it is primarily because we make them that way, and are prepared to pay the cost of doing so. The values which drive institutional design – which make us decide upon the respective sets of constitutive rules – are such that we are more willing to pay the cost of rigid rules in the one case (sport) than we are in the other (law). So Wendel is right: law is not baseball. The one is more tolerant and less clear than the other. But that difference flows less from the nature of the subject matter of the two domains than it does from choices we make when creating constitutive rules. The greater tolerance of what will count as acceptable legal practice is the result of specific and deliberate institutional design.

I turn to the external element of Applbaum's response to Rawls. Rawls realises, of course, that we can and do change the constitutive rules of practices such as baseball. Between 1889 and 1897 the number of 'called balls' that entitled a baseball batter to walk to first base changed four times, from nine to the current four; the number of balls in an 'over' in cricket changed from eight to the current six. Rawls argues, however, we cannot initiate these changes from within the practice. From there, all we can do is appeal to the rules of the practice. When we engage in the sort of evaluation that leads to change in the constitutive rules of the practice – and so leads to a change in the practice itself – we no longer act as practitioners engaged in that practice. Instead we take on a different office. As Rawls puts it:

> [I]f one holds an office defined by a practice then questions regarding one's actions in this office are settled by the reference to the rules which define the practice. If one seeks to question these rules, then one's office undergoes a fundamental change: one then assumes the office of one empowered to change and criticize the rules, or the office of a reformer ....[55]

---

55 Rawls, 'Two Concepts of Rules', p. 27.

Rawls argues, then, that practices can be evaluated, and arguments offered for their reform, but practitioners cannot engage in such evaluation and criticism qua practitioners. A baseball player who approaches the commissioner arguing that the game would be improved by the addition of a fourth strike isn't 'playing baseball'. He has abandoned the role of player for that of reformer. And of course Applbaum recognises that the Rawlsian model allows for external evaluation and practice revision. With this in mind, he identifies an obvious response to his objection to the Rawlsian approach.

> Because the possibility of external judgment of the entire practice is not denied by the argument of constituted description, the simplest reply is to show that, even if its conclusion is granted, the argument has no moral force and makes no moral difference.[56]

However, Applbaum does not think this is enough to rescue the Rawlsian model. Just as a player cannot act, qua player, other than as recognised by the constitutive rules of the practice (since if they do they stop being a player), so an external commentator cannot complain that a player, qua player, should have so acted. A sports commentator who criticises a player for failing to do something not permitted by the rules (the baseball batter for failing to convert fourth strike opportunities perhaps) can only be criticising the practice for failing to provide that opportunity – not the player. It makes no sense, on this account, to criticise Pakel's lawyer for failing to act, qua practitioner, in a way the constitutive rules of the practice did not recognise. If the rules of legal practice called upon him to plead the statute of limitation, the critic must either be criticising the practice, or calling upon Pakel's lawyer to abandon it. Applbaum takes this criticism one step further. Under the Rawlsian model external critics are all the more impotent, he argues, when confronted with morally questionable cases occurring within practices that are 'on the whole' justified. If external critics can only criticise practices, rather than particular actions, what are they to say about an 'on the whole' justified practice (such as law) which allows or requires morally questionable conduct, such as pleading a statute of limitations to allow a client to avoid a just debt, or casting doubt on the evidence of a truth-telling witness? They cannot criticise the practitioner, qua practitioner, for failing to do something not recognised by the practice, and if the practice is justified on the whole, they can't criticise that either. 'We do wish to pick out [the particular case] for moral criticism,' Applbaum writes:

> But if we grant the argument of constituted description, we can fault [the lawyer] only for failure to comply with the rules of a justified practice. ... So something does turn on the argument of constituted description; if a practice on the whole

---

56   Applbaum, *Ethics for Adversaries*, p. 89.

is justified, then actions constituted by that practice are immune from external moral criticism as long as they comply with the rules of the practice.⁵⁷

Applbaum offers a solution. Essentially, he thinks there are always 'multiple' descriptions of an action. Moral descriptions persist and may be used to question the constituted descriptions of law. But I think this is unnecessary. The Rawlsian model gives us all we need. Applbaum objects that the Rawlsian model renders particular actions constituted by an on the whole justified practice immune from external moral criticism as long as they comply with the rules of the practice. He may be right, but I think he gives too little weight to what the occupant of the office of external critic *can* do. Suppose the external critic believes that it is morally regrettable that the rules of the practice require advocates to plead a statute of limitations on behalf of a client seeking to avoid payment of a just debt in the absence of reasons to think the barred proceedings would be inequitable. They may be limited in what they can legitimately conclude about the practitioner. They cannot criticise the practitoner, qua practitioner, for failing to perform an action – refraining from advancing the defence – not recognised by the current practice. But they can argue that the practice ought to be changed, perhaps to allow recourse to the statute only where it would be inequitable to allow proceeding after a certain period. They can regret that the practice allowed the objectionable conduct. They might think all of this without thinking that the practice as it stands is 'on the whole' unjustified. They need not suppose that the untidy systems of rules and principles which constitute their complex legal system, generated over a long period, by different agents and collectives, motivated by varying social, moral and political concerns and pressures, is likely to be seamlessly coherent, all of a piece, and without flaw. They might even think that revising the institution to remedy the particular injustice would carry too high a price in other cases. In sum, they can do more than simply ask whether the action is an action under an on the whole justified practice.

The clean break and the possibility of multiple roles The possibility of external evaluation – coupled with the deliberate or inadvertently provided opportunity for 'internal' review provided by the practice rules of law – removes much of the force of Applbaum's critique of the Rawlsian model. I want to go a bit further, in a way that I hope will reinforce the structural model I have in mind, and make one of its virtues explicit. The Rawlsian model allows us to conceptualise an important feature of ethical legal practice. Often the 'external office of the reformer' is formally independent of legal practice: the offices of the Law Commissioners of many Commonwealth jurisdictions are an example. The model defended here, however, gives ethical reason to encourage and perhaps require lawyers themselves to participate more fully in law reform. A lawyer noticing that the statute of limitations has produced a result regrettable from the perspective of

---

57 Ibid., p. 90.

ordinary morality cannot act, qua advocate, other than the existing rules of the practice recognise. They must see the case through, helping their client secure their rights under the statute law. With the client's case complete, however, they might leave the role of advocate and take on that of reformer, perhaps writing to their local Law Commissioner, arguing the need for reform, which their legal expertise and familiarity with the particular case may have made especially clear. There are very obvious dangers here – the role of advocate and the role of reformer – might conflict: a current client may have organised their affairs in reliance on the unjust laws, and expect to maintain a professional relationship with the practitioner. Some practitioners may be prevented from advocating reform in some cases. But often there is likely to be no such current conflict. The Rawlsian model and the idea of role-differentiated obligation allows us to see how lawyers might move between two distinct roles, respecting both the demands of practices of which they are a part and the demands of ordinary morality which shape those practices.

This feature of the model allows a response to another aspect of the critique of the standard conception. One thread of the moral insensitivity strand focused on clients who come to lawyers seeking more than merely legal advice; their questions about estate-planning intended to solicit the lawyer's views on the fairness, rather than the enforceability, of the arrangements they have in mind.[58] Such clients will be unsatisfied by a response limited to the technical requirements of family protection legislation and the like. An adequate response, I characterised the critique as claiming, seems to require moral sensitivity and access to general morality apparently excluded by the standard conception and the idea of role differentiation. However, this particular thread of the 'moral insensitivity' strand of the critique is most powerful when directed at versions of the standard conception that deny to individuals who are lawyers (the point of the odd description will be clear in a moment) all access to the resources of the ordinary morality and their own moral experience: denies them access, that is, to the sorts of resources and experience one might draw upon when giving the sort of moral advice such clients seek. But the defence of the standard conception offered here is not committed to that position. According to that conception, as defended here, occupants of the lawyer's role are subject to a distinct set of role-differentiated obligations and permissions *when they act within their professional roles*. Qua lawyer, they may not appeal directly to the considerations of ordinary morality that justify that role. But the model has emphasised that ordinary

---

58 It seems likely that there is a connection between client expectations in these situations and the fact that roles are rarely purely 'social' or 'institutional' constructs. It is I think more obviously inappropriate to expect moral advice from the lawyer qua occupant of the institutionally constituted role, than of the lawyer qua occupant of the socially constituted role. While I have acknowledged that the lawyer's' role is neither purely one or the other, one might read some of the arguments in this book as reasons to shift the social expectations which generate the latter view of the role closer to that I think are or should be generated by the former.

morality does not disappear: the perspective of ordinary morality always remains available to reflective role-occupants. The ethical lawyer should, for instance, reflect upon the moral point of the role they fill, perhaps stepping into the role of reformer when the demands of that role seem to have come from the concerns of ordinary morality that drove its construction.

Furthermore, as the idea that they might occasionally have an obligation to step from their role as advocate to that of reformer suggests, the individuals who are lawyers may well occupy other roles. They might, for instance, occupy the role of 'friend' or 'confidant' or 'counsellor' (in the non-legal sense) to clients who come seeking more than legal advice. It is easy to imagine the client professional conversation that goes, roughly, 'Well, you could do that. The law is such and so. But my advice, as a friend, is to let this go.' However, lawyers should not imagine that these sorts of 'boundary crossings' are the norm. I suggested that there were obvious dangers in the idea that lawyers might move between the role of advocate and reformer, and I think that is a point to be made here too. There is I think no particular reason to think that legal training gives people the kind of expertise which makes them good moral advisors or counsellors (in the non-legal sense). Further, I think great care is required to ensure that clients are clear about the nature of the advice that is being given. It is too easy for clients to be confused about just what hat the person who is a lawyer is wearing in such conversations. A model of professional roles that makes the limits of those roles explicit, calling upon role-occupants to signal clearly what role they occupy at a moment, is an important element in the strategy of those concerned to guard against such confusion.

Kant's conflicted pastor Kant made a cameo appearance in the opening paragraph of this book, and we can turn to him here for a nice example that draws together the themes of the discussion in the last few pages. His question is 'What is enlightenment?', and his answer, in short, is that enlightenment is the capacity 'to use one's understanding without guidance from another'.[59] Enlightened individuals, he thinks, should have the courage to use their own understanding. It might seem that this is not an especially promising account in which to find support for a view that seeks to preserve robust role-differentiation, and to convince role-occupants that they will often be obliged to recognise the authority of role-obligation. However Kant takes what might seem a surprisingly tolerant view, not far from that advanced in this book. His example is a pastor, suffering what we would now call a crisis of faith, and sceptical about the doctrines he is required to expound to his congregation; sceptical we might say about the justification of his role-obligations. If the pastor aspires to enlightenment we might expect, given Kant's account of that state, that he should not act contrary to his own reason. But Kant draws a distinction between his entitlement to act of his own judgement 'as a

---

59   Immanual Kant, 'What is Enlightenment?', trans. L.W. Beck *Foundations of the Metaphysics of Morals and 'What is Enlightenment?'* (Indianapolis, 1959), p. 88.

scholar', and his entitlement to do so as a priest. A pastor, he writes,

> ...is bound to instruct his...congregation in accordance with the symbol of the church he serves, for he was appointed on that condition. What he teaches in consequence of his office as a servant of the church he sets out as something with regard to which he has no discretion to teach in accord with his own lights.[60]

Kant recognises that such obligations are in tension with his account of enlightenment. He argues, however, that they are required 'in many affairs conducted in the interest of community ... so that through an artificial unanimity the government may guide them toward public ends'.[61] And, more importantly, he insists, such role-obligations do not exclude the possibility, even the obligation, for individuals to step outside their roles and exercise the free reason which amount to enlightenment. Though the pastor must instruct his congregation in accordance with the symbol of the church when acting *as* pastor:

> ...as a scholar he has complete freedom, indeed even the calling, to impart to the public all of his carefully considered and well-intentioned thoughts concerning mistaken aspects of that symbol, as well as his suggestions for the better arrangement of religious and church matters. Nothing in this can weigh on his conscience.[62]

Dean Cocking and Justin Oakley are grudging and critical of Kant's attitude to the pastor. It is not enough, they write, to insist that he has an obligation to express his doubts about the church as a scholar while continuing to carry out his role-obligations. Allowing criticism of individuals for failing to publicise their misgivings about contentious aspects of their role in a nonprofessional context, they write,

> ... is not yet to allow that individuals are properly condemned for continuing to to fulfil those contentious role demands themselves, which, in the case of the priest, is condemnation Kant is plainly not prepared to make.[63]

But I am with Kant here. Suppose the pastor in question is the only one available to a community deeply reliant on his ministrations. They believe, rightly or wrongly, that they will be in mortal peril without the services he provides. Suppose he has contributed to this situation: he has taken the position, preached church doctrine, created the relationship upon which the parishioners now rely. In such circumstances, it seems to me, it might be sheer arrogance for the pastor

---

60 Ibid., p. 88.
61 Ibid.
62 Ibid.
63 Cocking and Oakley, *Virtue Ethics and Professional Roles*, p. 162.

to withdraw his services – at least until he can arrange for the concerns of his community to be met.[64] Kant's recognition that the conflicted pastor has both the capacity and the obligation to occupy more than one role seems an appropriate accommodation of the competing demands of role-obligation and individual enlightenment, and – we might add – ordinary morality.

Conclusion

This chapter began by offering an account of roles and role-obligations, proposing an understanding of roles as positions in social networks that bring with them specific sets of moral obligations that attach to those who come to occupy the positions. It offered a prima facie case for the conclusion that there are indeed role-differentiated obligations. But, even if accepted, the prima facie case left unanswered the most interesting questions about the moral significance of roles. The first was about the mechanics of role-obligations, about just how roles can generate distinct obligations. We considered a range of possible answers. I hope to have shown that, if we wish to preserve the prima facie conclusion, we must conceive of roles in terms of something like the Rawlsian approach. The picture which grants to ordinary morality the task of justifying institutions, but which allows that those institutions might generate independent obligations – answerable to ordinary morality only in the sense that their normative force depends upon their being obligations of a justified institution – allows us to 'give considerations of role-morality their proper weight without permitting them to simply override common morality'.[65] I responded to Arthur Applbaum's dramatically different reading of what I have called the Rawlsian model, according to which, far from allowing a balance between role-morality and ordinary morality, the model logically precludes moral criticism of particular actions within role. I have argued, however, that there are adequate responses to both what I have called the 'internal' and the 'external' aspects of Applbaum's case against the Rawlsian model. As an internal matter, practices such as law offer role-occupants far greater resources for 'internal critique' than Applbaum

---

64   Perhaps it matters whether the sceptical pastor's ministrations would be effective. Putting aside religious scepticism for the moment, officially, it seems they can be: '*Opus operatum; ex opere operato*: A technical phrase used by theologians since the 13th century to signify that the sacraments produce grace of themselves, apart and distinct from the grace dependent upon the intention of the person conferring the sacrament; the latter effect is designated by the phrase *ex opere operantis*. The phrase was officially adopted by the Council of Trent and used to signify the objective character of the sacraments as producers of grace in opposition to the subjectivism of the Reformers. According to Trent, therefore, the term *opus operatum* signifies that the correct use of the sign instituted by Christ produces the grace irrespectively of the merits of either minister or recipient.': *New Catholic Dictionary*: http://www.catholic-forum.com/saints/ncd06116.htm.

65   Luban, *Lawyers and Justice*, p. 128.

allows. The law itself allows broader review of role-acts than his criticism of 'practice positivism' recognises. Further, I have suggested that it is one of the virtues of the Rawlsian model that it allows us to see how role-occupants might have access to external resources for review of roles and their demands without undercutting the institutional significance of those roles. The model allows us to see, I have suggested, how lawyers might move between distinct roles, respecting both the demands of practices of which they are a part and the demands of ordinary morality which shape those practices.

I hope, in sum, to have offered substantial support for the prima facie case in favour of role-differentiated obligation. But of course this is not the only interesting question left unanswered by the prima facie case. In particular, the discussion in this chapter does not address the crucial questions, *should* we preserve role-differentiated obligations, and should we endorse the standard conception of the lawyer's roles? I turn to these questions in the next chapter.

Chapter 4
The Standard Conception and the Role of Law

Introduction

No sooner had we advanced the prima facie case for the conclusion that there were such things as role-differentiated obligations than we noted its limitations. Pointing out that we do encounter role-differentiated obligations does not tell us how entering a professional role might have the normative consequences claimed by champions of the standard conception, nor whether it should do so. Much of the previous chapter was addressed to the 'how' question. I argued that if we were to take the prima facie case seriously at all we should conceive of role-obligations in terms of Rawls' distinction between the justification of institutions and the justification of conduct within those institutions. We turn now to the 'should' question. This chapter begins to consider whether we should endorse the standard conception of the lawyer's role. I will argue that we should do so. Again, I believe that the conception is essentially the right way to conceive of the ethical obligations of lawyers. Those concerned with the ethics of the profession should regard lawyers acting in their professional capacities as subject to distinct, role-differentiated, obligations.

The argument that we should endorse the standard conception begins in this chapter with an appeal to the function of law. The point of the institution which supports a given role will feature significantly in any justification of that role and its role-obligations, whether we side with Luban or with a justificatory strategy based upon some version of the Rawlsian argument. The nature of the lawyer's role and the role-obligations it imposes depends upon the function of the role within the institution of which it is a part, and hence upon the function of that institution. On the Rawlsian account, an appeal to the moral significance of the institution and its role is likely to be the primary justification for establishing the institutional rules which settle the obligations of those within the institution.

I will suggest that the fundamental function of the institutions of law in modern constitutional democracies is to mediate between the range of views to be found in such communities on fundamental questions such as what constitutes human flourishing, what basic goals are intrinsically most worthy of pursuit, and what is the best way for individuals to live their lives. The law allows the advocates of very different views on these matters to live together despite their differences. The nature of the roles occupied by lawyers within the institutions of law is settled to a large extent by this mediating function of law. We will go on to examine the principles which make up the standard conception of law in light of this account of law and legal roles. For the most part, I will suggest, the approach supports the standard conception. We will see, however, that the appeal to the point of law gives us reason to reject readings of the conception as requiring lawyers to pursue 'hyper-zealously' every advantage obtainable for their clients through the law. I appeal to the role of law, this is to say, to defend a moderate version of the standard conception.

The standard conception and the role of law

Law and reasonable pluralism

We begin then with an account of the function of law. The institutions of law in Western democracies no doubt serve many functions: they are dispute resolution devices; they supply answers to coordination problems (they tell us, for instance, which side of the road to drive on); they secure the provision of certain public goods, such as health care and transport infrastructure; they allow conduct which would simply not be possible other than in institutional contexts (just as one cannot hit a six or a home-run without the institutions of cricket or baseball, nor can one incorporate a company without the institution of company law); they facilitate planning by treating certain kinds of undertakings or arrangements as enforceable; they identify certain forms of conduct as required or prohibited and lend the power of the state to better ensure compliance.

This is no doubt an incomplete list of the functions of the institutions of western law. Yet even in this abbreviated form it may seem so diverse as to render impossible a compelling appeal to law's function: how can one appeal meaningfully to 'the function of law' when it has so many functions? The answer is that a common and general function lies behind these more specific ones. John Rawls, writing in another context, points the way here as well. Rawls' recent work has been based on the premise that the citizens of modern democracies are and will remain sharply divided over fundamental questions such as what constitutes human flourishing, what basic goals are intrinsically most worthy of pursuit and what is the best way for individuals to live their lives. This 'plurality of conceptions of the good', Rawls concludes, is inevitable; it is 'the natural outcome of the activities of human reason under enduring free institutions'.[1]

Not all views about these fundamental matters count as reasonable. But even putting Nazis and nutters to one side (and conceding that they will not always be easy to identify), a plurality of reasonable views remains. In modern times, the claim goes, we have come to recognise a multiplicity of ways in which a fulfilled life can be lived, without seeing a hierarchy among them that we feel justified in enforcing. We have been obliged to acknowledge that even where we

---

1   John Rawls, *Political Liberalism* (New York, 1993) xvi.

believe that we have discerned the superiority of some ways of life over others, reasonable people may not share our view. Pluralism and reasonable disagreement are uneliminable features of the political landscape in modern constitutional democracies.

The challenge for such communities is to find a way that 'there may exist over time a secure stable and just society among free and equal citizens profoundly divided by reasonable though incompatible religious, philosophical and moral doctrine'.[2] A central part of the liberal answer to this question has been the adoption of a certain kind of neutrality as a political ideal. The members of a pluralist community, the idea goes, will often be able to agree on the structure of neutral institutions and practices even where they cannot agree on the right outcome of a policy question as a substantive matter. Fellow citizens may disagree deeply over, for instance, who should govern their country. It is likely they would never reach agreement on the substantive political questions that motivate their disagreement. But each may accept as fair a system which allows every view to be expressed, which allows representatives of every view to stand for office, which gives every person a vote, which allocates seats to representatives of the various positions in proportion to the percentage of votes cast in favour of that position, and so on. Procedures such as these are intended to ensure that all reasonable views are taken equally seriously and that none are preferred by the very structure of the procedures. Of course such practices cannot guarantee outcomes that will suit all the reasonable views. Often there will be no such universally acceptable outcome. There simply is no resolution of the abortion debate which will seem substantively correct to every reasonable disputant. The hope of liberalism, however, is that even those whose substantive preferences do not win the day on this or that occasion will have cause to accept as fair and binding the decisions of these institutions because they accept the procedures by which they were reached.

The institutions and practices to which a procedural understanding of neutrality give rise allow the creation of stable and just communities, despite the presence of a widespread diversity of conflicting and perhaps even incommensurable conceptions of the good. They do so by mediating between this diversity of substantive views and concrete decisions that communities must take. Joseph Raz, speaking of the practice of normally proceeding through the mediation of rules, makes the point when he writes, 'The practice allows the creation of a pluralistic culture. For it enables people to unite in support of some "low- or medium-level" generalisations despite profound disagreements concerning their ultimate foundations, which some seek in religion, others in Marxism or in Liberalism, etc'.[3]

How do procedures or rules mediate in this way? There are a number of aspects to the answer.

First, different and perhaps even incompatible views about how we should live often support common rules 'since different premises may lead to the same

---

2 Ibid., xviii.
3 Joseph Raz, *The Morality of Freedom* (Oxford, 1986) p. 58.

conclusions'.[4] We are familiar with social and political alliances that seem strange at first glance. Feminists and conservatives, for example, find themselves unlikely political bed-fellows in the debate over censorship. Though they hold dramatically different views on the justification of censorship, they (often) agree that pornography ought to be restricted or prohibited. Thus we have procedural consensus without substantive consensus.

Second, even where we do not have a fortuitous convergence of different views on common institutional responses, the procedural approach allows the advocates of diverse views to cooperate without abandoning their own views or embracing the views of others. Suppose we disagree about some option which will affect our future common action and that it has become obvious that each has given the other all the reasons they can imagine for favouring their view over the alternative. Our continued membership in a common community will sometimes require us to find a way of going on, of deciding what to do, despite our disagreement as to what ought to be done. Perhaps we toss a coin and you win. The toss changes the situation in an important way. If our discussion really was exhaustive, you could not give me any more reasons in favour of your view. After the toss, however, you can give me a new reason, namely the fact that the decision procedure we accepted has selected your preference. The normative force of *this* reason, however, does not depend upon me thinking that you were right about the substantive matter. I can accept it as a reason for action while continuing to hold on to my own view of what, from a substantive perspective, ought to have been done.

Of course, we do not settle our political disputes by the toss of a coin. The decision-making procedures which are the focus of the actual accommodations between competing conceptions of the good in our community are enormously complex. Instead of the straightforward coin-tossing procedure, we have a set of procedures which include the procedures for selecting governments, for making and interpreting law, for determining ownership of goods, and so on. As Kurt Baier writes:

> Although there seems to be no consensus on a conception of justice [in Western constitutional democracies], there is a consensus on something else, namely, on the procedures for making and interpreting law and, where that agreement is insufficiently deep to end disagreement, on the selection of persons whose adjudication is accepted as authoritative.[5]

Adherents of the various and diverse conceptions of the good that are represented in our communities cannot be expected to agree on any single conception of the good. They can agree, however, on the form of procedures that will give them,

---

4 John Rawls, 'The Idea of an Overlapping Consensus', *Oxford Journal of Legal Studies*, vol. 7 (1981) pp. 1–25, p. 9.

5 Kurt Baier, 'Justice and the Aims of Political Philosophy', *Ethics*, vol. 99 (1989) pp. 771–700, p. 775.

if not what they want, at least what they need.[6] Although we do not and will not agree on fundamental matters such as what constitutes human flourishing, what basic goals are intrinsically most worthy of pursuit and what is the best way for individuals to live their lives, we can agree on procedures which respect the diversity of views represented in the community, and which issue decisions with which we can live.

This section has addressed the role of law in pluralist communities. It began with the observation that the nature of roles and role-obligations depended upon the nature and function of the institutions of which they were a part. I have suggested that the institutions of law are designed and intended to mediate between the diverse range of views of what ought to be done, and particular decisions about what is to be done. That is the general function which lies behind the more specific tasks performed by the institutions of law; behind decisions about what public goods are to be secured, about which option is to be rendered salient to solve coordination problems, about which sorts of undertakings will receive the protection of law. These and the other specific tasks listed earlier are addressed by the institutions of law in order to allow people who have different views about such matters to live together despite their ongoing substantive disagreements. The role of the institutions of law, this is to say, is to allow there to 'exist over time a stable and just society among free and equal citizens profoundly divided by reasonable though incompatible religious, philosophical and moral doctrine'.[7]

Legal ethics and legal positivism

This account of the function of law is broadly positivist. Law is portrayed as mediating between the diverse range of views of what ought to be done which mark pluralist communities and particular decisions about what is to be done, and as doing so by providing procedural reasons for action which operate independently of the substantive reasons which bear upon the question of action at hand. Hence the account assumes that we can identify law and the reasons for action it provides in a particular case without settling our substantive moral disagreement about what we ought to do in that case; it assumes, that is to say, the separability of law and morality.

I remarked in Chapter 2 that one strand of the critique of the standard conception rested on scepticism as to the plausibility of the positivist account of law. At least some of these attacks are directed at caricatures of positivism, which come close

---

6   We should not be surprised that the theoretical issue here has been put more elegantly by the Glimmer Twins: 'You can't always get what you want. Oh no, you can't always get what you want ... but if you try sometime, well you just might find, you get what you need.' The Rolling Stones, 'You can't always get what you want', *Let it bleed*, (London, cat no. 4, 1969).

7   John Rawls, *Political Liberalism*, xviii.

to the blunt suggestion that positivism recognises no role at all for the moral evaluation of law. We should put aside such caricatures at the outset. Positivists have never doubted the possibility or the importance of inquiry into the morality of laws. Austin's iconic positivist maxim – '[T]he existence of law is one inquiry, whether it be or be not conformable to an assumed standard, is a different inquiry'[8] – insists that inquiries as to 'existence' and 'morality' be kept distinct, not that either should be neglected. Indeed, one influential argument for legal positivism turns precisely upon the idea that moral assessment of law is vital and is hampered by a failure to maintain a clear distinction between determinations of what the law is, and whether it is or is not moral. Failure to maintain the distinction, H.L.A. Hart argued, led to two contrasting errors: that of thinking that if something was law it was necessarily moral and that of thinking that if something was immoral it could not be law.[9] Both errors threaten to 'stifle criticism at its birth'. There are inevitably a number of distinct issues in any difficult discussion about how we should regulate a morally contentious issue. Imagining, on the one hand, that difficult moral issues are settled by settling the institutional status of a norm that bears upon them, is naive: it condemns us to a crude misrepresentation of our disagreement which would ignore much of what was really at issue. On the other hand, whatever the outcome of moral debate focused on the substantive issue – and it is unlikely to be clear-cut – we must also give proper weight to the status as law of any existing or proposed provision, with all of the institutional and practical significance that status carries. There is nothing here about rendering law immune from moral critique. Rather the aim is to make explicit that there are distinct issues to be addressed; that addressing one does not necessarily resolve the others.

Furthermore, positivism leaves open *how* such issues should be addressed. As the sketch of the functional account of law given in the last section suggests, there is nothing in positivism itself which entails that communities must settle on any particular institutional legal arrangement. What is distinctive about the positivist conception of law is not the *content* of the legal systems it endorses, but the place of morality as a reason for action for those subject to law. So for instance, as suggested earlier, there is nothing in positivism to suggest that we are stuck with the statute of limitations that allowed or required Pakel's lawyer to disregard Zabella's interest. There is no conceptual reason not to adopt a statute providing protection only in cases in which it would be inequitable to allow proceeding after a limitation period.

Perhaps the point in the last paragraph will seem to have taken us a long way from the acceptance of the opening point that positivism allows for the moral evaluation of law. It might seem that the requirement to determine whether, given some delay in instituting proceedings, it would be inequitable to allow proceedings to go ahead would require judges, and so the lawyers who put cases to them, to

---

8   John Austin, *The Province of Jurisprudence Determined* (London, 1832) p. 157.
9   H.L.A. Hart 'Positivism and the Separation of Law and Morals', *Harvard Law Review*, vol. 71 (1958) pp. 593–629, p. 597.

engage in moral reasoning in order to settle a claim under such an Act; to mean, that is to say, that we would have to settle a substantive moral disagreement about what we ought to do in order to settle what the law required or allowed us to do. And of course, the statute we are imagining, and so the challenge it poses to positivism, would not be novel or unusual. Many statutes, never mind constitutions and bills of rights, use moral or evaluative terms. New Zealand's Credit Contracts and Consumer Finance Act allows courts to 'reopen' oppressive credit contracts and provides that, for the purposes of the Act, 'oppressive means oppressive, harsh, unjustly burdensome, unconscionable, or in breach of reasonable standards of commercial practice' (s118). The key provision of a part of New Zealand's Companies' Act (s.174) protecting minority shareholders allows 'a shareholder... who considers that the affairs of a company have been...conducted in a manner that is ... oppressive, unfairly discriminatory, or unfairly prejudicial to him ... [to] apply ... for an order ... '. Similar 'morally laden' provisions will be found in every developed legal system. How can positivism accommodate them?

I argued in the previous section that the key function of law in pluralist communities is to provide answers to questions about what we were to do when we were divided over what, morally, we ought to do. Direct appeal to morality was ruled out, the suggestion went, because the members of communities such as ours were divided over what morality required. The suggested equitable statute of limitations, and the other provisions listed in the last paragraph, seem to refer to moral values, values that one might expect to be part of disputed ordinary or background morality. According to positivists, however, such provisions do not direct lawyers and judges to these terms *as* moral terms. Instead they direct them to legal resources, to see what those terms require and how the law has interpreted them. The prejudiced shareholder provisions of the New Zealand Companies Act are an illustration. The statutory remedy against oppression, unfair discrimination and unfair prejudice is relatively new. The Companies Act 1955 (s209) broadened the very limited common law remedies available to minority shareholders, giving a 'remedy against oppression'. It was in turn widened in 1980 by adding unfair discrimination and unfair prejudice. The change might have seemed a clear invitation to judges to engage in general moral deliberation in order to define the new terms, the more so since the United Kingdom report which gave impetus to similar amendments throughout the Commonwealth had explicitly said that the change was intended to give Courts 'power to impose ... whatever settlement the Court considers just and equitable'.[10] In fact, however, the judges who were handed this apparent invitation to appeal directly to ordinary morality did just what most lawyers expect judges to do: they looked for earlier cases which had used similar terms, working by analogy from related provisions to identifying criteria to govern the application of the new provisions, giving and creating a legal interpretation of the moral terms. The judge in the first case to come to the English House of Lords

---

10   Cohen Committee Report of the Committee on Company Law Amendment (1945) (Cmd 6659), para. 60.

under the new provision puts the approach very clearly, and connects it nicely to the role of lawyers while doing so. 'In my view,' wrote Lord Hoffman, 'a balance has to be struck between the breadth of the discretion given to the court and the principle of legal certainty. It is highly desirable that lawyers should be able to advise their clients whether or not a petition [under the new provisions] is likely to succeed.'[11] While noting the idea that it would be 'wholly undesirable' to define in advance of particular cases when an equitable remedy might be available, he immediately goes on to say,

> But that does not mean that there are no principles by which those circumstances may be identified. The way in which such equitable principles operate is tolerably well settled and in my view it would be wrong to abandon them in favour of some wholly indefinite notion of fairness.[12]

The *O'Neill* court went on to clarify the criteria for the application of the new remedy, saying, for instance, that continued majority control of a company in the face of an irreversible breakdown in relationships between shareholders is not on its own unfairly prejudicial to a locked-in minority and that disappointed expectations might ground unfair prejudice, but only if generated by promises or undertakings. The process has continued in subsequent decisions. The details of these criteria are not important for the current discussion. Rather, they are offered as an illustration of the manner in which moral terms become incorporated into law and are available to judges and lawyers under a positivist conception of law. Such considerations, either immediately or very quickly, function as legal rather than moral criteria. Their validity as terms of law, that is to say, turns not upon whether they would feature in some correct moral description of the case to which they are applied, but upon whether they have played a role in the justification of legal decisions: not upon their content, but upon their pedigree. Whether a moral term has a played such a role, and what role it has played, are matters of fact, not evaluation. It requires regard to the history of the legal institutions and practices to which judges and lawyers belong, not directly to moral discourse about fairness, oppression or good faith. It is, as positivists would say, a 'social fact', something that can be identified empirically rather than evaluatively.

I remarked that moral terms that appear in legislation become incorporated into law where they function as legal rather than moral criteria, 'either immediately or very quickly'. It might seem that this is a significant concession to the critic of positivism, who argues that legal judgment and legal advice require direct appeal to ordinary morality. What happens in the first case? Mustn't there be an initial decision in which judges are obliged to refer, not to the decisions of other judges, but instead to their own moral judgment? Practising lawyers – as opposed to philosophers of law – are likely to think that such cases are very rare, and I

---

11   *O'Neill* v *Phillips* [1999] 1 WLR 1092, 1099.
12   Ibid.

think they're right. One not need defend an implausibly formalistic or mechanical view of legal decision making to think that cases in which the deep well of law genuinely leaves judges with no recourse but their own moral assessment are very rare indeed. Typically there will be resources within a judge or lawyer's own jurisdiction, bearing in mind, as we see in the prejudiced shareholders cases, that they are not restricted to decisions using precisely the same terms in precisely the same cases, instead encompassing in addition analogous provisions and decisions.[13] And in the rare cases in which that search draws a blank, they look for persuasive guidance in analogous lines of reasoning in comparable jurisdictions. Just where they look, and what authority the decisions they find may have, is determined by the conventions of their jurisdiction. The upshot is that the 'artificial reason of law' has recourse to a vast body of material, interrogated by judges and lawyers asking whether the terms they are called upon to apply have, as a matter of fact, played a role in the justification of legal decisions.

And what of the now very rare cases in which all of this comes to nought, in which the case before the judge or lawyer is so unusual that there are no 'social facts' to be found among the vast body of law? Here, at the edge or penumbra of law, where there is simply no pre-existing law on the question at hand, it behoves the positivist to concede that judges are occasionally forced to act as legislators – forced, in Hart's terms, to exercise genuine discretion.[14] In these rare cases the judge does not identify pre-existing law, but fills a gap where none existed. The judge can only admit that they act 'beyond the law' and make the best moral decision they can. If such cases were common they would pose a serious challenge

---

13   Judicial attempts to develop property principles for the new resource 'petroleum' in the late 1900s provide an engaging illustration and give a sense of the breadth of resources analogical reasoning opens up to judges and lawyers. Judges in early petroleum cases looked to decisions concerning property claims to wild animals: *ferae naturae*. In *Westmoreland & Cambria Natural Gas Company* v *DeWitt*, 130 Pa.235, 18 A.724, 725, 5 L.R.A. 73 (1889), the Supreme Court of Pennsylvania remarked that: 'Water and oil, and more strongly gas, may be classed by themselves, if the analogy not be too fanciful, as minerals *ferae naturae*. In common with animals, and unlike other minerals, they have the power and tendency to escape without the volition of the owner. Their "fugitive and wandering existence within the limits of a particular tract was uncertain". Possession of the land, therefore, is not necessarily possession of the gas. If an adjoining, or even a distant, owner, drills his own land, and taps your gas, so that it comes into his well and under his control, it is no longer yours, but his.' The Westmoreland judge found that the ownership of petroleum depended on a 'rule of capture', citing a famous New York case *Pierson* v *Post* [1805] 3 Cal. R. 175, 2 Am Dec. 264 in which Pierson beat Post to a fox Post was chasing. Post claimed his pursuit entitled him to the fox but the court disagreed, finding that it was necessary to render the wild animal into one's possession or control in order to acquire rights in it. Similarly the Westmoreland court suggested that petroleum must be rendered into one's possession to acquire rights in it; it was not enough to show that it lay under one's property. Of course one might think that the analogy is 'too fanciful'.

14   Hart, *The Concept of Law*, pp. 254, 272–73.

to the positivist conception of legal reasoning. But they are rare, and, while they provide an authoritative ruling on the case at hand, the law they establish is open to review after more leisurely legislative consideration. And even without legislative intervention, from the point of the first ruling, normal transmission resumes: subsequent judges must appeal to the social fact of the legislating judge's decision, not to the soundness of their moral reasoning.[15] The first judge's ruling incorporates the moral term into law from which point it begins to function as a legal not a moral term.

We could almost stop here. As noted in Chapter 2, however, contemporary positivism is divided over just what is going on in cases of the sort I have sketched, and more particularly, is divided over just what role morality can legitimately play in such cases, and it will be useful to locate the preceding discussion within this debate. Since Hart's 1961 classic, *The Concept of Law*, positivists have tended to accept some version of the idea that legal systems rest upon a fundamental 'rule of recognition': a rule specifying the criteria of validity in a legal system and used by legal officials to determine which norms are norms of that system, rather than, say, norms of morality or norms of some other legal system. Importantly, for positivists, the rule of recognition of a particular jurisdiction is constituted by the actual practice of officials in deciding disputes about the validity of particular rules: we identify the rule of recognition of a jurisdiction by asking the empirical or factual question: 'What do the officials of that jurisdiction do when identifying law?' We can imagine two subsidiary questions. Having asked the core question, we might go on to ask: 'Do they appeal merely to the pedigree of a putative legal norm? Or do they also consider its substantive merits?' The divide within legal positivism is over what counts as an acceptable 'positivist' answer to the second question. It might seem that answering yes to that question in respect of some legal system would show that that system was not positivist, since its legal officials would consider the substantive merits of a norm in order to determine its legal validity. According to *inclusive* legal positivism, however, the only constraint on the content of a jurisdiction's rule of recognition is that it must rest on facts about the practice of officials. If it is true that the officials of a legal system consider the substantive merits of a norm in determining its legal validity, the rule of recognition for that jurisdiction will include substantive moral criteria.[16]

---

15   We should note throughout this discussion that there may be a significant difference between what lawyers and judges *do* and what they *say* they do. As Brian Leiter writes, '[P]ositivists must insist that we not be misled by judicial rhetoric...: non-pedigreed principles are not legally binding, but it is all too obvious why they should want to write their opinions *as if* they were.' Brian Leiter, 'Beyond the Hart/Dworkin Debate: The Methodological Problem in Jurisprudence', *American Journal of Jurisprudence*, vol. 48 (2003) pp. 17–51, p. 27.

16   See for instance W.J. Waluchow, *Inclusive Legal Positivism* p. 395: 'According to modern versions of Inclusive Positivism it is the accepted rule of recognition that determines which, if any, moral considerations figure in determinations of law. So *whether* morality

The model remains positivist, according to inclusive positivism, since the criteria identified by the rule of recognition have the status they do not because of their moral content – not because they promote human flourishing, or promote substantive conceptions of fairness, or what have you – but because, as a matter of fact, they are the criteria the officials of the jurisdiction employ to determine legal status. They can be identified, then, by purely empirical inquiry. Once incorporated via such a practice, however, the moral terms operate *as* moral terms: they allow, perhaps require, judges applying them to engage in 'regular' moral reasoning, looking to the content and not merely to the pedigree of the moral terms incorporated into law by the relevant inclusivist rule of recognition.[17]

According to *exclusive* legal positivism, by contrast, the concept of law precludes rules of recognition that allow reference to moral criteria in the determination of law. Instead, exclusive positivists argue, the criteria of validity specified by a rule of recognition must consist solely in facts about the sources or pedigrees of the putative legal norms. Exclusive positivism, this is to say, it demands a 'no' answer to the second subsidiary question. Joseph Raz has developed the most powerful argument for this claim,[18] and it is a version of the functional account of law offered in the previous section. Our concept of law, Raz argues, entails that it must be capable of making a coherent claim to authority. We can readily make sense of a legal system making such a claim unsuccessfully – perhaps because potential subjects took no notice – but we would not recognise as a potential legal system something that could not even potentially issue authoritative directives. What is required for a directive to be potentially authoritative? Among other things, according to Raz, it must be possible to identify the directive – to know what it is and what it requires – without recourse to the disputed considerations upon which it purports to adjudicate. Suppose, for instance, that we disagree about what period of delay would make it inequitable to commence proceedings. A statute of limitations that said simply that proceedings were barred if there had been an inequitable delay would be of no help. We are likely to be looking to the law precisely because we do not agree upon what would amount to such a delay. Hence such a statute would not be potentially authoritative. The statute itself could not settle our dispute. It would go unsettled, or would have to be settled by something else – perhaps some substantive moral view about inequitable delay or perhaps the judge's own view – and it would be that something else which was authoritative,

---

counts as in determinations of law is not itself a matter of morality. Rather it depends on which criteria of validity exist as a matter of accepted social practice within a legal system's rule of recognition. But there is nothing to prevent these criteria being moral in nature.'

17 Inclusive legal positivists keep faith with the core positivist notion that law and morality are conceptually distinct, since the possibility that morality is a criterion of legal validity in some jurisdictions is just that, a possibility; a contingent fact about the official practice in those jurisdictions. It could have been otherwise.

18 See especially Joseph Raz, 'Authority, Law, and Morality', *Monist*, vol. 68 (1985) pp. 295–324.

not the statute. According to Raz, this is precisely the implication of theories of law that require (for example, broadly natural law theories) or allow (for example, inclusive positivism) recourse to substantive moral criteria: such theories portray law as requiring resort to the very considerations the law is supposed to have authoritatively settled and hence do not capture the authority of law.[19]

We see the two versions of positivism in H.L.A. Hart's response to Ronald Dworkin. Hart argues that legal positivism can accommodate legally valid principles, such as the 'no person shall profit from their own wrong' principle that Dworkin argues determined the outcome of *Riggs* v *Palmer*. Hart makes two claims: first, that contrary to Dworkin some principles are valid in virtue of their pedigree. So, for instance, the *Riggs* v *Palmer* principle might be legally valid in a system by virtue of having featured in the justification of legal decisions in that system over a long period. Its validity here would depend upon its history, not upon the moral soundness of its content. And second, that there was nothing in the positivist notion of a rule of recognition to rule out content-based tests of legal validity, tests such as 'this rule is legally valid by virtue of being a requirement of fairness', which might allow recourse to principles which lacked pedigree. The first claim is consistent with exclusive positivism: it allows recourse to moral terms that have been incorporated into a legal system, but only by virtue of their pedigree, and it does not carry a commitment to the view that someone employing those terms would be allowed or required to engage in substantive moral reasoning. Judges and lawyers wielding the *Riggs* v *Palmer* principle, on this account, are likely to find a set of pedigreed criteria or tests for its application that do not require substantive moral evaluation. The second claim (and Hart endorsed both) is inconsistent with exclusive positivism: while the rule would only be available to judges and lawyers by virtue of having the appropriate pedigree, applying the rule would require substantive moral evaluation, working out what fairness was and what it required, as opposed to identifying a set of content independent application criteria.

How does this bear upon our discussion of the function of law and the standard conception of the lawyer's role? The functional account of the role of law offered above is broadly sympathetic to Raz's argument from authority, portraying law as mediating between the diverse range of views of what ought to be done which mark pluralist communities and particular decisions about what is to be done, and as doing so by providing procedural reasons for action which operate independently of the substantive reasons which bear upon the question of action

---

19 Hence Raz responds to Dworkin's view that the right answer to a legal question is that which coheres best with the institutional history of that jurisdiction (its statutes, decisions, and such) and provides the best moral justification of it, writing that '[m]y disagreement with Dworkin ... is that ... he makes the identification of a tax law, e.g., depend upon settling what a morally just tax law would be, i.e., on the very consideration which a tax law is supposed to have authoritatively settled' (Raz, 'Authority, Law and Morality', p. 310).

at hand. I have argued that we should prefer a conception of the lawyer's role that maintains a distinction between the reasons provided by law, and those provided by ordinary morality, because the point of law is to help us live together despite our ongoing moral disagreement: we do not agree on the moral criteria which might serve as criteria for the determination of law in content-dependent theories of law. The law allows us to live together despite our inability to do so. Hence, although we will not take the jurisprudential debate very far in this discussion, I am inclined to side with exclusive positivism. My suggestion is that the brief account of legal reasoning given above is more consistent with exclusive than with inclusive positivism. On that account, moral terms that appear in law do not direct judges to the resources of ordinary morality: they do not direct lawyers and judges to these terms as moral terms. Instead they direct them to legal resources, to see what those terms require and how the law has interpreted them, where that inquiry is an empirical inquiry into the legal pedigree rather than a moral inquiry into the content of those terms.

In a rare consideration of the significance of the debate between inclusive and exclusive positivism for legal ethics, Brad Wendel has come to the opposite conclusion about which of the two versions of positivism best explains legal practice, and hence best underpins an account of the ethical obligations of lawyers.[20] A short account of Wendel's argument and why I think it mistaken will help draw out some of the issues between inclusive and exclusive positivism and the significance of the debate for the model of legal ethics I defend. Wendel begins with a standard account of inclusive positivism, according to which it holds that 'moral principles may feature in a legal system in the sense that they are identified as part of law by the rule of recognition, as long as there is a conventional practice among officials of making decisions with reference to moral criteria'. Later he gives an example of 'inclusive positivism in action'; the rule from the regulation of police investigations, that a search may be unreasonable if the procedure 'shocks the conscience'.[21]

> A judge today who was asked to rule on whether a police practice 'shocked the conscience' would not be undertaking a freestanding moral evaluation, using only their capacity as a deliberating moral agent. Rather, the judge would refer to numerous decisions interpreting the 'shocks the conscience' test, which could probably be distilled into a series of principles or criteria that have the status of law, since they are conventionally referred to in the justification of legal decisions.[22]

---

20 W. Bradley Wendel, 'Legal Ethics and the Separation of Law and Morals', *Cornell Law Review*, vol. 91 (2005–2006) pp. 67–128.
21 A rule derived from *Rochin* v *California*, 342 U.S. 165 (1952): see Wendel, 'Legal Ethics and the Separation of Law and Morals', p. 104.
22 Wendel, 'Legal Ethics and the Separation of Law and Morals', pp. 104–105.

So far this sounds very similar to the account of inclusive positivism and the process of legal reasoning offered above. It is clear that there is an underlying disagreement between us, however, since Wendel offers the passage as an example of inclusive positivism in action, whereas I have suggested that a very similar example is more consistent with exclusive than inclusive positivism. The difference between us between us becomes clearer when Wendel suggests that the process of reasoning he sees in such cases is consistent with a hypothetical rule specifying the lawyer's role in counselling clients, according to which 'in rendering advice, a lawyer may refer to considerations such as moral, economic, social and political factors, *but only to the extent they are relevant to interpreting the law*'. This rule, he writes:

> is ... a concession to inclusive positivism. It permits a lawyer to provide advice which makes reference to moral considerations, *as long as those factors are relevant to the interpretation of law, and are not simply extralegal moral reasons that the lawyer thinks important*. [The rule] prohibits the lawyer only from offering 'freestanding' advice – that is, giving advice on moral, economic, social and political factors that do not bear on the application of legal rules to the client's situation. (My emphasis).[23]

But there seems to be a significant shift here. While Wendel emphasises that, according to the inclusive positivism, a judge is not licensed to engage in 'freestanding moral evaluation, using only her capacity as a deliberating moral agent', but would (and should) instead 'refer to numerous decisions ... which could probably be distilled into a series of principles or criteria that have the status of law, since they are conventionally referred to in the justification of legal decisions', it is not clear how his hypothetical rule imposes any such restriction. A rule which restricts judges and lawyers to 'moral, economic, social and political factors, but only to the extent they are relevant to interpreting the law', seems to leave a very large latitude for direct recourse to morality, even allowing the extra limitation posed by the rider that such factors may not 'simply [be] extralegal moral reasons that the lawyer thinks important'. Restricting judges and lawyers to considerations such as moral, economic, social and political factors, provided only that 'they are relevant to interpreting the law', seems to grant a much broader licence than that which would be generated by restricting them to those moral terms which have been rendered into legal terms through the sort of process in which clear and authoritative criteria for the application of the terms are specified by courts and legislatures.

The upshot is that I think Wendel's hypothetical rule is close to the spirit of inclusive positivism: it does license appeal to moral terms which have been incorporated into law, in the sense that they have been granted entry into law by an appropriate rule of recognition, and where, on Wendel's account, they function *as*

---

23 Ibid., p. 104.

moral terms, allowing substantive moral engagement. However, I am not convinced that his example of legal reasoning – the shocks the conscience case – requires or implies such a rule, and hence I am not convinced that the example supports inclusive positivism.[24] The example is informative, I think, but the reasoning of lawyers and judges in such cases can be captured, I think better captured, in an account according to which they are directed to content-independent application criteria for the ostensibly moral terms in which they couch their decisions and advice.

I began this section by remarking that the account of the function of law in the previous section was broadly positivist. We can now be a bit more specific and say that it is broadly in the tradition of 'exclusive legal positivism'. I noted in Chapter 2 that one strand of the critique of the standard conception of the lawyer's role rested on scepticism as to the plausibility of positivist accounts of law. As a strand of the critique of the standard conception, that scepticism is part of the general attempt to question the distinction that the conception seeks to draw between professional and ordinary morality, just as critiques of positivism, and especially exclusive positivism, question the distinction those theories seek to draw between law and morality. I do not imagine I will have advanced the jurisprudential debate between and within the major theories of law in this brief discussion. I do hope, however, to have given some reason to believe that positivism need not deny judges and lawyers access to moral resources, albeit to moral resources as they are incorporated into law in the guise of content-independent application criteria for the ostensibly moral terms which occur throughout law. Such an account, I think, comfortably describes legal practice, and better preserves the function of law as a device that mediates between inconsistent views of the good.

---

24 Wendel gives another example. His discussion occurs in a nuanced consideration of the ethical position of lawyers who counselled that torture was lawful. In that context Wendel considers the defence of necessity, roughly a defence which applies when an actor chooses to preserve a higher valued good at the expense of a lesser valued good, and argues that the defence reinforces the implausibility of exclusive positivism since it is 'impossible to talk intelligibly about a choice of evils without having some conception of the social values of various goods, and in order to make this determination, a legal official (as well as a citizen subject to the law) must reach out beyond the law, as it were, into the domain of ordinary morality' (Wendel, 'Legal Ethics and the Separation of Law and Morality', p. 103). Necessity, however, is a peculiar defence, arguably available when it is, for one reason or another, unreasonable to enforce the normal expectations of respect for law: it is asking too much of regular folk to expect punctilious respect for law when they have been adrift in an open boat for three weeks. But if that is a plausible account of necessity, then it is a poor example to motivate a discussion of the boundaries between legal and non-legal reasons for action, since necessity cases are precisely those in which extraordinary circumstances have eroded that boundary.

The role of law and the lawyer's role

I have claimed that one important strand in the justification of role and role-obligations relied upon the function of the institutions of which they were a part, and argued that the fundamental function of law in Western democracies is to mediate between reasonable but inconsistent views of what we should do as a community. I now return to the standard conception, aiming to draw the appropriate conclusions about the roles and role-obligations of lawyers from this account of the function of law, attempting to show how the principles that make up the standard conception – or modified versions of them – can be derived from this account of the role of law.

The principle of neutrality

Some of these derivations are obvious. Recall the principle of neutrality. It says that the lawyer must not allow their own view of the moral merits of the client's objectives or character to affect the diligence or zealousness with which they pursue the client's lawful objectives. The principle is explained by appeal to the fact of reasonable pluralism. Given the fact of reasonable pluralism we do not order our communities by direct appeal to any particular view of the good. Instead, we seek the support and cooperation of the advocates of a diverse range of views by undertaking, in effect, to appeal to the determinations of decision procedures structured to take all reasonable views seriously. Lawyers who calibrate their professional efforts according to their own view of the good – or indeed according to any particular view of the good – not only 'privilege' the view they favour and disenfranchise the view of the client, they undercut the strategy by which we secure community between people profoundly divided by reasonable but incompatible views of the good. Where legal rights are established by the procedure, decisions about what is to be done are to be settled by appeal to those rights, not by appeal to particular views of the good, still less any particular individual's views of the good.

In short the principle of neutrality recognises that it is not up to lawyers to determine what we will do as a community, what rights we will allocate and to whom. The complexity of the procedures upon which a pluralist community such as ours must rely means that lawyers do have tremendous power in this regard. Because of their legal expertise, they are better placed than any other group of citizens to work in and with our legal and political institutions. The principle of neutrality recognises this power and its potential for abuse. As remarked when we first encountered the principle, it guards against the possibility that someone might be denied rights allocated by a legal system because its lawyers find those rights or their allocation to that person morally objectionable. Since legal representation is at least sometimes necessary to secure legal rights, the lawyer or the community of lawyers could render the person's claim to their lawful rights worthless by refusing to represent them at all, or by making a less than zealous effort on behalf of an existing client. Given the function of law in pluralist communities, the principle of neutrality states an important and deeply moral obligation. It is a central part of an adequate legal ethics in such communities.

The principle of non-accountability

Similarly, the appeal to pluralism explains the principle of non-accountability, the principle according to which lawyers are not to be judged by the moral status of their client's projects, even though the lawyer's assistance was necessary to the pursuit of those projects. If we recognise that there are many plausible views about what interests should receive legal protection, we have reason to leave decisions about which ones are to be protected to procedures that recognise the fact of reasonable pluralism and that constrain the influence of individuals who happen to find themselves positioned to act as gatekeepers to the realm of legal rights. If these procedures do serve this mediating role then we cannot assume that lawyers identify or sympathise with particular rights or with their allocation to particular clients. Lawyers might have strong moral objections to a particular client's projects, but accept the importance of appealing to the procedurally allocated rights rather than to their own moral preferences. Furthermore, the appeal to pluralism gives us reason to hope that lawyers will not allocate their expertise in ways that will function as a de facto barrier to unpopular but protected views of the good. The principle of non-accountability removes one reason lawyers may have for refusing to act for clients whose moral views and legal goals do not accord with their own. In this guise, the rule is a defence for those who do take on unpopular cases. They may plead the rule in response to the mistaken assumption that they would not have taken on the case if they did not endorse the goals of the client. Thus the rule removes a barrier to such clients obtaining representation necessary to avail themselves of legal rights.[25]

The principle of partisanship

The derivation of the principle of partisanship, the remaining strand of the standard conception, may seem less obvious. How does the appeal to pluralism generate a duty to pursue the client's interests aggressively and single-mindedly all the way up to the limits of the law? Once again we can use David Luban as a focus for our discussion. He argues that the principle of partisanship cannot be justified by '[t]he argument...that the best way to guarantee that an individual's legal rights are protected...is to provide her with a zealous advocate who will further her interests'.[26] For current purposes, we can treat the rights-argument referred to in this passage as equivalent to the appeal to pluralism. Luban's claim, then, is that we cannot derive the principle of partisanship from the sort of arguments advanced in this chapter.

---

25 *Rondel* v *Worsley* [1969] 1 AC 191.
26 Luban, *Lawyers and Justice*, p. 74.

But I think that his conclusion is based upon a common mischaracterisation of the principle of partisanship that treats it as requiring lawyers to be more zealous than in fact it does require them to be. I think Luban is right when he says that the more zealous version of the principle cannot be derived from the sorts of arguments advanced in this chapter. But once the principle of partisanship is characterised in a more moderate form its derivation from the appeal to pluralism is reasonably straightforward.

Mere-zeal and hyper-zeal   What are these more and less moderate understandings of the principle of partisanship? According to one interpretation, the principle calls upon lawyers to exercise what I earlier called 'mere-zeal'. Merely-zealous lawyers are concerned solely with their clients' legal interests. They pursue those interests, 'without fear ... and without regard to any unpleasant consequences to [themselves] or to any other person'. On this account, the interests various codes require lawyers to 'fearlessly uphold ... without regard for personal interests or concerns'[27] are those interests protected by law, not simply anything which happens to be in the client's interests, let alone anything in which the client happens to be interested. It is often in our interest to have more than we are entitled to under law, and no doubt we are often interested in having more than our bare legal entitlement. But this is of no moment to the merely-zealous lawyer. Their professional obligation is to pursue the client's legal rights zealously. They are to be partisan in the sense that they must bring all of their professional skills to bear upon the task of securing their client's rights. But they are under no obligation to pursue interests that go beyond the law.

According to the alternative understanding, the principle of partisanship commits lawyers to what I called hyper-zeal, where the hyper-zealous lawyer is concerned not merely to secure their client's legal rights, but to pursue any advantage obtainable for their client through the law. 'My legal rights,' says Luban, 'are everything I am in fact legally entitled to, not everything the law can be made to give', but 'good' lawyers can almost always get me more than that to which I am legally entitled:

> Every lawyer knows tricks of the trade that can be used to do opponents out of their legal deserts – using delaying tactics for example, to make it too costly for an opponent without much money to prosecute a lengthy suit even though the law is on their side, or filing a nuisance claim carefully calculated to be cheaper to settle than defend.[28]

According to Luban and the tradition he draws from, the principle of partisanship *requires* lawyers to use these tricks to get their clients all that the law can be made

---

27   *International Code of Ethics,* adopted Oslo July 1956, amended Mexico, 1964, Clause 6.6.

28   Luban, *Lawyers and Justice,* p. 75.

to give. The standard conception, he implies, calls upon lawyers to secure the goals of mere-zeal, the defence of client's rights, by adopting the tactics of hyper-zeal: 'The no-holds-barred zealous advocate,' he writes, 'tries to get everything the law can give..., and thereby does a better job of defending the client's legal rights than a less committed lawyer would do.' But I think this is a mistake. I hope in the next few pages to show that the principle of partisanship requires lawyers both to be merely-zealous, and not to be hyper-zealous.

The derivation of mere-zeal   I begin with the derivation of mere-zeal. The duty of mere-zeal seems to flow from the appeal to pluralism in fairly straightforward fashion. Those arguments postulate a set of procedures which mediate between the diversity of views of the good and decisions about what is to be done. Individuals often require lawyers if they are to obtain the benefit of the procedures around which their communities are formed. They require lawyers to take advantage of the mechanisms which will allow them to have their property distributed a certain way after their death, to secure money over their property, to advance a defence when they are charged with an offence, and so on. The lawyers in these cases act on behalf of their clients. In effect, they do for the client things that the client would do for themselves if the legal system were not so complicated. If clients wish to avail themselves of the rights allocated to them under the legal system, their lawyers, insofar as they act on the client's behalf, must assist them to do so. That is what it is to act on the client's behalf with respect to the legal system.

Sometimes, of course, we feel uneasy about people who stand on their rights. Even if Pakel did have a legal right to avail himself of the statute of limitations, his decision to do so on the facts of the case show him to have been callous and nasty. But the appeal to pluralism shows that decisions about what is for the public good, about what sort of tax system we should have, about how long somebody can wait to seek a remedy in contract, about whether *this* defendant has *this* right, and so on, are things to be decided, not in private in the offices of particular lawyers, but in the public arena of politics where everyone can have a say, or in the public domain of the courts where reasons must be given and opportunities exist for challenge and representation. The arguments show that it is not up to individual lawyers to decide what interests will receive legal protection, what legal rights will be allocated to whom. That is the function of the procedures which make communities such as ours possible. Lawyers who fail to exercise mere-zeal, who take it upon themselves not to pursue legal entitlements available to their clients when their clients wish them to do so, privilege whatever moral view they are following in preference to that of their client and undercut the procedures which allow the advocates of a plurality of views to live together in communities.

Furthermore, though we often admire people who sacrifice their own interests for the benefit of others, the moral quality of these sacrifices depends crucially upon it being the rights-holder who makes the sacrifice. It hard to imagine the circumstances in which I act well by sacrificing some entitlement of yours, though there are many circumstances in which we think well of you for doing so. What is a virtuous act done by one person, is a vice done by another. R.E. Ewin puts this point this way:

> The client can, through the lawyer who is handling the negotiations, be generous, but for the lawyer to take it upon herself to act in that way without instructions from the client is for the lawyer to be 'generous' with what is someone else's, which is not to be generous at all. .. It is not simply that the lawyer *may* not be generous in that case; the lawyer *cannot* be generous.[29]

Lawyers who attempt to be generous by sacrificing their clients' rights – whether by not merely-zealously pursuing those rights or perhaps by simply not advising the client that the rights are available – display not the virtue of generosity, but instead a vice, 'something like arrogance':

> ... being so completely sure of the rightness of one's own views and the irrelevance of anybody else's, even the views of the person whose rights are at issue, that one simply forces one's views on the client.[30]

The problem of hyper-zeal We turn then to the problem of hyper-zeal. Luban suggests that the principle of partisanship commits lawyers to hyper-zealous advocacy, to pursuing not merely the client's legal rights, but all that the law can be made to give. And, of course, his is not an idiosyncratic view. Brougham's classic characterisation of the advocate as bound to pursue the client's interests 'at all hazards and costs to other persons', without 'regard [to] the alarm, the torments, the destruction which he may bring others', even to the extent that 'it should be his unhappy fate to involve his country in confusion'[31] surely takes us beyond mere-zeal and into the realm of hyper-zeal. In questioning Luban's linking of the standard conception and the principle of partisanship with the duty of hyper-zeal, then, we question a reading of the principle of partisanship which dates back at least to Brougham. Notwithstanding its pedigree, however, I do not think the attempt to pin a duty of hyper-zeal on the standard conception is warranted. Indeed, the appeal to pluralism allows us to see why lawyers do not have a duty of hyper-zealous advocacy.

Much of this chapter has been based upon the idea that the role of the lawyer is to allow clients to avail themselves of rights allocated to them by social institutions. If this is an accurate account of the role of the lawyer, it seems to follow directly that it is not their function to allow clients to satisfy interests beyond those allocated by law. Sometimes, of course, clients may wish to do so, and nothing thus far

---

29 R.E. Ewin, 'Personal Morality and Professional Ethics: The Lawyers Duty of Zeal', *International Journal of Applied Philosophy*, vol. 6 (1991) pp. 35–45, p. 39.
30 Ibid.
31 Nightingale, 1820–1821, p. 8.

entails that it is the function of the lawyers to prevent them.[32] But if we understand the lawyer as occupying a role in an institution, then we seem able to say at least that the demands that can be made on them must be demands to the 'resources' of the institutions of which they are a part. Lawyers occupy roles in an institution designed to allow pluralist communities by specifying what rights members of the community shall have. The role-obligations are framed by reference to the point of that institution. Hence lawyers have no special responsibilities to allow their clients to avail themselves of resources or benefits which lie outside the law. The lawyer's responsibility is to further the interests of the client, insofar as the institutional rights and duties of the client allow. The institutional framing of the lawyer's responsibilities means that the lawyer is not required to do just anything that would further the client's interests.

Some cases are simple. It may be that my interests would be served if the witness who saw me rob the bank was bumped-off, but it does not follow that my lawyer is thereby placed under a duty to bump-off the witness. And notice that this is true not just because it is illegal to bump-off witnesses. The lawyer has all the moral and legal reasons everyone has for refusing to advance my interest by bumping-off the witness, and a reason that only lawyers have: The lawyer can point to their role in an institution intended to ensure access to the rights allocated by law. I cannot require my lawyer to satisfy my interest in having the witness bumped-off, since that is not one of those rights. This is simply to say that the institutional rights of law structure the lawyer's responsibility. In their capacity as lawyer, they can and should respond to my request for help with these 'extra-legal' interests by pointing out that that is not their job. Their job is to act on the client's behalf, relative to the institutions of law.

Other cases seem more difficult. We saw some of Luban's examples earlier. Every lawyer, he said, knows tricks of the trade that can be used to do opponents out of their legal deserts, '…using delaying tactics for example, to make it too costly for an opponent without much money to prosecute a lengthy suit even though the law is on her side, or filing a nuisance claim carefully calculated to be cheaper to settle than defend.'[33] And he adds some others:

> The rules of discovery, initiated to enable one side to find out crucial facts from the other, are used nowadays to delay trial or to impose added expenses on the other side; conversely, one might respond to an interrogatory by delivering to the discoverer tons of miscellaneous documents to run up their legal bills or to conceal a needle in a haystack. Similarly, rules barring lawyers from representations

---

32 Saying that 'it is not the function of the lawyer to allow clients to satisfy interests beyond those allocated by law' is not the same as saying 'it is the function of lawyers not to allow clients to satisfy interests beyond those allocated by law'. The positioning of the negation is important.

33 Luban, *Lawyers and Justice*, p. 75.

involving conflicts of interest are now regularly used by adversaries to drive up the other side's costs by having the counsel disqualified.[34]

Luban complains that the principle of partisanship requires lawyers to use such tricks if they can advance their client's interests by doing so. These cases may seem more difficult than that involving the inconvenient witness, since the lawyers involved in them could be acting perfectly legally. And of course, it may be true that responding to the other side's interrogatory with tons of miscellaneous documents is the best way of serving the client's interests: Perhaps the client has a hopeless case. Still, though these cases are more difficult, the rights-argument gives us a response. As Luban describes some of these cases, the lawyer 'indulges in overkill to obtain as legal rights benefits that in fact may not be legal rights'.[35] Under this description, the rights-argument provides the lawyer with a response similar to that they gave when I wanted them to bump-off the inconvenient witness. The institutional rights of law structure their responsibility. Their job is to act on the client's behalf, *relative* to the institutions of law. It is not their job to pursue interests that are not protected by law.

We may also be able to develop this response a little by noting that an aspect of the role of helping clients to avail themselves of their legal rights is helping them ascertain what those rights are. And now we can respond that simply preventing a case coming before the decision procedures of our community, by abusing of the rules of discovery or conflict of interest, is not helping ascertain what rights a client may demand, even if it does further their interests. It is not doing the lawyer's job. It is preventing the job from being done. I have suggested that it is the role of lawyers to assist individuals to avail themselves of the rights allocated to them by their communities. This role does not generate obligations or permissions to avoid determinations of rights claims. Lawyers who abuse processes of discovery, for instance, to prevent a case coming to court, quite simply do not perform that role. An understanding of the duty of zealous advocacy that portrays lawyers as being allowed or obliged to use every lawful tactic to prevent the legal system addressing a case is simply mistaken. Note why it is mistaken. It goes wrong because it fails to see how the duties of lawyers are derived from a proper understanding of their roles. I am quite happy to concede that this may be a revision of the standard and well-pedigreed understanding of the standard conception. If it is, then so be it: it is one which gives a proper place to the moral considerations which inform the lawyer's role, while holding on to the idea that such roles are subject to role-differentiated obligations.

The upshot is that Luban is right when he says that the rights-argument does not support excesses of professional zeal. But since these *are* excesses, their failure to find support in the rights-argument is a mark in that argument's favour. By the same token, the fact that the more moderate version of the principle of partisanship can

---

34 Ibid., p. 51.
35 Ibid., p. 77.

be derived from the rights-argument is a reason to suppose both that the principle, in this form, expresses a genuine obligation on lawyers in pluralist communities, and that the standard conception has long been misunderstood as requiring more than acceptable zeal from lawyers.

Mere-zeal, hyper-zeal and abuse of process The discussion in the last few sections has relied upon two ideas: That not every lawful advantage that can be obtained through the law is a legal entitlement, and that the duty of zealous advocacy requires lawyers to pursue only their client's legal entitlements. The duty of zealous advocacy, this is to say, is a duty of mere- rather than hyper-zeal. I have argued for the distinction between legal entitlements and other advantages available through the law by appeal to the function of law: lawyers are not required to pursue every advantage available to clients through the law, the argument goes, because their professional roles are structured by the function of the institution to which those roles belong, and the function of that institution is to determine and protect legal entitlements, not to secure every possible lawful advantage. So much, I have argued, is consistent with a proper understanding of the standard conception of the lawyer's role.

There is an obvious objection to this model: how are we to know what counts as mere-zeal and what counts as hyper-zeal? I hope to have said something in response to this legitimate concern – lawyers should reflect upon the point of law and of their role – but of course I appreciate that that leaves a good deal unsaid. I am not very optimistic about the prospects of anyone developing what would in effect be a theory of interpretation that would provide a knock-down answer. The line between mere-zeal and hyper-zeal will no doubt be unclear in some cases (though as always in such cases we should not suppose the absence of clear lines between concepts renders those concepts unusable). Notoriously there are no clear lines between baldness and hirsuteness, but, most of the time, we wield the two concepts without difficulty.[36] Given the likely difficulties facing any attempt to provide a satisfactory answer to the interpretative question, however, I want to try another approach.

It seems to me that there are important parallels between the distinction between mere- and hyper-zeal on the one hand, and, the jurisdiction to prevent abuse of process on the other, such that the latter jurisdiction shows us both that lawyers and

---

36 We can distinguish between someone who is bald and someone who is not. Suppose I'm not. Each day from now on I pluck out one hair. Eventually I will be bald. But what particular hair made the difference? For any hair nominated, surely one less wouldn't matter. But if that's true, then why wasn't I bald before I plucked out the hair before that? There's always only one hair's difference between me from day to day. But now I must be bald now (or hirsute at the end of the process) since there's only one hair's difference between me now and me tomorrow and so on. Paradoxically, we believe both a) that the states of affairs at either end of the process are clear, and b) that there's no clear distinction between them. This is paradoxical, but still, a) is true.

judges can maintain the distinction between mere- and hyper-zeal and something about its content. Bluntly, I think the abuse of process jurisdiction goes a long way to answering the interpretative question about the mere-zeal hyper-zeal distinction by showing that lawyers already draw a substantially similar distinction. There are no bright lines between abusive and non-abusive use of process either, of course, but lawyers and judges maintain the jurisdiction by doing those things lawyers and judges do: putting arguments, consulting precedents and statutes, drawing out implications of the point of particular bodies of law, and so on. If this is right, and if I am right about the parallels between the jurisdiction and distinction between mere- and hyper-zeal, we have an 'ostensive' argument for the distinction we want: we can point at the abuse of process jurisdiction and say 'like that'.

The most obvious reason for thinking that the doctrine of abuse of process might be helpful in this context is the similarities between judicial formulations of the doctrine and its significance, and the argument advanced above which appealed to the function of law. Bluntly, the courts have given a *functional* account of abuse of process. An abuse in this context consists in 'a party using court proceedings and procedures for a purpose unrelated to the objectives which the court process is designed to achieve'.[37] 'The focus in such a suit is on the purpose for which the proceedings exist.'[38] We might equally say that the focus is on the *function* of the procedures. So in *Grainger* v *Hill*,[39] the case that is the source of the tort of abuse of process, a writ of arrest was issued under a mortgage of a ship. The plaintiff's intention was not in fact to avail himself of his rights under the mortgage, but to bring pressure on the defendant to surrender the ship's register – something quite outside the mortgage. Tindal CJ said 'that the process of the law has been abused, to effect an object not within the scope of the process'.[40] Abuse of process, this is to say, consists in using legal procedures to pursue 'collateral advantages',[41] or for 'ulterior purposes'.[42]

My suggestion is that there is a useful analogy between these 'ulterior purposes' or 'collateral advantages' and the advantages available though the law which are other than legal entitlements. Of course, lawyers should not regard themselves as allowed, let alone required, to abuse the processes of the legal system, and just what will count as an abuse of process is to be determined by reference to the purpose or function of the procedures in question. The abuse of process

---

37 *White Industries (Qld) Pty Ltd* v *Flower & Hart* (a Firm) (1998) 156 ALR 169, 239.
38 *Williams* v *Spautz* (1992) 107 ALR 635, 639.
39 *Grainger* v *Hill* (1838) 4 Bing. (NC) 212; [132 ER 769].
40 Ibid., 221; 773.
41 In Re *Majory* [1955] Ch 600: '... court proceedings may not be used or threatened for the purpose of obtaining for the person so using or threatening them some collateral advantage to himself, and not for the purpose for which such proceedings are properly designed and intended' per Lord Evershed MR, at 623.
42 *White Industries* v *Flower & Hart*, 231.

jurisdiction requires lawyers to identify the proper object of legal proceedings, by reference to the function of those proceedings, and then to restrict their advocacy to the pursuit of those objects. This is essentially the same test, and the same outcome, as that recommended in the argument from the function of law given above. Thus the abuse of process jurisdiction is an illustration both of our ability to distinguish between legal entitlements and other advantages available through law, and of the use of that distinction to restrict legitimate advocacy. Lawyers may legitimately restrict themselves to merely-zealous advocacy, where that is to say that they must zealously pursue their client's legal entitlements, but need not not zealously pursue every advantage – we might say every collateral advantage – that the law can be made to provide.

Thus, I propose an analogy between the functional argument for distinguishing between mere- and hyper-zeal and the abuse of process jurisdiction. We can begin to explore this analogy by noting a very general respect in which the abuse of process jurisdiction echoes the functional account of the limits of legitimate advocacy. The echo becomes apparent when we consider the common recognition of the need for caution in the exercise of the jurisdiction. Sir John Donaldson MR gives the classic statement when he says that the jurisdiction 'falls to be exercised with care and discretion and only in clear cases', because '[i]t must never be forgotten that it is not for solicitors or counsel to impose a pre-trial screen through which a litigant must pass before he can put his complaint or defence before the court'.[43] To the same effect, the judge in a recent Australian case remarks upon 'the tension' between the jurisdiction and 'the important right of a person to have a case conducted in the courts irrespective of the view which his or her legal adviser has formed about the case and its prospects of success. The courts must be open to any party who claims that he or she has been wronged and seeks to vindicate a right or to compel the enforcement of an obligation'.[44] In describing the tension in these terms, these judges indicate that the elements the abuse of process jurisdiction seeks to balance – crudely, the prevention of abuse on the one hand and the principle that lawyers may not act as gate-keepers to legal rights on the other – are the very ones which have structured the legal ethics debate itself. The two inquiries address essentially the same questions; they seek to balance the same elements.

The analogy and the claim as to its usefulness to the attempt to specify the ethical limits on advocacy are also supported by more detailed attention to the jurisdiction. We saw that the most challenging cases for the attempt to limit zealous advocacy seemed to be those in which lawyers were called upon to pursue *lawful* but ethically objectionable goals for their clients. I suggested that we might secure the appropriate limitation by appeal to the function of law. The abuse of process jurisdiction seems helpful here as well. For although the plaintiff in *Grainger* v

---

43   *Orchard* v *South Eastern Electricity Board* [1987] QB 565, 572 per Sir John Donaldson MR.

44   *White Industries* v *Flower & Hart*, 231.

Hill[45] wanted something to which he had no claim, the ulterior purpose or collateral advantage which lies behind an abuse of process need not itself be illegal or improper. The question is rather whether the purpose or advantage is a proper goal of the particular proceedings. In *Williams* v *Spautz*,[46] for example, the respondent had been dismissed from his position as a university lecturer. Spautz immediately commenced proceedings against the university seeking a declaration that his dismissal was invalid. Over the next 10 years, he also issued 'an extraordinary number of proceedings', the majority criminal prosecutions, against those he took to have had a role in his dismissal. Among the 30-some criminal informations laid by Spautz were the three alleging criminal defamation against Williams and two others, which were the subject of the current case. The trial judge found, and the High Court agreed, that the 'predominant purpose of Dr Spautz in instituting and maintaining the criminal proceedings ... was to exert pressure upon the University ... to ... agree to a favourable settlement of his wrongful dismissal case'.[47] The criminal proceedings were held to be an abuse of process, not because there was anything improper about Spautz's goal of seeking to have his dismissal reviewed, or because there had been any improper conduct in the course of the proceedings, but because it was not proper for Spautz to use criminal defamation proceedings, designed and intended to determine whether an accused had committed an offence, for the ulterior purpose of convincing the university to reconsider his dismissal. The proceedings were an abuse of process because they were used for a purpose other than that for which they had been designed and intended, notwithstanding that the ulterior purpose was itself proper, or even that it was possible that Spautz might have won the criminal defamation cases had they been prosecuted to a conclusion. The abuse of process doctrine, then, supports the idea that appeal to the function of law may allow lawyers to decline to pursue every lawful advantage available under law.

Further, a recent abuse of process case has made clear that lawyers cannot shelter behind the wishes of their clients when accused of abuse of process. In *White Industries* the respondent law firm had acted for a plaintiff in earlier proceedings against White Industries.[48] White won this earlier case and were awarded costs, but the plaintiff had gone into liquidation just before the end of the 150-day trial. White argued that the law firm's conduct of the earlier case was an abuse of process, and that the firm should pay the award of costs. The Federal Court agreed. They found that Flower & Hart had issued proceedings against White on behalf of their client, alleging fraud, negligence and breach of the Trade Practices Act (which prohibits misleading or deceiving conduct in the course of trade) believing from the outset that their client could not win. The partner in

---

45 *Grainger* v *Hill* (1838) 4 Bing. (NC) 212 [132 ER 769].
46 *Williams* v *Spautz* (1992) 107 ALR 635.
47 Ibid.
48 *Caboolture Park Shopping Centre Pty Ltd* (In liquidation) v *White Industries (Qld) Pty Ltd* (1998) 45 FCR 224.

charge of the case wrote to the client, suggesting the heads of proceeding, before continuing, 'I do have to make clear that you could not win any litigation if put to the test.'[49] Neither the firm nor the client were unduly bothered by this prognosis, however, since neither was interested in winning. The proceedings were bought not to have the allegations determined, but to gain a temporary bargaining stance and delay inevitable payment of money owed to White by the client. The proceedings were issued, that is to say, for an ulterior purpose. The firm argued, among other things, that they had done no more than follow their client's instructions to 'to take every point, fight everything and make life difficult for White and its legal advisers'. Their client, they said, was an experienced litigant and wont 'to take a small prospect of success and convert it into an impregnable case…'.[50] But the Federal Court found that it was not sufficient 'simply to say – he was doing what his client wanted'. Indeed, Goldberg J continued:

> The fact that Mr Herscu [the client] had a robust approach to litigation, did not believe anything was impossible and was unconcerned about entering litigation with limited prospects made it all the more important for Flower & Hart to have regard to the manner in which it instituted and conducted proceedings on his behalf and on behalf of his companies and to be conscious of its duty to the court.[51]

White Industries is relevant in another regard as well. I suggested earlier that we might strengthen the conclusion that the duty of zeal does not require or allow lawyers to pursue every possible lawful advantage available to clients, by noting that it was an aspect of the role of helping clients avail themselves of their legal rights to help them ascertain what those rights were. Given this, I suggested, the functional approach allowed us to conclude that simply preventing a case coming before the decision procedures of a community was not doing the lawyer's job. It was preventing the job being done. *White Industries* supports this contention. Goldberg J says this:

> I do not consider that it is a legitimate purpose for the institution of a proceeding in this court that the purpose of the proceeding is to postpone, delay or put a barrier in front of a claim of another party and the payment of an amount due in respect of that claim. The purpose of the proceedings in a court of law is to vindicate a claimed right…. It is not part of the legal processes of this Court that its process and procedures be used as an instrument of oppression so as to frustrate the bringing, and expeditious disposition of a legitimate claim.[52]

---

49 *White Industries* v *Flower & Hart*, p. 180–183.
50 Ibid., p. 177.
51 Ibid., p. 250.
52 *White Industries* v *Flower & Hart*, p. 249.

The abuse of process jurisdiction bears upon our discussion in another way as well. Critics of the standard conception maintain that existing limitations on zealous advocacy are insufficient to prevent lawyers acting unethically. Although the principle of partisanship is subject to 'the established constraints on professional behaviour', writes Luban, those concerned with the ethical conduct of lawyers should take no comfort from this limitation, since it 'still leaves plenty of latitude for practices that some may find unjust'.[53] We have already seen one response to this complaint. It was an implication of the earlier discussion of the role of law that whether practices should be allowed could not be settled by the fact that 'some may find' those practices unjust. Given that law mediates between reasonable but inconsistent views about what we should do as a community, inevitably some of the time, some of the people will find some of the legal accommodations unjust. So much follows from the earlier discussion of the role of law in pluralist communities. If we show the link between the abuse of process jurisdiction and the function of law, and support the claims for the significance of that link for the limits of legitimate advocacy, we may have produced another response to Luban's dismissal of existing constraints. If the jurisdiction to prevent abuse of process allows courts to restrict lawyers to merely-zealous advocacy we will have shown it to be a more significant constraint on legal practice than Luban's dismissal allows.

A fictional application: The artists and the nasty landlord

An example, suggested by Austin Sarat and discussed by a number of commentators, may help to bring this discussion together.[54] An artists' cooperative had become a source of pride for the small town in which it was located. The cooperative was located in a building which was bought by an out-of-town developer. The legal profession in the town was divided between 'old-timers' and 'new-arrivals'. The developer was represented by one of the latter, who did the legal work involved in raising the rent above the means of the cooperative, which eventually moved out and disbanded. The old-timers were apparently appalled by the conduct of the new-arrivals. They believed, we are told, that 'real professionals' would have tempered the client's conduct for the good of the community. Justin Oakley and Dean Cocking offer this case as in itself a criticism of the standard conception. They write this:

> While the developer no doubt had a legitimate claim to develop their property, the lawyer's pursuit of this claim, uninhibited by its violation of other conflicting,

---

53 Luban, *Lawyers and Justice*, p. 12.
54 The case is described and discussed by David Luban in 'Smith Against the Ethicists' *Law and Philosophy*, vol. 9 (1990–1991) pp. 417–433, pp. 427–430 and by Dean Cocking and Justin Oakley in 'Doing justice to the lawyer's role', p. 79.

commensurate legitimate claims, seems to fall short of, and unjustifiably claim a stance of immunity from, the claims of ordinary broad-based morality.[55]

But a brief foray into 'broad-based' moral and political theory provides another perspective on the case. Imagine a community, not unlike our own, in which we find a range of views about property. Some people think that being a source of pride to your community gives you a property claim to the building in which you live or work. Others think that the owners of such buildings are those who have exchanged other property for them and who have had title transferred and registered in their names. The people of this community are likely to find themselves in community-threatening disputes. We can imagine that they will see a need to decide which view of property, or more likely which compromise between these and other views represented within the community, is to recognised and protected.

Suppose that after careful debate and consideration of all the possible views they settle on something fairly close to the latter view. A system of property is instituted which allows those who have paid for property to insist upon transfer of title, and to deal with their property as a public system of property laws allows. This is not to say that owners under this system can do anything they like with their property: in this system, as in many (actual) others, they cannot alter the property without town-planning permission, or use the property for just any purpose. Perhaps some members of the community favoured a system that would have granted owners these sorts of freedoms, but their preferences did not carry the day. Following the example of many other communities, for instance, this one recognises that tenants too have certain kinds of property rights, and it specifies, in particular, that owners cannot evict tenants without giving specified periods of notice. Unfortunately, in the way of such things, the property system of this community is such that most people require expert assistance to ensure that their rights under the system are protected.

The case allows us to make a number of points. It suggests that the property systems of such communities are ways of allowing community between people with different substantive views. On this view the role of the property experts in protecting the claims under the system is a deeply important moral and political role. People who help others avail themselves of institutional rights need not apologise for what they do. Often their communities depend precisely upon the role they fulfil. Suppose some significant portion of the property system experts in a town advocated one of the views which was not preserved in the final public system of property laws, though it influenced the compromise. So confident are these experts of the correctness of their view that they are quite undeterred by the failure of that view to win fuller protection in the property system adopted by their community. They do various things to implement their own view – ranging from counselling clients about the moral iniquity of the system to refusing to represent those who seek to avail themselves of their publicly allocated rights. Should we

---

55 Cocking and Oakley, 'Doing justice to the lawyer's role', p. 79.

admire such experts? It is surely not obvious that we should. In the extreme case, their conduct threatens to revive the very disputes which led to the public property system at the outset. It shows a spectacular moral arrogance, especially in a case such as Sarat's, where it is surely at least not obvious that the system of rights which allows the developer to evict the tenants is unreasonable. They seem to abuse their position as de facto gatekeepers to the enjoyment of publicly allocated rights. They impose a significant burden on people who need expert assistance, who must now run the risk of finding themselves represented by an expert who does not sympathise with the system or perhaps with its allocation of these rights to this claimant.

Cocking and Oakley suggest that these sorts of conclusions follow only if the outcome of the system is substantively just. They think those who endorse the conclusions for which I have argued have unrealistic views about how close an approximation to the 'ideal system' actual systems tend to be. But there is nothing in the case that supposes that the property system is ideal. Indeed, it portrays legal systems as the products of compromises and trade-offs between the views represented in the communities they govern. Often it will seem to almost everybody that the adopted system is second best. If there is insufficient consensus on what best would be, however, and if we are not prepared to impose our views on others, second best may be the best we can do in the actual world. The moral obligation here is to the less than ideal system and to those who rely upon it and the community it makes possible.

One of the striking things about the easy case, is that while one can see how the property system might have been different, the actual system does not seem to be patently morally unacceptable. Cocking and Oakley's sanguine acceptance that even in this easy case, lawyers acting for the owner 'violated ... other conflicting, commensurate legitimate claims' and 'fell short of, and unjustifiably claim a stance of immunity from, the claims of ordinary broad-based morality' shows just how far one might be led astray by concentrating on one's own views of the moral good. To do so is to ignore the moral good of public institutions.

Far from being troubled by the Sarat's case, then, I think it allows us to see how the law functions, to appreciate the proper role of lawyers, and to see again that the role-differentiated conception does not render the role of lawyers amoral let alone immoral. The case shows again why lawyers have moral grounds to take their roles seriously.

Chapter 5
The Standard Conception and the Client-Professional Relationship

Introduction

I was concerned in the previous chapter to argue that the role of law in pluralist communities had significance for the ethical obligations of lawyers working within those communities. More particularly, I claimed that an appreciation of the role of law should lead us to prefer the standard conception's account of the lawyer's ethical obligations over less role-differentiated alternatives. In this chapter I continue the defence of the standard conception, but turn attention from the broader social context and function of law to the nature of the relationship between lawyers and their clients. I shall suggest that the nature of those relationships gives us another reason to reject accounts of the lawyer's role that diminish the significance of role-differentiated obligations. I shall argue, that is, that the nature of the relationship between lawyers and their clients should lead us to favour some version of the standard conception.

The relationship between clients and professionals

I begin by setting out the relevant features of the relationships between clients and professionals. There are a number of such features that seem especially significant to our inquiry:

The imbalance of expertise and power

First, professionals almost always have specialised knowledge and expertise, which their clients lack. The physician has a specialised knowledge of medicine and human health, which allows them to diagnose and treat illness. The lawyer has specialised knowledge of the 'artificial reason of law'.[1] They either know what

---

1   The phrase is taken from Lord Coke's famous reply to James I's claim that since law was founded upon reason, the King could decide cases as well as judges: '[T]rue it was,' said Coke, 'that God endowed his Majesty with excellent Science, and great Endowments of Nature; but his Majesty was not learned in the Laws of his realm of England, and Causes which concern the Life, or Inheritance, or Goods, or Fortunes of his Subjects, are not to be decided by natural Reason but by the artificial Reason and Judgement of Law, which Law

rights their client has, or how to go about determining what they are. They know how the complex mechanisms of law must be operated to ensure that their client's lawful interests are protected and furthered.

The imbalance of expertise between the client and the professional gives rise to an imbalance of power, generating a de facto monopoly over many professional services. Few clients could perform complex professional tasks for themselves. It is unrealistic, for instance, to expect many non-professionals to find out enough about the law and its procedures to effectively pursue their own interests or the interests of others. This de facto monopoly is often reinforced *de jure*, by regulation making it unlawful to practise as a lawyer without being a member of the appropriate professional body. Many jurisdictions, for instance, require even fairly routine legal services – wills, probate applications, real estate transactions, uncontested marriage dissolutions, and the like – to be handled by lawyers. Thus clients typically have little real choice as to whether to consult a professional. They will be either unable to help themselves or be prohibited from doing so if they could.

People do manage to get by without consulting lawyers. Some people avoid the law altogether, and some of those who do not manage to do that represent themselves despite the difficulties. But in general the possible costs of not consulting a lawyer are so high that lay-people effectively have no choice in the matter. Both because of their specialised knowledge and expertise, and because of their institutional power, professionals can do things for clients – things that clients must have done – that clients cannot do for themselves.

The importance of the matters about which clients consult professionals

Second, the matters about which clients consult professionals such as physicians and lawyers are typically of considerable importance to the client. We see professionals about matters such as our health, our social and political rights and the security of the assets upon which we rely to provide for ourselves and those who depend upon us. The importance of such matters both reinforces the power of professionals – there is normally a considerable cost to simply ignoring the needs to which professionals cater – and makes it important that those matters are addressed expertly and diligently.

Of course, we do use the term professional in trivial contexts. We speak of professional sports players, for instance, to distinguish them from their amateur counterparts. But the sense of 'professional' in these sporting contexts is not the same as that we employ when speaking of professionals such as lawyers, physicians and engineers. Rugby players who play the game for nothing are not professionals, but physicians who donate their expertise are no less professionals

---

is an Act which requires long Study and Experience, before that a Man can attain to the cognizance of it ...' *Coke Reports* (1738), 63, 65 (pt. 12, 4th edn 1738), reprinted in 77 *Eng Rep* 1342, 1343 (1907).

than their colleagues who charge. It is a somewhat interesting question whether there could be a profession, in the sense that medicine and the law are professions, which dealt with trivial matters. I suspect not, but it is not a question we need to settle here. It seems clear enough that when we see professionals such as lawyers and physicians, we typically see them over matters that are important to us.

The opacity of professional diligence and expertise

Third, the ability of clients to assess the expertise or diligence with which professionals pursue the professional task is often limited. From the client's perspective, a considerable 'opacity' surrounds the professional's work. My physician tells me that I am ill and should undergo a course of treatment. Often, no matter how carefully I enquire into their professional methods, I must simply accept their word for that. The engineer tells me that a dam built in a specified manner will be safe. I cannot assess the engineering information myself. I must simply accept that they know what they are talking about. My lawyer tells me that if I follow the instructions they provide, and have them execute the arrangement in question, my property will be safe from business creditors. I must simply accept their advice.

Perhaps it will seem that clients can easily remedy this opacity by seeking a 'second opinion'. No doubt this is an option that sometimes operates as a genuine check upon professional competence and diligence. But we should not over-estimate its usefulness. For one thing, it will often be expensive. Having borne the cost of consulting one professional, clients may be understandably reluctant to consult another over the same matter. For another, just as clients cannot reliably judge the diligence or expertise with which a professional pursues their interests, nor can they reliably judge when a second opinion would be appropriate. The opacity of professional expertise and diligence itself makes it difficult for clients to know when they *should* seek a second opinion. And the second opinion may not help much in any event, since the second professional's diligence and expertise will be no less opaque to the client than that of the first. One commentator summarises the client's position in these terms:

> In a professional relationship ... the professional dictates what is good or evil for the client, who has no choice but to accede to professional judgement. Here the premise is that, because he lacks the requisite theoretical background, the client cannot diagnose his own needs or discriminate among the range of possibilities for meeting them. Nor is the client considered able to evaluate the calibre of the professional services he receives.[2]

---

2   E. Greenwood, 'Attributes of a profession', *Social Work*, vol. 2 (1957) pp. 45–55, p. 45.

Professionals have knowledge and expertise that the client lacks. That makes it difficult if not impossible for the client to do the original task without consulting the professional, and it makes it equally difficult if not impossible for the client to assess how well the task has been done – whether in order to judge the need for a second opinion, or to assess the accuracy of a second opinion if one is sought. I cannot check everything my professional does: I would need to be a 'professional-of-all-trades' to do so.

The limited nature of the relationship between clients and professionals

The three features set out so far are, I think, fairly commonly taken to be distinctive of the relationship between clients and professionals.[3] I believe that there is another important feature, which does not appear in the standard characterisation of such relationships. Professionals and clients, typically, enjoy only limited relationships. The client is likely to know very little about the professional as an individual. I know my physician *is* a physician – he has his degrees on his surgery wall – and I know a few other things about him garnered from our conversations and from the photographs on his desk.[4] But I know almost nothing about his personal life or his personal moral views. I do not know what he values; I do not know what motivates him; I do not know his views on the fundamental questions we encountered in the previous chapter as to what constitutes human flourishing, what basic goals are intrinsically most worthy of pursuit, and what is the best way for individuals to live their lives.

Popular portrayals of professionals often suggest otherwise, and people speak as though community members almost always know their professionals very well indeed. Popular literature is full of examples of the local physician who has delivered most of the children in the district and whose own life is as well-known to his patients as theirs are to him. More recent television shows about professionals invariably disclose both professional and private aspects of their characters' lives, and a significant portion of their plots rely upon a simple blurring of the professional and the private. But whether this is or was typical, it is not the reality for most contemporary clients. Most of us deal with professionals we hardly know at all. We know *that* they are professionals and little else. Yet we walk

---

3   Note, however, that there is little consensus on which features are common to the professions or indeed, on whether there are common features at all. I do not intend to enter into this debate. The features of typical client-professional relationships are not offered as part of a definition of 'professional', but as features typically encountered in client-professional relationships. As to the definitional debate, however, it seems likely that 'professional' is a family-resemblance term: see Ludwig Wittgenstein, *Philosophical Investigations* 1953, para. 66.

4   Though, since almost all physicians seem to have photographs of children on their desks, one wonders whether the photographs are supplied along with white coats and stethoscopes.

into their offices or surgeries and – sometimes literally, sometimes figuratively – lay ourselves and our children before them.

Ethics and the client-professional relationship

Relationships between clients and professionals, then, are typically characterised by these four features: an imbalance of expertise and power, the importance of the matters about which clients consult professionals, the client's limited ability to assess the professional's expertise or diligence and the client's limited knowledge of the professional as a person. The features make relationships between clients and professionals quite remarkable. Given these features, the clients of professionals are typically obliged to rely upon relative strangers for things of considerable importance when they cannot assess the expertise or diligence with which their interests have been pursued. What follows for the ethical obligations of lawyers from this analysis of relationships between clients and professionals?

Significance for particular obligations

First, the nature of the client-professional relationship explains many of the particular ethical obligations to which lawyers are subject. Full treatment of these obligations would include an account of duties such as confidentiality and conflict of interest. For current purposes, however, an obvious but fundamental example will suffice to make the point.

The analysis of the client-professional relationship just offered highlights the grounds for regarding such relationships as paradigmatically fiduciary. It is necessary, though not sufficient, for a fiduciary relationship that one party, the fiduciary, has dominance or ascendancy over another who must nevertheless repose confidence or trust in the fiduciary. In such circumstances, the law may impose duties upon the fiduciary in order to prevent the abuse of the confidence. It does so as a matter of course in lawyer-client relationships: '[T]he reposing of trust by the client is automatically assumed', so that the relationship 'automatically gives rise to the [fiduciary] duty'.[5] The discussion of lawyers as fiduciaries anticipates many of the features highlighted above. Consider the following passage from Story's classic equity text:

> The situation of the attorney or solicitor puts it in his power to avail himself not only of the necessity of his client, but of his good nature, liberality and credulity to obtain undue advantages, bargains and gratuities. By establishing the principle

---

5   *Sim* v *Craig Bell and Bond* [1991] NZLR 535, 543 per Richardson J. See, as well, New Zealand Rules of Professional Conduct for Barristers and Solicitors, Rule 1.01: 'The relationship between practitioners and client is one of confidence and trust which must never be abused.'

that while the relation of client and attorney is in full vigor the latter shall derive no benefit to himself ... [the law] supersedes the need of any inquiry into the particular means, extent and exertion of influence in a given case; a task often difficult, and ill supported by the evidence which can be drawn from any satisfactory sources.[6]

In this passage we find recognition of the imbalance of power and expertise ('The situation of the attorney or solicitor puts it in his power to avail himself ... '), of the importance of the issues and the lack of choice as to whether to consult a professional (' ... of the necessity of his client ... '), of the opacity of professional expertise and diligence ('... a task often difficult, and ill supported by the evidence which can be drawn from any satisfactory sources ... '), and of the appropriateness and point of publicly accessible standards of professional conduct ('By establishing the principle...[the law] supercedes the need of any inquiry ... '). Similar themes are to be found in the many other treatments of the lawyer as fiduciary.[7]

Equity imposes a number of specific duties in response to the treatment of the client-professional relationship as fiduciary: the duties to protect and further the client's interests, to avoid conflicts of interest, to maintain confidences, to refrain from using the relationship for personal gain, to act with absolute fairness and openness toward the client. All these duties flow from the classification of the relationship as fiduciary, which flows in turn from the identification within those relationships of the features set out in the previous section. The upshot is that, given the nature of their relationships with clients, lawyers should regard themselves as bound by antecedently-specified rules of conduct designed to protect clients who are vulnerable to them, who are obliged to rely upon them and who cannot assess the diligence or expertise with which they carry out their tasks. This is to say that the nature of the client-professional relationship favours the standard conception of the lawyer's role, which is concerned to secure just this model of professional obligation.

Significance for the standard conception

The analysis of client-professional relationships offered above has more general significance for the ethical position of lawyers as well, which significance we can see by comparing such relationships with others in which we commonly make ourselves vulnerable. Perhaps there is nothing very remarkable about our decisions to make ourselves vulnerable to professionals. After all, we constantly make ourselves vulnerable to friends, to lovers, to family members, and so on: we bare our souls to our lovers, we rely on family members and we trust our

---

6   J. Story, *Equity Jurisprudence* (1918) 14th edn. Vol. 1, Section 433.

7   See, for instance, *Bray* v *Ford* [1896] AC 44, 51-2, per Lord Herschell (Deemed expedient to lay down positive rules protecting clients); *Green and Clara Pty Ltd* v *Bestobel Industries Pty Ltd* [1982] WAR 1 at 6 (difficulty of proving that a fiduciary has improperly used his position).

friends with our children. Perhaps our decisions to make ourselves vulnerable to professionals are neither more nor less remarkable than our decisions to make ourselves vulnerable to these more 'natural' intimates. But I believe that it is remarkable that we so commonly make ourselves vulnerable to professionals. It is remarkable because our relationships with intimates such as friends and lovers differ from our relationships with professionals in ways that bear precisely upon the wisdom of making ourselves vulnerable.

When we make ourselves vulnerable to our friends we have grounds – our intimate or personal knowledge of the individual to whom we are vulnerable – to make assessments of what that person is likely to do. The intimacy of our relationship gives us access to their motivations, to their priorities, to their views on the fundamental questions noted in the last chapter, and so forth. This knowledge explains our willingness to place ourselves in their hands. From time to time, I trust my friend Hugh with my children's welfare. An important factor in my willingness to do so is the fact I know enough about him, about what he cares about, about what he is likely to do in the face of an offer to abandon my children and go for a beer, to feel secure that my children will be safe with him.[8]

Most of us do not have this kind of detailed knowledge about our professionals. Yet we leave ourselves (and our children) vulnerable to them in ways that are not dissimilar to the ways we leave ourselves vulnerable to friends, partners, family-members and other 'natural' intimates. If I am right that one important reason we happily make ourselves vulnerable to these intimates is our knowledge about them, our knowledge about what they value and what they are likely to do, then if it is to make sense to adopt similar positions of vulnerability to our professionals, we need similar knowledge about them – we need grounds to judge what they value, what they care about, what they are likely to do. If we cannot make these assessments by reference to our knowledge of the character of our professionals we need another way.

Given the nature of the relationships between clients and professionals, these interests in obtaining grounds to trust our professionals should lead us to favour the standard conception and the idea of role-differentiated obligation. The adoption and promulgation of a distinct and public professional morality is a way of making the ethics of the profession available in a way that the personal ethical views of its members cannot be. Of course, clients get the benefit of this 'public ethics' only if it is indeed given priority over personal ethics in members' dealings with the public. The client need only know that the professional is a role-occupant, and what values the professional role requires the professional to adopt; to know what values at least should govern the professional's conduct in the relationship.

---

8   I do not mean to suggest that all of these relationships involve 'decisions' to make ourselves vulnerable. My children's vulnerability to me is a natural and almost unavoidable incident of being my child. But the child's position may be unusual. I do choose my friends, I do choose when to make myself vulnerable to them, and normally I will choose to do so only after I have the kind of knowledge of them remarked upon in the text.

Thus the nature of the relationship between clients and professionals supports the standard conception and the idea of role-differentiated obligation. They offer just this 'public' account of professional ethics.

This argument from the nature of the relationship between clients and professionals turns upon the idea that the client is vulnerable to the professional, given the imbalance of power and the opacity of diligence and expertise which normally accompany client-professional relationships, and given the fact that the personal ethical views of professionals are rarely available to clients. Sometimes, of course, these features are absent. Sooner or later every lawyer will experience the rather uncomfortable consultation in which the client clearly knows more than the lawyer. The client may have incorporated or wound up dozens of companies, or divorced as many spouses, and seek only the signature of a member of the bar on the appropriate form – a form to which the client is both keen and able to direct the lawyer. In such cases, there seems little imbalance of expertise and only a slight imbalance of institutional power. In addition, of course, some people do know their professionals' personal moral views. They may have chosen their lawyer because she is a member of their congregation, or because she is a friend. Perhaps the personal life and views of the small town lawyer are well known about the district, and the big city lawyer may have gone out of his way to publicise his own ethical views.

But I do not think such cases detract from the general argument. Even if it is true that some clients suffer no particular inequality of power and expertise, and even if some clients know the ethical views of their professionals well, these relationships cannot be adopted as the 'standard'. To do so would be to impose an enormous and unpredictable burden upon those clients not so situated. This is not just a matter of catering to the majority, though of course most clients do not enjoy the degree of expertise or intimacy that marks the anomalous cases. Rather, it is to recognise that an arrangement which assumes equality of expertise and power and close personal relationships between clients and professionals would severely disadvantage typical clients, who know little about law and less about their lawyers as individuals, while benefiting the anomalous clients only marginally. Ideally, any client should be able to walk into any lawyer's office and know the ethical principles that will govern the lawyer's conduct. It is not reasonable – not least because it is probably impossible – to expect clients to make the kinds of inquiry which would allow professionals to conduct their professional lives by appeal to their personal views. To do so would be to place an extraordinary burden on the weaker party to an already unequal relationship.

Charles Fried: The lawyer as the client's 'special purpose friend'

I suggested in the last section that we could usefully compare client-professional relationships with those enjoyed with more natural intimates such as family-members, lovers and friends. I was concerned to highlight the differences between the two kinds of relationships. Though we make ourselves vulnerable to lawyers and friends alike, the relationships are significantly different. Typically we lack the sort of knowledge about our professionals which explains our willingness to make ourselves vulnerable to our friends.

Charles Fried also compares lawyers with friends in an attempt to defend the standard conception of the lawyer's role. According to Fried, the key question in the legal ethics debate is, 'How can it be that it is not only permissible, but indeed morally right, to favour the interests of a particular person in a way which we can be fairly sure is either harmful to another particular individual or not maximally conducive to the welfare of society as a whole?'[9] His answer to this restatement of Macaulay's question starts from the observation that there are other familiar cases in which we take ourselves to be entitled to exercise just this sort of moral favouritism or 'agent-relativism', namely, in our dealings with family and friends. If we can see why the special preference for the interests of family and friends is justified, Fried maintains, we will find the justification for the analogous obligations and permissions within professional relationships.

Fried considers and rejects utilitarian justifications for giving priority to friends and family. Such justifications would only allow us to prefer the interests of family and friends if we promoted the general good by doing so. 'But,' insists Fried, 'we are not required, indeed sometimes not even authorized' to make this inquiry as to whether we promote the greatest good for the greatest number by distributing our efforts and affections unevenly: when we decide to care for our children, to assure our own comforts...we do not do so as the result of a cost-benefit inquiry...'[10] Fried's non-utilitarian account of such relationships proceeds from the premise that the very idea of morality – even by utilitarian lights – requires that we are able 'to posit choosing, valuing entities'.[11] Fried believes that we can do so only if we take ourselves to have a kind of moral priority: a 'responsible, valuable, and valuing agent ... must first of all be dear to himself'.[12] And now, armed with an appropriately valued self, we can relate to others in the way an adequate morality requires. The moral agent should 'generalize and attribute in equal degree to all persons the value which he naturally attributes to himself'. Therefore, Fried concludes:

> ... it is not only consonant with, but also required by, an ethics for human beings that one be entitled first of all to reserve an area of concern for oneself and then move out freely from that area if one wishes to lavish that concern on others to whom one stands in concrete, personal relations.[13]

---

9   Fried, Charles 'The Lawyer as Friend: The Moral Foundations of the Lawyer-Client Relation', *Yale Law Journal.* Vol. 85 (1976) pp. 1060–1089, p. 1066.
10   Ibid., p. 1067.
11   Ibid., p. 1069.
12   Ibid.
13   Ibid., pp. 1070–71.

At this point Fried takes himself to have shown how it can be morally right to favour the interests of a particular person even though doing so threatens harm to another or is not maximally conducive to the common good. Pace the utilitarian, relationships such as friendship are valuable not because they promote some other value such as the common good or the greatest happiness of the greatest number, but instead in their own right, or as an end in themselves, because they are an essential precondition of morality itself. And now Fried argues that this justification for the preference of some individuals over others can be applied to the relationship between the lawyer and the client. It is permitted and perhaps required for the lawyer to prefer the interests of the client over the interests of others, even when doing so fails to promote the general good or threatens harm to another, because the lawyer is the client's 'special purpose friend': 'As a professional person,' writes Fried, 'one has a special care for the interests of those accepted as clients, just as his friends, his family and he himself have a very general claim to his special concern.'[14]

Many of the conclusions Fried goes on to draw from the friendship analogy are similar to those advanced in this book. Considering the question why we should allow the lawyer the obligations and permissions of friendship, for instance, he offers a familiar appeal to the role of law. 'It is,' he writes, 'because the law must respect the rights of individuals that the law must also create and support the specific role of the legal friend.'

> For the social nexus has become so complex that without the assistance of an expert advisor an ordinary layman cannot exercise that autonomy which the system must allow him. Without such an advisor, the law would impose constraints on the lay citizen (unequally at that) which it is not entitled to impose explicitly.[15]

Similarly, although he does not employ the language of mere- and hyper-zeal, he believes that the friendship analogy gives him a response to the concern that lawyers may be required to go beyond the law for their clients. The lawyer is the client's friend 'relative to the legal system', hence it is false, he writes, 'to assume that the lawyer fails to have the proper zeal if he does for his client only what the law allows'.[16] Again, this seems not dramatically different from the position on hyper-zeal defended in this book.

However, there is at least one important difference between our strategies. To see the difference and its significance, note that once Fried has advanced his analogy between friendship and the lawyer-client relationship, it does not seem to do a great deal of work. Most of Fried's arguments are similar to those just sketched: they appeal to the role of law, or the complexity of legal institutions, or

---

14 Ibid., p. 1073.
15 Ibid, p. 1067.
16 Ibid., p. 1081.

to the idea that we might attribute wrongs to institutions rather than to individuals who occupy roles within those institutions. In the end, if Fried convinces us that lawyers are not committed to what I have called hyper-zealous advocacy, for instance, it is not because of the friendship analogy. It is because he mounts a compelling independent argument by appeal to the role of law.

Furthermore, Fried's attempt to defend a very close analogy between lawyers and friends may actually be counterproductive. Most responses to his argument attack the analogy, claiming, for instance, that 'we do not expect gross immorality of our friends', and that 'we don't think much of the moral quality of friendship that can be bought, even if Fried's suggestion does catch the idea of law as the second oldest profession'.[17] But there are important lessons to be gained from the comparison of friendships and client-professional relationships. Fried's insistence upon the analogy distracts from those lessons.

I suggested earlier that what stood out in the comparison of friendships and client-professional relationships were similarities between the vulnerabilities we assume in the two cases, notwithstanding that the intimate knowledge which marks friendships is absent in relationships with professionals. The comparison of the two sorts of relationships is not significant because of a close analogy between friendships and client-professional relationships. Indeed, it is the disanalogous degree of knowledge that is crucial. Given the similarity of the vulnerability, we can look to friendships for guidance as to what features we need to build into professional relationships to protect clients. We can see what it is about relationships of friendship that explains our willingness to make ourselves vulnerable in those relationships. And from here, it is useful to conceive of many of the ethical constraints upon professionals as aimed at reproducing in professional relationships the central features of those more intimate relationships in which the vulnerability of the client would more naturally be found. We can understand these features as designed to turn the professional into the client's 'artificial' and 'special purpose' friend. If we take this view of the comparison of friendships and client-professional relationships, we need not be surprised that in many respects they differ, in the role of the fee for instance, or in the failure of the client to have reciprocal feelings of loyalty for the lawyer. These matters trouble Fried and prompt criticism of his analogy, but they are quite irrelevant to an approach that asserts the usefulness of the comparison for the purposes of institutional design. Fried's attempt to show that the professional is allowed to prefer the interests of the client, not because of institutional structure, but by virtue of the moral character of friendship itself, distracts from the real and valuable lesson to be drawn from the comparison of lawyers and friends.

---

17   R.E. Ewin, 'Personal morality and professional ethics: The lawyer's duty of zeal', *International Journal of Applied Philosophy*, vol. 6 (1991) pp. 35–45, p. 44.

Chapter 6
Virtue Ethics, Legal Ethics and Harper Lee's *To Kill a Mockingbird*

Introduction

I suggested earlier that we could usefully regard the various strands of the critique of the standard conception as linked by a common ambition to weaken the distinction the conception seems to draw between professional and general morality. Gerald Postema, for instance, argues that by divorcing lawyers from 'the resources of a broader moral experience' the standard conception makes it impossible for lawyers to preserve their sense of moral responsibility. Hence Postema argues for a new conception of the lawyer's role which 'achieves a fully integrated moral personality' and 'allows the lawyer to bring his full moral sensibilities to play in his professional role.'[1]

At this point, the legal ethics debate connects directly with one of the most striking features of contemporary moral philosophy – the rediscovery of Aristotle and virtue ethics. At the heart of this renaissance is the idea that moral deliberation and justification cannot proceed deductively through the application of general principles to particular cases. Aristotle supposes that the phenomena with which ethical inquiry is concerned are marked by mutability, indeterminacy and particularity, such that they can never be unproblematically subsumed under general principles of right action. His view of the limitations of general principles of right action led him to stress the importance of 'practical judgement' (*phronesis*), a practical reasoning skill which is neither a matter of simply applying general principles to particular cases nor of mere intuition. *Phronesis* is a complex faculty in which general principles and the particularities of the case both play a role.[2] The *phronemos* relies upon his judgement to identify the right thing to do in light both of principles and the exigencies of the particular case. This emphasis upon judgement brings the character of the practical reasoner to centre stage. We cannot look to general principles to settle the right thing to do. Rather, we must look to the character – or virtues – of those doing the judging.

Although the Aristotelian model once dominated normative theory, including legal theory, it fell into disfavour around the time of the scientific revolution.

---

1 Postema, 'Moral Responsibility in Professional Ethics', p. 64.
2 'Practical wisdom is not concerned with universals only; it must also recognize particulars, for it is practical and practice concerns particulars': Aristotle, *Nichomachean Ethics*, 1141b14-16.

Recently there has been a dramatic return to Aristotle. Though it is difficult to characterise virtue theory so as to capture all that has been gathered under that rubric, and though the renaissance is still in its infancy, so that it is not yet clear what contemporary virtue ethics will look like in its mature form, it will do for the moment to understand a virtue theory as one which holds that judgements about the character of persons, independently of assessments of the rightness or the value of the consequences of their actions, are what is most fundamental in moral evaluation. A flavour of the new wave of virtue theory, understood in this rather broad fashion, may be gained from John McDowell who maintains that morality is 'uncodifiable', and writes that 'one knows what to do (if one does) not by applying universal principles but by being a certain sort of person: one who sees situations in a certain way'.[3] Similarly, Martha Nussbaum says that '[t]he conception of ethical theory on which I rely is, roughly, an Aristotelian one',[4] while arguing for the priority of perception over rules and claiming that 'to confine ourselves to the universal is a recipe for obtuseness.'[5]

Gerald Postema and other significant contributors to the legal ethics debate belong squarely within this Aristotelian renaissance. Postema's new conception of the lawyer's role is essentially Aristotelian. It rejects the idea that lawyers might look to appropriate rules or principles of right action for moral guidance in favour of a view based on the claim that '[i]n professional contexts there is much need for practical judgement in this Aristotelian sense'.[6] Similarly, Anthony Kronman's charts and attempts to revive a once dominant professional ideal which portrayed the good lawyer as Aristotle's *phronemos*: not a mere technician but a person of practical wisdom and public spiritedness.[7]

I think this turn to virtue or character-based approaches in legal ethics is a mistake. I shall argue that the approach has only a limited contribution to make to a proper understanding of lawyers' ethical responsibilities and that the standard conception is basically correct. Indeed, I shall argue that as virtue- or character-based approaches are currently defended within the legal ethics debate, taking them seriously would make lawyers less rather than more likely to fulfil their professional ethical obligations.

For the most part I am going to tackle these questions in a somewhat unusual but I hope engaging manner. Some of the most interesting discussion of the significance of virtue- or character-based ethics for lawyers has found support in

---

3   John McDowell, 'Virtue and Reason' in Stanley G. Clarke and Evan Simpson, *Anti-Theory in Ethics and Moral Conservatism* (Albany, 1989) pp. 87–109, p. 105.

4   Martha Nussbaum, *The Fragility of Goodness: Luck and Ethics in Greek Tragedy and Philosophy* (New York, 1986) p. 10.

5   Martha Nussbaum, '"Richly Aware and Finely Responsible": Literature and the Moral Imagination', in Clarke and Simpson, *Anti-Theory*, p. 122–134, p. 126.

6   Postema, 'Moral Responsibility in Professional Ethics', p. 68.

7   Anthony Kronman, *The Lost Lawyer: Failing Ideals of the Legal Profession*, (Cambridge, Mass., 1993).

Harper Lee's marvellous novel *To Kill a Mockingbird* and its lawyer hero Atticus Finch. Though I think *Mockingbird* does provide useful insights into the ethical responsibilities of lawyers, I will argue that the novel does not support the turn to virtue ethics. Before turning to Atticus, however, I address a more radical anti-rule or principled, character-based ethics defended by Hubert and Stuart Dreyfus.

Character-based ethics and the nature of moral reasoning

According to Hubert and Stuart Dreyfus, not only do 'moral experts' not use principles or rules in their reasoning, they cannot do so – either in the process of moral deliberation or in giving an account to others of why and how they have made particular judgments.[8] I will claim that this cannot be an adequate account of ethical expertise. Ethics, I will suggest, is an ineluctably public endeavour. The possibility that one's ethical choices could be justified and explained in terms of reasons which are at least coherent, if not convincing, is not an optional matter. It is a constitutive element of ethical practice. The doubts here go to the adequacy of certain kinds of particularist virtue theories *as ethical theories*.

The Dreyfuses set out to give an account of the phenomenology of moral reasoning. They target what they call the intellectualist tradition which they think has emphasised the role of deliberation and appeal to rule and principle in moral reasoning to the neglect of the possibility 'that our moral consciousness expresses itself chiefly in everyday ethical comportment which consists in unreflective, egoless responses to the current interpersonal situation.'[9] They aim to remedy this neglect by defending an account of 'expertise' in general which they then apply to ethical expertise. It seems, they write:

> ... that beginners make judgements using strict rules and features, but that with talent and a great deal of involved experience the beginner develops into an expert who sees intuitively what to do without applying rules and making judgements at all. The intellectualist tradition has given an accurate description of the beginner and of the expert facing an unfamiliar situation, but normally an expert does not deliberate. She does not reason. She does not even act deliberately. She simply spontaneously does what has normally worked and, naturally, it normally works.[10]

They use drivers and chess players as examples. So we are said to teach people to drive by breaking driving down into a number of features which can be

---

8 Hubert L. and Stuart E. Dreyfus 'What is Morality? A Phenomenological Account of the Development of Ethical Expertise' in David Rasmussen, (ed.), *Universalism and Communitarianism* (Cambridge, Mass., 1990) pp. 237–264.
9 Ibid., p. 239.
10 Ibid., p. 243.

recognised even by raw beginners: the beginner driver is taught the rule 'when the speedometer points to 15km/h, change out of first gear'. Advanced beginners – the next stage – begin to note or are taught additional components of the situation in which the skill is exercised, and they use these situational aspects to develop maxims of action: so the advanced-beginner driver learns to use engine noise as well as speed to decide when to change gear. At the next level – competence – the practitioner chooses plans by which they select, on grounds of relevance to the plan, some of the features and aspects they have learned and which are relevant to that plan. Here we find detached planning, conscious assessment of elements salient with respect to the plan, and analytical rule-guided choice of action. The use of plans of action introduces an emotional component because choosing plans in the absence of rules is stressful. Next, moving from competence to proficiency:

> Having experienced many emotionally laden situations, chosen plans in each, and having obtained vivid, emotional demonstrations of the adequacy or inadequacy of the plan, the performer involved in the world of skill 'notices', or 'is struck by' a certain plan, goal or perspective. No longer is the spell of involvement broken by detached conscious planning. The proficient performer, immersed in the world of skilful activity *sees* what has to be done but must [still] *decide* how to do it.[11]

With sufficient experience with a wide enough variety of situations the proficient performer decomposes these situations into subclasses, each of which shares the same action or tactic, allowing an immediate intuitive response to each situation, so:

> The expert driver, generally without any awareness, not only knows by feel and familiarity when an action such as slowing down is required; they know how to perform the action without calculating and comparing alternatives. They shift gears when appropriate with no awareness of their acts. On the off ramp their foot simply lifts off the accelerator. What must be done, simply is done.[12]

If the skill model is correct, and if everyday ethical comportment is a form of expertise, the Dreyfuses conclude, 'We should expect ethical expertise to exhibit a developmental structure similar to that just described. On analogy with chess and driving it would seem that the budding ethical expert would learn at least some of the ethics of her community by following strict rules, would then go on to apply contextualised maxims, and, in the highest stage, would leave rules and principles behind and develop more and more refined spontaneous ethical responses.'[13]

---

11 Ibid., p. 242.
12 Ibid., p. 243.
13 Ibid., p. 244.

Perhaps enough has already been said to show that Dreyfus and Dreyfus think deliberation and reflection have only a very small role in moral reasoning, and then only during rehearsals for the real show or activity. It will be worth picking this theme out a little more clearly, however, since it is what I'm particularly interested in. The Dreyfuses take it to be an implication of their view that 'an expert *cannot* improve future performance by abstract reflection on previous situations, actions and outcomes'.[14] The most important reason they give for this, for current purposes, is that 'detached reflection asks what it was about a previous action that made it satisfying or regrettable. This is like asking the competent chess player to figure out what principles of chess explain why a master made a particular move or which neglected ethical principles explained why one felt regret in an ethical situation. But, they write, 'As we have seen in the case of chess, in the next situation when one applies the principle one may well lose the game, or, in the case of ethical action, still feel regret. This is not because it is difficult to determine which features define membership in the right similarity set, nor because it is hard to find the principles that lead to expert action. Rather, as far as anyone knows, there just aren't any such features and principles.'.[15]

There is a possibly significant caveat to all of this dramatic particularism. The Dreyfuses concede that even experts might deliberate in some cases: 'A chess master confronted with a chess problem, constructed precisely so as not to resemble a position that would show up in a normal game, is *reduced* to using analysis. Likewise an ethical expert when confronted with cases of "life-boat morality" may have to *fall back* on ethical principles.'.[16] For my purposes it will do to draw attention to the way in which even where a role for principles is acknowledged it is only in novel or extreme cases, and, as the ranked or graded model implies, the Dreyfuses think such strategies inferior: the chess master is *reduced* to analysis, the ethical expert *falls back* on principles. Indeed the Dreyfuses continue explicitly: 'But since principles were unable to produce expert behaviour for the competent performer, it should not be a surprise if falling back on them produces inferior responses. The resulting decisions are necessarily crude since they have not been refined by the experience of the results of a variety of intuitive responses to emotion laden situations and the learning that comes from satisfaction and regret.'[17]

It seems to me this is to get ethics quite wrong. One way to approach that conclusion is to draw attention to some disanalogies between driving and chess on the one hand and moral reasoning on the other. In driving and chess success does not depend upon being able to tell others why one has acted as one has. Putting aside problems of driving coordination, so concentrating on the Dreyfuses' own driving examples – such as successfully negotiating a curved motorway exit – success in driving, in the sense of simply successfully changing gears, negotiating

---

14   Ibid., p. 245.
15   Ibid., p. 246.
16   Ibid., p. 248.
17   Ibid.

corners and the like, does not require that I can explain to others why I acted as I did, does not require that others can accept that I have acted for the right motives, that they can engage in debate about what I have chosen to do and why. But that is precisely what ethics does require. The possibility of dialogue and discussion are non-optional components of an adequate ethics. Without its possibility we are not engaged in ethics at all. And now the claim is that an account which makes *expertise* at an endeavour amount to acting in a way which seems to defeat the point of the endeavour itself cannot be right. Note that this is an objection to the idea that on the Dreyfuses' account the expert *cannot* make use of principles, cannot engage in dialogue in a way which would help others to understand why they had chosen to act as they did. It is an objection to the idea that doing so involves taking a step back down the levels of expertise.

I do not think the acknowledgments toward the end of the account for some role for deliberation help: though I applaud the idea that one can't do ethics effectively 'from the life-boat', I reject the suggestion that only in such cases can the giving of reasons have a proper place. In the end the idea is that ethics is an ineluctably and necessarily public activity in which the ability to explain one's reasons for action to others is not a mere and inferior 'optional extra' to be tolerated in certain odd and rare cases. It is what the activity is about at its core not merely at its periphery or when called upon *in extremis*. It cannot be right that in its finest manifestation ethical reasoning renders ethical reasons opaque.

I turn now to Harper Lee's *To Kill a Mockingbird*. Advocates of virtue ethics have claimed that Atticus Finch, the lawyer hero of the novel, is the *phronemos*, who shows us that a good lawyer relies upon their wisdom rather than upon rules or principles of right action. Though I think *Mockingbird* does provide useful insights into the ethical responsibilities of lawyers, I argue that the novel does not support the turn to virtue ethics. Indeed, I think Atticus's lesson is that we should not abandon rules and principles in favour of character. On the contrary, Atticus shows why we should be wary of relying upon at least certain versions of virtue ethics in the legal ethics context.[18]

To Kill a Mockingbird: an overview

In the simplest terms, *To Kill a Mockingbird*[19] is the story of the trial of a black man, Tom Robinson, for the rape of a white woman, Mayella Ewell, in racist Alabama in the 1930s. Appointed to defend Tom, Atticus Finch takes the task seriously, and in doing so draws upon himself and his children the slurs and taunts

---

18   I give a fuller versions of the following discussion in 'Legal ethics, virtue ethics, and Harper Lee's *To Kill a Mockingbird*' in *Challenges to Legal Ethics and Legal Practice* (ed.) Kim Economides (Oxford, Hart Publishing, 1998) pp. 39–60, and 'Lawyers, Ethics and *To Kill a Mockingbird*' *Philosophy and Literature*, vol. 25 (2001) pp. 127–141.

19   Harper Lee, *To Kill a Mockingbird* (London, 1960).

of neighbours. At trial he proves that Tom could not have raped Mayella, showing her attacker to have been left handed with two good arms while Tom had lost the use of his left arm in a cotton gin accident. The plain implication of the evidence is that Mayella's father, Bob Ewell, beat her after seeing her with her arm around Tom's waist. Yet Tom is convicted nonetheless. The verdict does not surprise Atticus. Racism, 'Maycomb's usual disease', has made it a forgone conclusion. Atticus tells Tom that they have a good chance on appeal, but Tom refuses to be comforted: 'Good-bye, Mr Finch,' he responds, 'there ain't nothing you can do now, so there ain't no use tryin.'[20] Sure enough, shortly afterwards, Tom is killed, shot 17 times while trying to climb a prison fence in full view of guards. Atticus describes the event as showing that Robinson was 'tired of white men's chances and preferred to take one of his own',[21] though it reads as easily as suicide and some commentators assume it was murder.[22] Robinson's death completes one story in *Mockingbird*: an innocent black man has been falsely accused, wrongfully convicted and killed.

Tom's story occurs in the middle parts of the novel, flanked by another. A central figure in this other story is Arthur 'Boo' Radley, the Finch's mysterious neighbour. He has been kept a recluse inside his family's house for close to 25 years, and has not been seen since stabbing his father with a pair of scissors about 15 years into this period of isolation. The Finch children – Scout, a 9-year-old tomboy, and Jem, a 12-year-old boy – regard Boo as a bogey man and they play what seem to them dangerous games of brinkmanship with him. The reader sees that Boo is not as the children perceive him. He is a gentle person – he leaves gifts for the children, he wraps a blanket around Scout as she watches a fire in the cold, he attempts to mend the trousers Jem has torn and abandoned in flight from a raid into the Radley property.

The two stories – Tom's and Boo's – come together at the end of the novel. Walking home from a school pageant the Finch children are attacked by Bob Ewell. Scout is saved by her pageant costume. Jem is knocked unconscious and has his arm badly broken. They are saved by a mysterious rescuer who turns out to be Boo Radley. Boo kills Bob Ewell. In what will be an important moment for my account of the novel, Atticus ultimately decides to go along with the Sheriff's recommendation that they do not charge Boo over Ewell's death. Instead, Atticus and the Sheriff adopt the fiction that Ewell fell on his knife.

---

20   Lee, *To Kill a Mockingbird*, p. 258.
21   Ibid., p. 260.
22   Monroe Freedman treats the episode as showing Atticus's naïveté: 'You can believe this improbable story [that Tom was broke into a blind, raving charge in a hopeless attempt to climb over the fence and escape], as Finch purports to. But I believe (and Harper Lee appears to believe) that Tom was goaded into a desperate, futile run for the fence on threat of being shot where he stood': Monroe Freedman, 'Atticus Finch - Right and Wrong', *Alabama Law Review*, vol. 45 (1994) pp. 473–482, p. 478.

Each of these stories is a vehicle for the moral fable which runs through *Mockingbird*. In the simplest terms still, this is a fable of innocence confronting evil and learning from the experience. Scout, the narrator, personifies the theme. Her childish innocence is a crucial part of her narration. The senselessness of the racism and class divisions which rent Maycomb is highlighted by her genuine lack of comprehension, just as her inability to comprehend Tom's conviction makes explicit the senselessness of justice being destroyed by prejudice. Scout finds all of these things mysterious, and through her eyes readers too are invited to cast aside any jaundice or resignation that may dull the impact of what is, after all, a tragically familiar story. Scout's innocence wanes during the course of the novel. It gives way, however, not to prejudice but to informed goodness and tolerance. The transformation is most evident in her attitude to Boo. At the beginning of the story she regards him as an outsider and misfit, legitimately tormented and feared. The novel closes with her taking his hand to lead him home and seeing that things look the same from the Radley porch as they do from her own.

Much of the credit for Scout's moral development is owed to Atticus. He is a loving, patient and understanding father who consciously and conscientiously guides his children to virtue while respecting them as individuals capable of judgment and decision. He teaches them compassion and tolerance, advising them to 'step into the shoes' of others. Atticus treats everybody, regardless of class or colour, with respect. He is courageous, both in the sense which leads him to zealously pursue Tom's defence despite knowing that it will not succeed, and in the more straightforward sense evident when he arms himself only with a newspaper though anticipating a confrontation with a lynch mob. In sum, Atticus's is a voice of decency, wisdom and reason, courageously speaking out against bigotry, ignorance and prejudice.

Mockingbird and legal ethics

Mockingbird's three great moments for legal ethics

There are three moments in *Mockingbird* of particular significance to lawyers and legal ethics. The first occurs in Atticus's summation to the jury. One often hears, he remarks, that men are created equal. On some construals the assertion is simply ridiculous: as a matter of fact, people are not born equally smart or equally wealthy. But, says Atticus:

> … there is one way in this country in which all men are created equal – there is one human institution that makes a pauper the equal of a Rockefeller, the stupid man the equal of an Einstein and the ignorant man the equal of any college president. That institution, gentlemen, is a court. It can be the Supreme Court of

the United States or the humblest J.P. court in the land, or this honourable court which you serve. Our courts have their faults, as does any human institution, but in this country our courts are the great levellers, and in our courts all men are created equal.[23]

The passage requires no further elucidation. It is as plain a statement of the role of courts as one could hope for. Whatever inequalities people suffer outside the court, within it they are to be treated as equals.

The second great moment occurs after Tom's death. Mr Underwood, the editor of the local newspaper, has published a courageous editorial condemning the death as sinful and senseless, likening it to the 'slaughter of songbirds'.[24] Initially, Scout is puzzled by the editorial: how could Tom's death be sinful when he had been granted due process of law and vigorously defended in an open court. But she continues:

> Then Mr Underwood's meaning became clear: Atticus had used every tool available to free men to save Tom Robinson, but in the secret courts of men's hearts Atticus had no case. Tom was a dead man the minute Mayella Ewell opened her mouth and screamed.[25]

Again, the meaning of the passage seems clear: Tom was convicted, despite the evidence, because he had not been tried in a court of law at all. His trial had been conducted 'in the secret courts of men's hearts'. These courts were governed not by presumptions of equality and innocence, but by the prejudices and bigotry that comprised Maycomb's usual disease. Atticus's plea to the jury, to ensure that Tom was tried in the public courts of law, had been ignored, and Tom had been convicted and killed as a result.

In his summation Atticus makes clear his commitment to the ideal of a rule of law – where a rule of law is to be understood precisely as rule by public standards rather than by the private wishes and inclinations of individuals. In Scout's explication of Mr Underwood's editorial we have a further elucidation of that commitment. An innocent man has died because a jury chose to try him secretly by their own standards rather than by those of the public system of law. Thus far, then, the message of *Mockingbird* to lawyers seems to be that they should fight for and maintain commitment to the rule of law rather than to the rule of individuals. They should honour and protect the public judgements of courts, not only in preference to, but also from the private judgements of individuals.

The third moment occurs in the novel's last few pages, when Tom's and Boo's stories come together. Bob Ewell has attacked Atticus's children as they walk home through the woods after dark. Ewell has been killed. Initially all that is

---

23 Lee, *To Kill a Mockingbird*, p. 227.
24 Ibid., p. 265.
25 Ibid., p. 266.

clear is that the children have been attacked and that their attacker lies dead, 'a kitchen knife stuck up under his ribs'.[26] Atticus thinks that Jem has killed Ewell, wresting the knife away during the attack, and he simply takes it for granted that Jem will go before a court, though he will be acquitted since 'it was clear cut self defence'.[27] Mr Tate, the sheriff, interrupts, telling Atticus that Jem did not stab Ewell; that he fell on his own knife. Atticus assumes Tate is trying to hush up what has happened to protect Jem, and refuses to go along with the subterfuge. But soon Atticus realises that it is not Jem that the sheriff is trying to protect. Boo Radley killed Ewell, and it is Boo who will be spared a trial by the fiction that Ewell fell on his own knife. It would, Tate maintains, be a sin to bring Boo before a court:

> To my way of thinking taking the one man who's done you and this town a great service an' draggin' him and his shy ways into the limelight – to me, that's a sin. It's a sin and I'm not about to have it on my head. If it was any other man it'd be different. But not this man. I may not be much, Mr Finch, but I'm still sheriff of Maycomb county, and Bob Ewell fell on his knife.[28]

Atticus sits, looking at the floor for a long time before finally raising his head and saying to Scout, 'Mr Ewell fell on his knife. Can you possibly understand?' Scout's response demonstrates that she understands perfectly well that there has been a decision to accept a fiction. 'Yes sir,' she says, 'I understand. Mr Tate was right. Well, it'd be sort of like shootin' a mockingbird, wouldn't it?'[29]

These three episodes pose an obvious challenge. In the first two we have a clear message in favour of the rule of law, put quite specifically as a warning about the danger of deciding upon guilt or innocence within the 'secret court's of men's hearts' rather than by the public processes of the courts of law. But this seems to be exactly what Atticus countenances in the final episode. Atticus and the sheriff have decided that Boo should be spared a trial. They have tried him in the secret courts of their own hearts and declared him innocent, and their decision is endorsed by Scout: to try Boo would be like shooting a mockingbird. What was a wicked thing in Tom's case is a good thing in Boo's case.

Mockingbird and the return to virtue

The challenge has not gone unnoticed. For the most part commentators applaud both Atticus's position in his summation and his decision to spare Boo. Indeed, the apparent inconsistency in Atticus's responses in the two episodes is taken to show his praiseworthy character and his laudable attitude toward the law. Claudia

---

26 Ibid., p. 294.
27 Ibid., p. 300.
28 Ibid., p. 304.
29 Ibid.

Johnson writes at length of Atticus's respect for law, before commenting on the Ewell/Radley decision:

> Despite Atticus's respect for the law, he believes that reason must prevail when law violates reason. In the case of Boo Radley's killing of Bob Ewell, law is proven inadequate, because on occasion reason dictates that laws and boundaries must be overridden for justice to be done. Circumstances must override honour; a human being's needs must supersede principle.[30]

Here the apparent inconsistency between Atticus's views in Tom's and Boo's cases is taken to illustrate Atticus's 'wisdom' or practical judgement. He is not a mere automaton mindlessly following the law wherever it may lead. Where following law would defeat justice, Atticus is prepared to abandon law in order to preserve or further more fundamental values. And even though Thomas Shaffer describes Atticus's decision to adopt a fiction over Ewell's death as a mistake, he does not think it diminishes Atticus as a hero. Rather, it shows us precisely 'how a good man makes a doubtful choice' and once again reminds us of the importance of character, since the episode demonstrates 'that more is involved than whether the choice is sound in principle'.[31]

These authors take the importance of *Mockingbird* to lie in its demonstration of the importance of the character of practitioners in professional ethics. In effect, they render Atticus's character coherent by subsuming his conduct under the notion of 'judgement'. His conduct may well be inconsistent when viewed from the perspective of this or that general principle or rule of right conduct, but this just shows the inadequacy of principle or rule-governed approaches to ethical conduct. This response to *Mockingbird* is part of the wider rediscovery of Aristotle and virtue ethics. It presents Atticus as the *phronemos*, an expert practical reasoner sensitive both to general principle and the particularities of cases. Atticus is one who knows what to do not by applying general principles, but by being the sort of person he is, by having the sort of character he has. Atticus recognises that confining himself to general principles such as those he defended at Tom's trial would be a recipe for obtuseness. Again, his lesson for us is the priority of character over rules and principles.[32]

---

30 Claudia Johnson, 'Without Tradition and Within Reason: Judge Horton and Atticus Finch in Court', *Alabama Law Review*, vol. 45 (1994), pp. 483–510, p. 499. See as well, Timothy Hall who, arguing for the ethical centrality of character, defines character by reference to Atticus, and concludes that Atticus allows us to see and teach how virtue and character guide the practice of law: Timothy Hall, 'Moral Character, the Practice of Law and Legal Education', *Mississippi Law Review* (1990) pp. 511–525.

31 Thomas L. Shaffer, 'The Moral Theology of Atticus Finch', *University of Pittsburg Law Review*, vol. 42 (1981) pp. 181–224, p. 196.

32 So Thomas Shaffer writes: 'One thing you could say about Atticus is that he had character…We say that a good person has character, but we do not mean to say only

Not all lawyers and commentators have been so ready to praise Atticus. Most influentially, Monroe Freedman has argued that Atticus was hardly a man to be admired since, as a state legislator and community leader in a segregated society, he lived 'his own life as the passive participant in that pervasive injustice'.[33] Though there is plainly disagreement between Freedman and the Atticans, as he dubs his opponents, there is also an important point of agreement. Both take it that Atticus's suitability as a role model for lawyers is to be settled by his character. Freedman argues against giving Atticus the job on the grounds that he is not the mythical figure portrayed by the Atticans: Atticus does not take on Robinson's defence willingly but only when appointed by the court. Atticus admits that he had hoped 'to get through life without a case of this kind'.[34] Atticus excuses the leader of a lynch mob as 'basically a good man' who 'just has his blind spots along with the rest of us'.[35] Atticus sees that 'one of these days we're going to pay the bill' for racism, but hopes that payment, and so justice for blacks, will not come during his children's lifetimes.[36] Freedman argues, then, that Atticus's character makes him unsuitable as a role model.[37]

---

that he believes in discernible moral principles and, under those principles, makes good decisions. We mean also to say something about who he is and to relate who he is to his good decisions. When discussion proceeds in this way, principles need not even be explicit. We can say, '"How would Atticus see this situation?"' or '"What would Atticus do?"' rather than, '"What principles apply?"' Thomas L. Shaffer, *Faith and the Professions* (Provo, Utah, 1987), p. 5. Note the similarity with Anthony Kronman's character-based account of the 'outstanding lawyer': ' – the one who serves as a model for the rest – is not simply an accomplished technician but a person of prudence or practical wisdom as well. It is of course rewarding to become technically proficient in the law. But earlier generations of American lawyers conceived their highest goal to be the attainment of a wisdom that lies beyond technique – a wisdom about human beings and their tangled affairs that anyone who wishes to provide real deliberative counsel must possess. They understood this wisdom to be a trait of character that one acquires only by becoming a person of good judgment, and not just an expert in the law ... When we attribute good judgment to a person, we imply more than that he has broad knowledge and a quick intelligence. We mean also to suggest that he shows a certain calmness in his deliberations, together with a balanced sympathy toward the various concerns of which his situation (or the situation of his client) requires that he take account. These are qualities as much of feeling as of thought.' Anthony Kronman, *The Lost Lawyer*, pp. 2 and 16.

33   Monroe Freedman, 'Atticus Finch, Esq., R.I.P.', *Legal Times* (24 February 1992) p. 20.
34   Lee, *To Kill a Mockingbird*, p. 98.
35   Ibid., p. 173.
36   Ibid., pp. 243–244.
37   Monroe Freedman, 'Atticus Finch – Right and Wrong'.

An alternative reading of the three moments: Atticus as a tragic figure

I think there is a more natural reading of these passages which shifts attention from Atticus's character altogether. I believe that we should regard Atticus as a tragic rather than a wise figure, and that by doing so we unearth a very different lesson about the moral responsibilities of lawyers. *Mockingbird* has at least some elements of tragedy: an innocent man falls victim to evil despite the best efforts of the novel's hero. Atticus's story, too, is tragic. He is a man who regards the rule of law as of tremendous importance. He presents his arguments in its favour to the jury with passion and all of his professional ability, recognising that the life of an innocent man rests upon his success. But he fails and Tom dies. When a decision over Boo is required, Atticus is struck by the similarities between the cases. Boo's case is hauntingly familiar to Atticus. Both Tom and Boo are mockingbirds: innocents whom it would be sinful to harm. Both Tom and Boo are 'outsiders': Tom because he is black and Boo because he is simple and has lived as a recluse, isolated from the dominant community. And, of course, Atticus is cast as protector of both men. In each case, an outsider must rely upon the dominant community to ignore the fact that they are outsiders. In Tom's case it did not do so despite Atticus's best efforts. When confronted with the fact that Boo stabbed Bob Ewell, Atticus must decide whether he will allow another outsider to face that threat. In Boo's case he has the power to do what he tried and failed to do in Tom's case. When faced with the possibility of another tragedy in Boo's case, Atticus's faith in the rule of law, and perhaps his courage as well, fail him. He cannot bear the possibility that he will be party to the 'death' of another mockingbird. In the end Atticus abandons a principle that he has passionately defended, in terms of which he has understood himself, which has to a large extent secured his unique and valuable role in Maycomb. That is the stuff of tragedy: a principled man has been confronted by the inability of principles by which he understands himself to resist evil, and realises that he cannot risk another loss. He abandons the principles and adopts a fiction. Whether or not it is wicked to try people in the secret courts of men's hearts now depends upon which men's hearts.

Understanding Atticus as a tragic figure provides us with an explanation of what happened in Boo's case. We need not strain for an interpretation that makes Atticus's conduct consistent: it was not consistent. It is not that Atticus was throughout acting as the *phronemos*, an eye firmly on substantive principles of justice and fairness. He was a more accessible figure, who tragically though understandably was not prepared to risk a vulnerable person who was effectively in his care having so recently seen how his legal system mistreated another similarly placed outsider.

It is important not to misunderstand the significance of interpreting Atticus as a tragic figure. The point is not to brand Atticus as less than admirable and *therefore* as unsuited to the job the Atticans would give him. I propose the reading of Atticus as a tragic figure as an alternative to the conclusion that Atticus deliberated as an Aristotelian *phronemos* and as an alternative to the assumption shared by both sides of the debate that his significance for legal ethics is to be settled by reference to his character. Cast as a tragic figure, Atticus has a very different message for us from that which he conveys as a wise figure. We are not meant to *admire* what he does qua tragic figure; rather, we are meant to be struck by the gravity of his loss. Viewed as a tragic figure his message is one about the value of the principles he has abandoned, not one about the desirability of regarding them as disposable, or trivial, or burdensome.

Challenges to Atticus as *Phronemos*: Boo's case

A tenacious Attican might claim that even if Atticus did abandon the principles he defended in Tom's case, the decision to do so was a wise one, and does not show Atticus to have acted other than as a *phronemos*. But there are reasons to reject this assessment. Some of these reasons are specific to Boo's case: they undercut the claim that Atticus's decision in Boo's case was a wise one. I examine these 'Boo-specific' issues in this section. Other reasons to reject the assessment are more general, having to do with the social roles of law and lawyers. I turn to these more general issues in the following section.

Perhaps the most striking Boo-specific feature in this context is the fate from which Atticus and Sheriff Tate are attempting to save Boo. In portraying Atticus as a tragic figure I suggested that he could not bear the thought of being party to the death of another mockingbird. The talk of 'death' is rhetorical. The rhetoric is warranted if we seek to characterise the phenomenological structure of Boo's case for Atticus. It is the appropriateness of 'death' in this context which explains why Scout speaks so effectively when she likens putting Boo on trial to 'shootin' a mockingbird'. But the reference to death *is* rhetorical. None of the parties to the decision to spare Boo seem to think that there is any very real chance Boo will suffer Tom's fate. They take it for granted that he has committed no crime and that he will be acquitted. It is not even the trauma of the trial which is foremost in Atticus's or the Sheriff's minds. Sheriff Tate makes this clear when he says to Atticus: '… maybe you'll say it's my duty to tell the town all about it and not hush it up. Know what'd happen then? All the ladies of Maycomb includin' my wife'd be knocking on his door bringing him angel food cakes. To my way of thinkin', Mr Finch, taking the one man whose done you and this town a great service an' draggin' him and his shy ways into the limelight – to me, that's a sin.'[38]

The worst Sheriff Tate can imagine for Boo is that he will be besieged by grateful Maycomb ladies. Now plainly neither Scout, Atticus nor the Sheriff think this a trivial matter for Boo. Given Boo's shy ways this public attention would be an ordeal. But surely this cannot be an appropriate ground upon which to reject what on anybody's reading of the novel is a fundamental principle of justice. This is to suggest that Atticus made a mistake in Boo's case. He did so, I have

---

38 Lee, *To Kill a Mockingbird*, p. 304.

suggested, because his deliberations were dominated by the perception that Boo was, like Tom, an outsider. But while Boo was indeed an outsider, he was an outsider of a very different sort to Tom, and the difference was both plain and important. We see it illustrated starkly in the Sheriff's very different responses to Boo and Tom. After a somewhat perfunctory investigation of each episode, he immediately arrests Tom, with no apparent qualms about the reliability of the Ewells' accusation. He does not, for instance, think it necessary to obtain medical evidence of the assault, an omission to which Atticus draws critical attention at the trial. Yet he decides on the spot to adopt a fiction to spare Boo a trial, evidencing a sensitivity to Boo quite absent from his dealings with Tom. Atticus says not a word about the Sheriff's apparent change of heart, but it shows that Boo was not the same sort of outsider as Tom. As compared with both Tom Robinson and Bob Ewell, Boo is a privileged outsider, but Atticus seems not to have noticed, or to have given too little weight to this fact.

There are other reasons to wonder how well Atticus deals with Boo's case. It does not seem to occur to him that the involvement of his own children in Boo's case is a reason to insist upon a public response. His gratitude to the man who saved his children is surely understandable and one can see that a parent in his position would be loathe to be the very one to insist that his children's rescuer be put through a public trial and, in Boo's case, the ensuing ordeal of displays of public gratitude. By the same token, however, surely the involvement of his own children should have led him to be especially careful about trying Boo in the secret court of his own heart. It is also striking that no 'middle grounds' are canvassed. There is no discussion of the possibility of putting Boo on trial and forbidding Maycomb's ladies from bombarding him with angel cakes for instance. And nor is there any discussion of whether the public has a legitimate interest in knowing what has happened. It is surely only a little churlish to point out that Boo had already had special consideration from the legal authorities, and that it was far from obvious that it had been to his benefit. 'According to neighbourhood legend', at least, he had been released into his father's custody rather than being sent away to a state industrial school after some youthful high jinks. While his fellow hooligans 'received the best secondary education to be had in the state; one of them eventually working his way through to engineering school in Albany', Boo was not seen or heard of for 15 years.[39] He did not come to public attention again until he gratuitously stabbed his father with a pair of scissors. Again, he received special consideration: after a period in the local cells he was once more released into his family's custody rather than being sent for psychiatric help, his father insisting 'no Radley was going to any asylum'.[40] By the time of the episodes recounted in *Mockingbird*, Boo has been held a recluse in his family home for some 25 years! Surely one need not be terribly hard-hearted to think that the local community has an interest in knowing that a person with Boo's history had been

---

39 Ibid., p. 11.
40 Ibid., p. 12.

about with a honed kitchen knife, no matter how much Ewell deserved his fate or how clearly Boo had merely been trying to prevent a crime. And equally, one might wonder whether Boo would have been better served precisely by bringing him out of the shadowy world he had occupied for so long.

We have seen that Thomas Shaffer also describes Atticus's decision to spare Boo as a mistake, though he thinks it is one which shows 'how a good man makes a doubtful choice', and once again reminds us of the importance of principle, demonstrating 'that more is involved than whether the choice is sound in principle'.[41] But I think that Sheriff Tate had it right when he said:

> Mr Finch I hate to fight you when you're like this. You've been under a strain tonight no man should ever have to go through. Why you ain't in bed from it I don't know. But I do know that for once you haven't been able to put two and two together.[42]

There is of course a link between this reading of Atticus's decision in Boo's case and the interpretation of him as a tragic figure. He makes a poor decision in Boo's case because his focus on the common themes between the cases prevents him paying sufficient detail to the particularities of Boo's situation. Indeed, the considerations, and Atticus Finch's response to them, may be regarded as a further defence of the reading of Atticus as a tragic figure. It is difficult to believe they would not have moved 'Atticus the wise', but we might expect 'Atticus the tragic' to respond just as Atticus Finch responds. This, however, is not their only significance. They also speak to the difficulty even a character like Atticus will face from time to time in making decisions in particular cases, and in this role are reasons to be wary of the character approach in general. If even Atticus cannot avoid the sort of understandable cognitive dissonance which seems on reflection to mark his deliberations in Boo's case, then we should favour an alternative approach which places less emphasis upon the particular judgements of individuals. A rule or principle-based approach, though not of course eliminating the need for judgement, is such an alternative.

There is another point to be drawn from this discussion. Behind much of it has been the idea that the decision to spare Boo would have been more reasonable had there been a genuine risk that Boo would have suffered Tom's fate. I have suggested that the facts of Boo's case simply do not support that conclusion. But suppose for a moment that I am wrong about that. Suppose, that is, that Boo's status as an outsider would have led a Maycomb jury to convict him unjustly of wrongdoing in the death of Bob Ewell. What lesson should we take from *Mockingbird* on this reading? Not, I think, that lawyers should admire and emulate Atticus's alleged attitude to rules and principles. On the contrary, on this reading it would be precisely the jury's disregard for public principles of justice in favour

---

41 Shaffer, 'The moral theology of Atticus Finch', p. 196.
42 Lee, *To Kill a Mockingbird*, p. 303.

of private prejudice which led to the injustice in Tom's case. Once again, on the reading of the novel that supposes a genuine risk of a serious injustice in Boo's case, Atticus's lesson is one about the *importance* of rules and principles, not one about their triviality.

Challenges to character-based approaches to legal ethics

The role of law

I remarked that there were two sorts of reasons to doubt that Atticus's decision in Boo's case was a wise one, some specific to Boo's case and others which were of more general import. In this section I turn to the reasons of the second sort. These are reasons to think that we should reject the character-based approach to legal ethics itself, quite apart from the grounds for thinking Atticus was led astray in Boo's case. They will be familiar. They are essentially applications of the arguments given in Chapters 4 and 5.

The appeal to the role of law in Chapter 4 proceeded from the idea that the most significant fact about modern Western societies was the existence of a plurality of reasonable views of how one should live. A central part of the liberal response to this fact has been the establishment of procedures and institutions that aspire to an ideal of neutrality between the reasonable views represented in the communities to which they apply. The members of a pluralist community, the idea goes, will often be able to agree on the structure of neutral institutions and practices even where they cannot agree on the right outcome of a policy question as a substantive matter. Of course, these institutions and practices cannot guarantee outcomes that will suit all the reasonable views: often there will be no such universally acceptable outcomes. The hope of liberalism, however, is that even those whose substantive preferences do not win the day on this or that occasion will have cause to accept the decisions of these institutions as fair and just. At the very least, they must have reason to believe that their views have been taken seriously and that the decision procedures have not simply turned the individual preferences of some members of the community into public policy to be imposed on all.

Precisely these sorts of general political concerns lie behind the requirement that individuals are to be tried by public standards in public courts rather than by private or secret tribunals. Why object to trials in the secret courts of men's hearts? Not because we are worried about whether or not we have the right men's hearts. Rather, because a crucial part of the role of law in pluralist communities is to allow individuals to *see* the mechanisms by which public decisions are made and to *see* that those mechanisms have indeed been used in particular cases. Liberal community, so understood, is undercut by those who insist upon appeal to their own substantive views of the good rather than to the procedures. Appeals to individual judgement are likely to be conceptually confused as well: to suppose it legitimate to override public process when it conflicts with private judgement is to ignore the fact that it is the inappropriateness of appeal to private judgement which leads us to adopt public decision processes in the first place.

Atticus had it right in his summation to the jury. A commitment to tolerance and equality, a readiness to 'walk in another's shoes', leads to decision procedures which render trial within the secret courts of men's hearts illegitimate. Atticus's decision to spare Boo a public trial is a mistake not just because it fails to take account of the particular facts of Boo's case, but because it undercuts the role of law in securing community between people who hold a range of diverse and reasonable views. This view about the role of law in pluralist societies has consequences for the ethical obligations of lawyers. They act improperly when they substitute their own judgements for those of the procedures, acceptance of which makes pluralist community possible. An appreciation of the role of law should lead us away from rather than towards a character-based approach to legal ethics. The issue is not whether we have the right men's hearts, but whether any individual's heart will do.

Anthony Kronman: The Lost Lawyer

This discussion provides a response to a recent and important contribution to the legal ethics debate. Anthony Kronman has argued that the legal profession is in the grip of 'a spiritual crisis which strikes at the heart of [the lawyer's] professional pride' and threatens the very soul of the profession itself.[43] The crisis has resulted from the demise of a professional ideal – the ideal of the 'lawyer-statesman' – which portrayed the outstanding or model lawyer as, in essence, Aristotle's *phronemos*: not a mere technician but a person of practical wisdom possessed of a range of honourable and more or less peculiarly legal character traits. This Aristotelian professional ideal served as a model for lawyers for the better part of two centuries, providing compelling reason to believe the various 'law-jobs' worthwhile. With its demise lawyers have come to regard law as an essentially technical discipline requiring no particular character or virtue on the part of its leading practitioners, judges and teachers. Kronman aims to revise and revive the Aristotelian ideal in the hope that 'we may ... find a foundation for the belief that to be a lawyer is to be a person of a particular kind, a person one may reasonably take pride in being'.[44]

As the 'lawyer-statesman' epithet suggests, Kronman takes lawyers to have a significant leadership role. In the political sphere, the lawyer-statesman seeks a certain kind of political integrity, namely, one which obtains despite the existence of significant and ineradicable conflict. The lawyer-statesman directs us to a condition of political wholeness in which 'the members of a community are joined by bonds of sympathy, despite the differences of opinion that set them apart on

---

43 Kronman, *The Lost Lawyer*, p. 2.
44 Kronman, 'Practical Wisdom and Professional Character', p. 208.

questions concerning the ends, and hence the identity, of their community'.[45] By establishing bonds of fellow feeling among the members of a community – bonds based upon a willingness to sympathise with the interests and concerns of others within the community – political fraternity helps to counteract the destructive forces posed by groundless yet identifying choices which confront both individuals and communities.

The discussion of the role of law and lawyers given above allows us a better account of these matters. First, note that the 'procedural' story is directed precisely at securing political community in the face of ongoing substantive dispute. The neutral institutions of political liberalism aim to give us ways of going on as a community which take the reasonable views represented within our midst seriously, and which assure even those whose personal preferences have failed to carry the day that neither they nor their views have been ignored. Law is an essential part of the effort to secure stable and just political community between the advocates of diverse views of the good.

Given this role, the procedural approach provides a response to Kronman's spiritual crisis as well: on the procedural account the various law jobs are extraordinarily important in pluralist communities and hence are ones in which lawyers can and should take pride. One might think, indeed, that some such story would be a source of considerably more comfort to lawyers than Kronman's – it tells them, after all, that what most of them are doing has moral and political value. It seems not unlikely that any current crisis of morale would be made worse by Kronman's conclusion that contemporary lawyers belong to the generation that killed the lawyer-statesman. The lesson for legal ethics, I believe, is not that lawyers need to throw over the rule- and principle-based model of professional ethical obligation, but that they should be brought to appreciate the significance of the social roles they serve, and to understand and take pride in fulfilling the duties that flow from those roles.

The client-professional relationship

In Chapter 5 I argued for an analysis of the client-professional relationship which I said supported the standard conception of the lawyer's role. We can relate that analysis to *Mockingbird* by noting a difference between Atticus's position and that of most contemporary lawyers. *Mockingbird* is importantly the story of an intimate community. A good deal of the book is concerned to place Atticus and his family within Maycomb, to show how he and his forebears came to the town, and

---

45   Kronman, *The Lost Lawyer*, p. 93. It is no coincidence that Kronman appeals to historical examples of the lawyer-statesman, just as the Atticans appeal to the fictional figure of Atticus. Both are led to 'define' the *phronemos* ostensively, since they are suspicious of the possibility of doing so by appeal to anything like 'principles' of deliberation or good character. The use of such principles would threaten to undercut the suppositions of the character approach.

to show that the neighbours and the community know him well. As a result, we might suppose, Atticus's professional relationships have much in common with relationships such as those between family members or friends. But this is not typical. We do not tend to know our lawyers as the Maycomb folk know Atticus. Nonetheless, we often, of necessity, place ourselves in positions of vulnerability to our professionals in a way and to an extent which we would typically reserve for much more intimate relationships. In these latter relationships we have grounds – our intimate or personal knowledge of the individual – to make assessments of the character of the person to whom we are vulnerable, their motivations, their priorities, and so forth, which explain our willingness to place ourselves in their hands. But because most of us do not have this kind of detailed knowledge of our professionals – because most of us do not live in Maycomb or anywhere much like it – we cannot rely upon the character of our professionals as we rely upon the characters of friends. This is to say that the clients of professionals typically rely upon relative strangers, to whom they stand in relationships of considerable inequality of expertise, for things of importance, when they cannot reliably assess or constrain the diligence or expertise which the professional applies to the task. The result is that the 'character aspect' of the virtues approach makes it inappropriate for professional and legal ethics. Clients do not have access to information about the character of their professionals in a way which would make it reasonable to ask them to place themselves in positions of vulnerability in reliance upon character-based considerations.

Few people manage to get through their lives without requiring the services of a professional. Given the analysis of professional-client relations sketched here and defended in Chapter 5, it is important not only that professionals are ethical, but also that clients and potential clients have some way of knowing the ethical stance of practitioners even though they do not know them or their moral views personally. The adoption and promulgation of a distinct professional morality is a way of making the ethics of the profession public as the personal ethics of its members cannot be. Clients get the benefit of this 'public ethics', however, only if it is indeed given priority over personal ethics in members' dealings with the public. The client need only know what values the professional role requires the professional to adopt, and that the professional is a role-occupant, to know what values at least should govern the professional's conduct in the relationship. In a different world, perhaps one characterised by the positive communal aspects of life in Maycomb, we may not need these guides to the ethical views of our professionals. But Maycomb, both thankfully and sadly, is not our world.

Virtue ethics and rules

The discussion in this chapter has concentrated on an interpretation of virtue ethics according to which it gives priority to character over rules and principles. The concentration seems justified given the particular content of the debate about

Mockingbird. Certainly, this is the issue between Shaffer and Freedman, and McDowell and Nussbaum seem to have a 'character-based' model of virtue ethics in mind when they speak of the 'priority of perception over rules' and the idea that 'one knows what to do (if one does) not by applying universal principles but by being a certain sort of person: one who sees situations in a certain way'.[46] As I remarked at the outset, however, the virtue ethics renaissance is still in its infancy. Contemporary virtue ethics has still to find a final form. One of the issues currently under discussion is whether virtue ethics can give greater weight to rules and principles than is proposed by the particular advocates we have discussed. Dean Cocking and Justin Oakley think it can do so. They argue that discussion of virtue ethics which focuses upon character misses the point. There is, they maintain, 'no reason why virtue ethics must hold that the character of the moral exemplar whose actions determine what is right for us cannot have internalised and be guided by certain principles'. Indeed, they recommend a 'plural value view' under which:

> … virtue ethics construes the character of the virtuous agent as governed by a variety of principles, ranging from the general to the very specific, which are importantly informed, justified, and constrained by broad-based values and by particular role, relation, and practice-sensitive features. The alleged opposition, then, between an ethics of character and one of principle is rendered misguided and obsolete.[47]

Similarly, Rosalind Hursthouse responds to the charge that virtue ethics 'does not tell us what to do', by arguing for a version of virtue ethics which appeals, not directly to the character of virtuous agents, but instead to 'virtue-rules' such as 'act honestly', 'do not act uncharitably' and so on, derived from the virtues and vices, which are to be 'enumerated, as the deontologist's rules have been'.[48] Virtuous agents, on this account, will be possessed of character traits or dispositions to act according to such rules. The response, writes Hursthouse,

> … amounts to a denial of the oft-repeated claim that virtue ethics does not come up with any rules … We can see now that it comes up with a large number; not only does each virtue generate a prescription – act honestly, charitably, justly – but each vice a prohibition – do not act dishonestly, uncharitably, unjustly.[49]

Of course, this strategy poses an obvious difficulty for virtue ethics. As Hursthouse writes, '…if the virtuous agent can only be specified as an agent

---

46 John McDowell, 'Virtue and Reason', in Clarke and Simpson *Anti-Theory in Ethics and Moral Conservatism* (1989) pp. 87–109, p. 105.

47 Cocking and Oakley, *Virtue Ethics and Professional Roles*, pp. 82–83.

48 Rosalind Hursthouse, 'Normative virtue ethics' in *How Should One Live? Essays on the Virtues* (ed.) Roger Crisp (Oxford, 1996) pp. 19–36, p. 25.

49 Ibid., p. 23.

disposed to act in accordance with moral rules, as some have assumed, then virtue ethics collapses back into deontology and is no rival to it.'[50] William Frankena suggests some such thing when he proposes that we 'regard the morality of duty and principles and the morality of virtues or traits of character not as rival kinds of morality between which we must choose, but as two complementary aspects of the same morality.'[51] Hursthouse resists this collapse. Even if virtue ethics were to generate the very same rules as deontology, she suggests, still the deontologist and the virtue ethicist would understand those rules and their application very differently. The 'theoretical distinction between the two approaches,' she writes, 'is that the familiar rules, and their application in particular cases, are given an entirely different backing.' Whereas the deontologist supposes that one should not lie because to do so would be to breach the rule 'do not lie', '[a]ccording to virtue ethics, I must not lie, since it would be dishonest, and dishonesty is a vice…'.[52]

I have some reservations about this strategy for securing the distinction between Hursthouse's virtue rules and the more familiar deontologist's version. Hursthouse seems to walk a very fine line. If the dispositions to follow the rules are very robust – so that a virtuous agent never or almost never appealed directly to the 'entirely different backing' – then the view does seem to collapse into deontology. If the dispositions are less robust, however, so that the agent though disposed to follow the rules is more ready to appeal directly to the virtues – if the entirely different backing is closer to the surface – then the rules seem less secure. One wants to know, in other words, under what circumstances would Hursthouse's virtuous agent appeal directly to the 'entirely different backing' rather than to the rule?

For current purposes however, I do not think we need to settle the issue. The preceding arguments against character-based virtue ethics – the appeal to the role of law and to the nature of the client professional relationship – concentrated upon the idea that what matters in law is a public statement of the rules and principles which will govern the conduct of the professional. Hence, I have no quarrel with a version of virtue ethics which gives sufficient priority to rules of conduct to allow the clients of professionals to rely upon those rules to determine how the virtuous agent will conduct themself; to determine what values will govern the professional in their dealings with the client. I have no quarrel, that is, with a version of virtue ethics that portrays the virtuous lawyer as possessing the virtue or disposition to take the rules of conduct seriously. If virtue ethics can allow rules this priority – whether because of its general account of virtue and the virtuous agent, or because of its view about the appropriate virtues in the particular context (a virtue ethicist might accept the arguments against character-based ethics and think that the virtuous lawyer, at least, should treat the rules of conduct very robustly) – then the ground or backing of this priority does not seem especially important.

---

50 Ibid.
51 William K. Frankena, *Ethics* (Englewood Cliffs, NJ, 1973) p.65.
52 Hursthouse, 'Normative virtue ethics', pp. 27–28.

Chapter 7
Detachment, Distance and Integrity

Introduction

In Chapter 2 I attempted to lay out the strands of the critique of the standard conception. A number of strands of the critique were motivated by concerns about 'detachment' or 'professional distance', and the threats these phenomena pose to personal integrity. According to Gerald Postema, the standard conception portrays the role-occupant as a mere witness, a detached bystander, to situations in which they are personally and significantly involved. Kazuo Ishiguro's butler, Mr Stevens, sees everything through the norms of his role, and is as a consequence unable to respond as an individual to Miss Kenton or to his father, or to see that ordinary morality calls upon him to protest as his employer is duped by his Nazi guests. The crisis of morale that grips the legal profession is due in part, according to another strand of the critique, to the 'moral schizophrenia' role-differentiation often involves. Montaigne may be comfortable that he can fill the office of the Mayor of Bordeaux without moving his own finger, but most of us are likely to find this sort of division more taxing, morally and psychologically if not metaphysically, the more so if our professional selves are called upon not merely to witness, but to advocate on behalf of causes to which our lay-selves are deeply opposed. These strands of the critique seem to raise concerns about the ways in which the standard conception calls upon professionals to distance themselves from their lay-persona, from the claims of ordinary morality, from the circumstances in which they act, from the people they engage with when acting as role-occupants. It seems to require, in sum, that lawyers acting under the standard conception sacrifice their integrity.

In subsequent chapters I have defended a modified version of the standard conception. My hope, of course, is that it can provide responses to the various strands of the critique. In this chapter I explore the capacity of my version to respond to these concerns about distance, detachment and integrity. I proceed from the idea that lawyers are not merely passive recipients of professional norms or instruments of client preferences; the aim from the beginning has been to provide lawyers themselves with moral reasons to take their roles seriously. The key to a response to the cluster of concerns about integrity lies, I think, in the moral engagement this approach assumes. For morally engaged professionals, I propose, there is no essential conflict between personal integrity and recognition of the authority of role-obligations. In a bit more detail, I offer an account of integrity resting on the simple idea that whether or not a person has integrity depends crucially upon whether they have engaged in a process of sincere and thorough critical reflection upon their situation and been prepared to embrace the recommendations of that reflection. Reflective role-occupants, I hope to show, can give proper weight to the role-differentiated norms of their role without sacrificing their integrity.

An important part of my defence of this simple idea is an examination of three influential accounts of integrity, according to which integrity requires or consists in the maintenance of autonomy, or an integrated self, or fidelity to identity-conferring commitments or ground projects. Each of these views identifies something – autonomy, integration, identity – that is important to integrity. However each faces significant difficulties. Integrity, I will argue, cannot be autonomy as the autonomy view understands that notion, and, as many others have pointed out, the integration or identity views too readily grant integrity to those who hold fast to views or sets of views which are integrated or identity conferring but also morally obnoxious. We can significantly reduce these difficulties, however, and so hold onto the intuition that the views in question do identify things important to integrity, if we read them in light of the requirement for sincere and thorough reflection. Integrity is not autonomy, or integration, or identity, and certainly none of these things alone – each of the views 'reduces integrity to something that it is not'[1] – but these are the sort of things to which a person of integrity should have proper regard in a process of sincere and thorough reflection, and it is this process of reflection which underpins integrity, not the particular outcome or focus identified by any of the views discussed.

This may sound very abstract, more about the concept of integrity than about the position of role-occupants faced with demands to distance themselves from their lay-persona, from the claims of ordinary morality, from the people they engage with when acting as role-occupants. The idea, however, is that the process of reflection which underpins integrity will lead lawyers of integrity to traverse something approaching the model of legal ethics offered in this book, and that that model addresses the problems of distance, detachment and integrity on a number of fronts: it seeks to minimise the conflict between the demands of role morality and those of ordinary or broad-based morality by limiting the excesses of advocacy; it offers a model of professional roles which, while insisting on a 'clean break' between role morality and broad-based morality, nonetheless recognises the contribution of ordinary morality at the point of institutional design; it offers a moral argument for the particular differentiated demands of the lawyer's role, suggesting that there are reasons of ordinary morality to take those demands seriously; and it shows that lawyers have a professional moral obligation to engage in a constant

---

1   Cheshire Calhoun, 'Standing for Something', *Journal of Philosophy*, vol. 42 (1995) pp. 235–260, p. 235. Calhoun remarks that each of the conceptions she identifies 'ultimately reduces integrity to something else to which it is not equivalent – to the conditions of unified agency, to the conditions for continuing as the same self, to the conditions for having a reason to refuse cooperating with some evils' (p. 235). It will be obvious that my account of integrity is much influenced by Calhoun's influential treatment, not least by this methodological observation.

process of law reform, aimed at promoting fit between the lawyer's role morality and broad-based morality. And now my suggestion is that the model really does have the resources to respond to the troubling concerns about distance, detachment and integrity. There is nothing in the notion of integrity which should lead us to deny it to a lawyer who reflects upon the nature of their role and its grounding in ordinary morality, who sees why it generates role-differentiated obligations and permissions, who accepts those permissions and obligations, appreciating the ways in which they call upon them to depart from ordinary morality, and who accepts that they may be called upon from time to time to occupy the related role of critic. Role-occupants, this is to say, can recognise the authority of role-differentiated norms without sacrificing their integrity. I turn, then, to the alternative accounts of integrity, aiming to find support for my 'reflective' reading of that virtue.[2]

Integrity as autonomy

I begin with what I have called the autonomy view of integrity. I approach the view in a slightly roundabout way, by responding to a book which made a splash in political philosophy in the 1970s. In his influential *In Defense of Anarchism*, Robert Paul Wolff argued that there was an irreconcilable conflict between legitimate authority and the moral autonomy of the individual.[3] Seeing why Wolff was mistaken allows us to see how many critics of the standard conception are mistaken about the conflict between personal integrity and the recognition of role-demands. According to Wolff, a state enjoyed legitimate authority only if it had a right to command those subject to it, and its subjects had a correlative obligation to obey its commands. Wolff used the term 'obey' in a strict sense. Acting consistently with a state's commands – 'complying' in Wolff's terms – was not sufficient to show obedience. Subjects obeyed commands only when their motive for acting one way rather than another was the fact that they had been commanded to do so. Obedience in this sense, Wolff argued, was inconsistent with autonomy. The autonomous person, he argued, assumed responsibility for her actions, where doing so 'involve[d] attempting to determine what one ought to do, and that ... [laid] upon one the additional burdens of gaining knowledge, reflecting on motives, predicting outcomes, criticizing principles, and so forth.'[4] Wolff thought that the autonomous person could never legitimately obey a command; never legitimately perform an act merely because it had been commanded. To do so would be to

---

2   I have restricted discussion to the autonomy, integration and identity views since I think they suffice to draw out what I think is important about integrity. I think the sorts of points to make, however, could be drawn out of almost all of the significant accounts of integrity to be found in the literature. All give an important place to critical reflection, and that, rather than the particular substantive view a particular account favours, is what matters for integrity.

3   Robert Paul Wolff, *In Defense of Anarchism* (New York, 1970).

4   Ibid., p. 12.

surrender autonomy, and so the very basis of one's status as a moral agent: 'When I place myself in the hands of another.' he wrote, 'and permit him to determine the principles by which I shall guide my behavior, I repudiate the freedom and reason which give me dignity.'[5]

Wolff's understanding of autonomy and its significance has much in common with the idea of integrity as it appears in many discussions of moral and, more particularly, professional, obligation. Like Wolff's autonomous agent, the person of integrity in this strand of the literature is motivated by *their own* principles and decisions, taking on the 'burden of gaining knowledge, reflecting on motives, predicting outcomes, criticizing principles, and so forth'. And, just as Wolff concluded that this understanding of autonomy was inconsistent with authority, so contributors to the professional ethics debate have concluded that integrity interpreted in this way is inconsistent with recognition of the authority of role-demands. Having given an account of integrity along the lines just summarised, Sharon Dolovich appeals to the obligation to maintain client confidentiality and continues:

> From the perspective of integrity, the confidentiality rules ... deny lawyers the possibility of exercising their own judgment and acting consistently with their own moral commitments to decide when disclosure is warranted. Such strictures ... force the lawyer to give preference to the interests of clients even when doing so conflicts with the lawyer's most strongly held moral commitments, short circuiting the process of deliberative judgment by dictating the outcome, whatever the lawyer might conclude on the basis of his own moral sense to be the right course of action. In this way a lawyer's own moral character and moral judgment become irrelevant, not just in the larger scheme, but to her own actions. She acts on the basis of some other actor's dictates, not her own.[6]

Further, she continues, following such rules:

> ... trains lawyers over time to suppress the exercise of their own moral judgment and the accompanying traits of moral integrity ... Those who adhere mechanically, without reserving to themselves the obligation of assessing *in each case* the moral appropriateness of the rule's dictates, can expect to see ... the traits that comprise integrity ... atrophy with disuse.[7]

It is easy enough to see why someone concerned to preserve the possibility of integrity within roles might be drawn to the autonomy model of integrity. The model places the problem of integrity at just the right place for those, such

---

5 Ibid., p. 72.
6 Sharon Dolovich, 'Ethical Lawyering and the Possibility of Integrity', *Fordham Law Review*, vol. 70 (1979) pp. 1629–1687, p. 1674.
7 Ibid., emphasis added.

as Dolovich, who see the problem of integrity as essentially a conflict between integrity and the acknowledgment of the authority of the role. But Wolff was wrong about the conflict between autonomy and authority, and so are those who paint a straightforward conflict between integrity and the recognition of role-demands. There is nothing new in disagreeing with Wolff – contemporary critics were legion[8] – but it is useful to look back at his argument from the perspective of more recent work in the philosophy of law and practical reasoning. In short, my claim is that Wolff's autonomy/authority antinomy is generated by a mistaken view about practical reasoning – a view his critics tended to share – and about the way a class of reasons for action, such as rules, feature in such reasoning. Wolff's model implies that the autonomous agent cannot legitimately use such reasons, but they are so central to any life that involves cooperation and commitment that no account of autonomy that puts them beyond the pale for the autonomous agent can be right. Far from being *inconsistent* with autonomy, they are just the sorts of strategies likely to appeal to a reflective autonomous agent committed to 'attempting to determine what ... to do, and [shouldering] the additional burdens of gaining knowledge, reflecting on motives, predicting outcomes, criticizing principles, and so forth.'[9] So what was Wolff's view of legitimate, autonomous, practical reasoning? Consider the following example, which Wolff offered in explanation of his view (emphasis in the original):

> If someone in my environment is issuing what are intended as commands, and if he or others expects those commands to be obeyed, that fact will be taken into account in my deliberations. I may decide that I ought to do what that person is commanding me, and it may even be that his issuing the command is the factor in the situation that makes it desirable to do so. For example, if I am on a sinking ship and the captain is giving orders for manning the lifeboats, and if everyone else is obeying the order *because he is the captain*, I may decide that under the circumstances I had better do what he says, since the confusion caused by disobeying him would be generally harmful. But insofar as I make such a decision, I am not *obeying his command;* that is, I am not acknowledging him as having authority over me. I would make the same decision, for exactly the same reasons, if one of the passengers had started to issue 'orders' and had in the confusion come to be obeyed.[10]

---

8   See, for instance, Harry G. Frankfurt, 'The Anarchism of Robert Paul Wolff', *Political Theory*, vol. 1 (1973) pp. 405–414; James P. Sterba, 'The Decline of Wolff's Anarchism', *Journal of Value Inquiry*, vol. 11 (1977) pp. 213–217; Mike W. Martin, 'Reason and Utopianism in Wolff's Anarchism', *Southern Journal of Philosophy*, vol. 18 (1980), 323–334; M.B.E Smith, 'Wolff's Argument for Anarchism', *Journal of Value Inquiry*, vol. 7 (1973) pp. 291–306; Michael S. Pritchard, 'Wolff's Anarchism', *Journal of Value Inquiry*, vol. 7 (1973) pp. 297–302.
9   Wolff, *In Defence of Anarchism*, p. 12.
10   Ibid., pp. 15–16.

According to Wolff the compliant passenger in this story retains autonomy, even though he does as the Captain orders, and even though he regards the order as 'the factor that in the situation that makes it desirable to do so'. He retains autonomy, it seems, since the Captain's order features in his reasoning only *indirectly*. The order creates circumstances – the conduct of other, obedient, passengers – which lead him to judge that getting into the lifeboat is the right thing to do. We might as well think of the order as an approaching wave that causes the other passengers to rush for the boats, and leads the autonomous passenger to think he would create dangerous confusion by failing to follow suit. The wave plainly lacks authority, but nonetheless it generates reasons to act one way rather than another. And so it is with Captain's order. The status of the order *as an order* is irrelevant to its status as a reason for action for the autonomous passenger. One way to put this is to say that the compliant passenger acts solely on the balance of reasons, having himself determined where that balance lies. The captain's order affects the balance of reasons by influencing the conduct of other passengers, generating reasons that are added to the balance, but the order itself does not provide the agent with a reason for action.[11] Wolff's agent retains autonomy if and only if he acts solely on the balance of reasons.

But I do not think this can be the right way to understand autonomy. Some practical reasoning involves appeal to the balance of reasons, but some does not. Earlier I discussed the ways in which the members of a community who disagreed over what ought to be done might nevertheless agree to cooperate under rules specifying what would be done. Agreeing to cooperate under rules in this manner amounts to accepting that the rules provide reasons for action which function independently of the balance of reasons that bear upon the questions those rules address. We accept the rules as reasons for action without believing that the action they require is what would have been recommended by direct appeal to the balance of reasons. And a good thing too, since often it will be our inability to agree upon

---

11   Later, Wolff explicitly makes his point in terms of the weight of reasons for action: 'I ... deny that there are, or could be, states which are legitimate in the sense that the validity of their laws constitutes, in itself and independently of considerations of long-run considerations or side effects, a reason *of any weight at all* for complying with those laws. That is to say, when a man (or a woman) is attempting to decide whether to comply with a law, he may reasonably take into account the impact of compliance…on his own interests (including the chance of punishment etc); the moral significance of the effects on others of his particular compliance…; the larger, and more distant, consequences to himself and others of the impact of his compliance…on the institutions of law and state, the patterns of social interaction in general, the respect for law, *etc. etc. etc. But*: when all this has been weighed in the balance ..., if someone says to him. "Furthermore, this is a *legitimate* state…and *that fact should count all by itself* for something in your deliberations" then I say, no, that is never a good reason – that is never a reason which deserves to be given any weight at all.' Wolff, 'Reply to Professors Pritchard and Smith', *Journal of Value Inquiry*, vol. 7 (1973) pp. 303–306, pp. 303–304.

what the balance of reasons requires that leads us to accept the mediation of a system of rules at the outset.

Perhaps this will seem to beg the question against Wolff. He might accept some such analysis of rule-governed behaviour, but deny that the autonomous agent could legitimately accept the reasons for action provided by rules so understood. The response becomes less plausible, however, once one notices that rules are only one, perhaps particularly clear example of a pervasive *mode* of practical reasoning that involves or generates similar non-weight based reasons for action. When I agree to follow a rule, I allow those I cooperate with – including those who may make themselves vulnerable to me (who perhaps invest time and material repairing my car in return for my undertaking to pay them when they're done) – to know that they are not vulnerable to case-by-case calculations of the balance of reasons when it is time for me to pay. When I use the practice of promise I tell promisees that, *ceteris paribus*, I will do as I have promised, not what I think best come performance time. When I sign on to a superannuation scheme which has me paying a percentage of my income into a fund which I cannot access even if I decide 10 years later that I *really* want a bigger, more beautiful, yacht, I intend to protect myself from the consequences of changing my mind on the basis of some future assessment of the balance of reasons: I tie myself to the mast of my current vessel in recognition of my weaknesses in such matters. The upshot is that we should reject Wolff's understanding of autonomy, and the treatments of personal integrity which echo it, because it rules out not just cases in which there is a genuine external or heteronomous threat to an agent's ability to 'be the author of their own life', but also many central strategies that apparently paradigmatically autonomous agents use to write the life they want. No understanding of autonomy or integrity that restricts an agent to case-by-case assessments of the balance of reasons can be right.

Before turning to alternative understandings of autonomy, it is perhaps worth noting that Wolff himself seems to have come close to the same conclusion, albeit without acknowledging the tension between it and his central argument for an irresolvable conflict between autonomy and authority. An autonomous agent, he thought, could properly recognise the authority of at least one form of government, 'unanimous direct democracy', in which every citizen votes on, and is able to veto, every law. Under such a system, writes Wolff,

> … every member of society wills freely every law which is actually passed…
> Since a man who is constrained only by the dictates of his own will is autonomous, it follows that under the directions of unanimous direct democracy, men can harmonize the duty of autonomy with the commands of authority.[12]

But suppose my community, a unanimous direct democracy, is considering enacting a controversial law. The debate is long and intense. Initially, at time t_1, I

---

12   Wolff, *In Defence of Anarchism*, p. 23.

am deeply opposed to the law. Confronted with powerful arguments, I change my mind. Come referendum day, t_2, I cast my vote in favour of the law. Yet I continue to wonder whether I have done the right thing. A week after the referendum, at t_3, having carefully considered the balance of reasons for and against the law (factoring in the effects of my vote at t_3), I have completely changed my mind, and am deeply (though perhaps not irrevocably) opposed to the law. Can Wolff's autonomous agent acknowledge the authority of the law at t_3? It would seem that he cannot. His assessment of the balance of reasons at t_2 should be irrelevant at t_3 other than as it bears (like the Captain's order) on the balance of reasons at the later time, when he thinks the balance of reasons count against the law. Were he to follow the law at t_3, he would be obeying, not complying. But Wolff thought a law generated by a referendum in a unanimous direct democracy was different: it was one of the laws 'freely willed (at t_2) by every member of society'. Let's not worry about whether this is a conclusion Wolff's argument allows him to draw (surely it is not). For now, we can simply note that the unanimous direct democracy exception leads to Wolff to acknowledge that autonomous agents can after all legitimately recognise non-weight based reasons for action. The autonomous agent is entitled (and required), Wolff concludes, to accept the law passed at t_2 as a reason for action at t_3 even though, at t_3, he judges the balance of reasons to recommend otherwise. It is not hard to see why Wolff wants to allow the unanimous direct democracy exception.[13] If practical reasoning strategies involving non-weight based reasons are central to the lives of autonomous agents, then Wolff needs to make a place for them. Such strategies, I have suggested, are certain to appeal to a reflective autonomous agent 'attempting to determine what ... to do, and [shouldering] the additional burdens of gaining knowledge, reflecting on motives, predicting outcomes, criticizing principles, and so forth'. But they are not available to the autonomous agent as that agent is understood by Wolff, or to the agent with integrity as that agent is understood by those who follow the autonomy model of integrity.

This conclusion suggests that we should reject the autonomy model of integrity, at least as that model seems to be understood by writers such as Dolovich. Properly understood, autonomy itself does not prevent a role-occupant acknowledging the force of reasons for action generated by the rules which constitute the roles they take on: they can, without threat to their autonomy and integrity, acknowledge the authority of the role norms to which they are subject. More positively, the analysis highlights the call upon autonomous agents, and so persons of integrity,

---

13 Though it is not at all clear why Wolff limits the exception to laws produced by referenda in unanimous direct democracies. Many decisions based on careful contemporaneous considerations of the balance of reasons purport to restrict an agent's autonomy at a subsequent time: promises, commitments, consents, undertakings to abide by the rules of a procedure, may all be just as surely and purely an act of will as our agent's decision to vote for the controversial law at t_2. If an autonomous agent can be bound by his previous decisions in the unanimous direct democracy case, why can't he be bound by these previous decisions as well?

to reflect upon the reasons for action that motivate them. That reflection is unlikely to lead them to endorse only weight-based reasons for action. The autonomous agent will often choose to eschew case-by-case weight-based reasoning about what to do, accepting that prior autonomous decisions to promise, to commit, to accept systems of rules, have made recourse to such reasons illegitimate. Wolff's account of autonomy goes wrong when it fails to see that the kind of reflection it correctly emphasises as an element of autonomy need not issue in only one form of legitimate reasons for action. We can hold on to its appreciation of the need for such reflection for both autonomy and integrity, without accepting its narrow view of the range of reasons for action which might legitimately be endorsed by such reflection. That will lead us to the idea that integrity requires not autonomy as Wolff or Dolovich understand that notion, but some form of reflective oversight of one's reasons and conduct.

Ishiguro's Mr Stevens illustrates the point. One reason to think Mr Stevens lacks integrity is his failure to engage in or accept the demands of such reflection. For all his philosophical ruminations upon what it is to be a great butler, Mr Stevens finally concedes, teary-eyed to a stranger, that if Lord Darlington chose a misguided life path, 'he chose it, he can say that at least' whereas, 'I can't even claim that … I can't even say I made my own mistakes. Really – one has to ask oneself – what dignity is there in that?'[14] The book ends with Mr Stevens rather easily persuaded by the stranger's advice not to brood on the past, to see that 'the evening's the best part of the day', and so deciding to brush up his bantering skills to please his new Lord and to return to the butler's role. The ending is meant to be a sad sign of Mr Stevens' continuing lack of integrity – another missed opportunity to list alongside his failure to declare his love for Miss Kenton, go to his father's deathbed, or confront his employer about his anti-Semitism – because his conclusion that the life of the bantering butler is after all not a bad way to make the most of the 'remains of the day' is implausible, a sign that he has not *really* asked himself what dignity (or, for current purposes, integrity) requires. On this reading, Mr Stevens lacks integrity in part because he lacks autonomy, but he lacks autonomy not because he follows the norms of his role, or chooses to return to them, but because he does so with no genuine reflection or engagement upon their point or value.[15]

---

14   Ishiguro, *The Remains of the Day*, pp. 243–245.

15   Notice that one might accept this account of integrity, and perhaps of Ishiguro's point, while rejecting the final assessment of Mr Stevens. His assessment of the value of the bantering butler's role might be right. It turns upon the judgment that bantering might after all not be such a foolish thing, 'particularly if it is the case that in bantering lies the key to human warmth' (Ishiguro, *The Remains of the Day* pp. 243–245). Of course, we might doubt that, and doubt that the dry and emotionally challenged Mr Stevens will be able to pull it off, but we will have already conceded that whether Mr Stevens has 'autonomy integrity' turns not upon whether he decides to accept the norms of the butler's role, but upon the quality of the reflection that leads him to do so.

Integrity as integration

The integrated-self view of integrity proceeds from the idea that 'integrity' is related to 'integration, the unification of parts', and so understands integrity as 'the integration of 'parts' of oneself – desires, evaluations, commitments – into a whole.'[16] The person of integrity is 'undivided ... '[17]; he 'keeps his self intact'.[18] Harry Frankfurt's treatment of freedom and responsibility is often used to support the integration view.[19] I have strong (first-order) desires to lie a-bed in the morning. Nothing wrong with that, you might think. But what if I desperately wished it were not so? What if I had strong (second-order) desires to be the kind of person who leapt out of bed and worked for an hour before breakfast and a five-mile run? I would then be someone whose first- and second-order desires were in conflict, and such conflicts can be a source of misery: I do not leap out of bed but nor do I lie there savouring the moment. Instead I am tormented by my desire to have different desires, not to be the kind of person who has the desires I have. And it might not end there. I might have (third-order) desires not to have the (second-order) desires not to have my (first-order) desires. Perhaps I wish I were a more spontaneous person, less influenced by popular maxims about the virtues of early-risers and more comfortable simply giving in to at least those of my first-order desires which would, at worst, have me remain in my warm bed a little longer. To be a person of integrity, on this account, is to bring these different levels of desires, and the actions they generate, into harmony; to integrate competing desires into a single ordering, abandoning desires that cannot be brought within the integrated hierarchy, and wholeheartedly endorsing the remainder. The person who has achieved self-integration, on Frankfurt's account:

> ... no longer holds himself at all apart from the desire to which he has committed himself. It is no longer unsettled or uncertain whether the object of that desire – that is, what he wants – is what he really wants.[20]

For Frankfurt this is more than a matter of achieving a harmonious soul. On his account, the 'mere wanton' who fails to deliberate and decide which of their desires they want to be volitionally effective, simply acting on whichever desire happens to be psychologically strongest at a moment, lacks a self altogether. Self-integration requires integrating competing desires into a single ordering, separating

---

16   Calhoun, 'Standing for Something', p. 235.

17   Lynne McFall, 'Integrity', *Ethics*, vol. 98 (1987) pp. 5–20, p. 7.

18   Gabriele Taylor, 'Integrity', *Proc. Aristotelian Society* supp. vol. 55 (1981) pp. 143–159, p. 148.

19   Harry G. Frankfurt, 'Freedom of the Will and the Concept of a Person', *Journal of Philosophy*, vol. 68 (1971) pp. 5–20, and 'Identification and Wholeheartedness' in Frankfurt *The Importance of What We Care About* (Cambridge, 1988) pp. 150–176.

20   Frankfurt, 'Identification and Wholeheartedness', p. 170.

some desires from the self and relegating them to 'outlaw' status and it is, Frankfurt writes, these acts of ordering and of rejection – integration and separation – that create a self out of the raw materials of inner life'.[21] Hence the conditions that threaten integration, and so integrity, also threaten the very existence of a self.

The integration view seems to lie behind many concerns about integrity and roles. I remarked above that one reason to think Ishiguro's butler lacked integrity was that he lacked autonomy. We might also think he lacked integration: we think him a tragic figure because we don't believe he wants to be the kind of person who cannot declare his love for Miss Kenton, or who takes pride in serving soup rather than going to his father's deathbed, or who really endorses the value of the bantering butler. He does not, we suspect, really have the higher-order desires to have the lower-order desires he has or claims to have. Montaigne may be able to maintain indifference to what he does in the role of Mayor, but, if he can, it is at the cost of his integrity, where integrity requires integration and wholeness, that one not be divided.

Notice however, that even if we accept that Mr Stevens and Montaigne lack integrity understood as integration, and take the view to explain why we think them pathological characters, there seems little reason to leap to the same conclusion about role-occupants in general. The account of role-obligation defended in this book suggests that there are moral reasons for role-occupants to take the obligations of their roles seriously; that the clash between the demands of ordinary morality and role-morality might be much less dramatic than is commonly supposed, especially if the duty of zeal is properly interpreted as a duty of mere- rather than hyper-zeal; that lawyers should take pride in their roles given the contribution of law as conceived under the revised standard conception to the viability of pluralist communities; and that role-occupants are encouraged to both consider the need for and take active steps toward institutional reform to diminish the gap between role and ordinary morality. We do not need to suppose that any lawyer accepts all of these suggestions, or that the suggestions, even if accepted, eliminate all the tensions between role and ordinary morality. However, whatever one thinks of Mr Stevens and Montaigne, and without imagining that this defence of the standard conception amounts to a knockdown response to critics, one can imagine role-occupants reasoning, in Frankfurt's terms, that there are higher-order reasons to respect the lower-order demands of roles. We might find it hard to accept that Mr Stevens wants the first-order desire he claims to want, but it seems less obvious that a lawyer might not want, and want to want, to recognise the authority of role-demands.

The formalism objection The idea, then, is that the process of critical reflection upon a role, its justification and its demands, will often lead role-occupants to have higher order desires to recognise the authority of those roles. But it has often been thought that integration-integrity faces a particular problem in this regard:

---

21   Ibid.

one might have integration-integrity, it seems, even if one's role is not, all things considered, morally justified. The 'formalism objection' points out that integration-integrity imposes formal rather than substantive constraints on integrity. The view says nothing directly about the content of the desires and volitions which are to be bought into harmony. Prima facie, then, someone might have integration-integrity even though their desires and volitions fall short of a moral ideal.

The formalism objection has led some commentators to conclude that the integration view cannot give an adequate account of integrity; that whatever integration-integrity is, it is not really 'integrity'. Damian Cox, Marguerite La Caze and Michael Levine ask us to:

> ... [i]magine a person who sells used-cars for a living and is wholeheartedly dedicated to selling cars for as much money as possible. Such a person will be prepared to blatantly lie in order to set up a deal. The person may well be perfectly integrated in Frankfurt's sense, but we should feel no temptation at all to describe them as having exemplary integrity.[22]

Other commentators accept that one might understand integrity in something like the terms proposed by the integration view, but insist that one can only attain integration-integrity if one's desires and volitions are morally admirable. These commentators understand integration-integrity in a way that rules out the formalism objection. Justin Oakley and Dean Cocking's argument that role-occupants can attain 'Aristotelian psychic harmony' in the face of role-demands for professional detachment only if their roles serve morally worthwhile ends appears to take this route: unless the role-demands for detachment serve morally worthwhile ends, role-occupants will not have integrity or psychic harmony.[23] I address this response first, before turning to that which takes the formalism objection to show that we should reject the integration view of integrity.

Cocking and Oakley set out to show how an Aristotelian 'virtue ethics approach to professional roles offers a promising analysis of the morality of professional detachment.'[24] The approach, they write, '... is well known for its emphasis on the importance of psychic harmony and personal integrity in a good human life and this might be suggested as a reason for thinking that virtue ethics could provide a promising general account of how to avoid the ... perils of detachment.'[25]

Aristotle's remarks on psychic harmony do seem particularly relevant here. When our beliefs, desires and emotions are in harmony, he maintains, they 'speak

---

22 Damian Cox, Marguerite La Caze and Michael Levine, 'Integrity', *Stanford Encyclopedia of Philosophy* (online) Edward N. Zalta, (ed.), (2005) pp. 1–17.
23 Cocking and Oakley, *Virtue Ethics and Professional Roles*, pp. 137–151.
24 Ibid., p. 138.
25 Ibid., p. 139.

with the same voice' about what we value.²⁶ Those who lack this psychic harmony are 'at variance with themselves...their soul is rent by faction, ... one element in it...grieves when it abstains from certain acts while the other part is pleased, and one draws them this way and the other that, as if they were pulling them in pieces...to be thus is the height of wretchedness'.²⁷ It will be clear why Cocking and Oakley's discussion falls where it does in the current treatment of integrity: to have Aristotelian psychic harmony as Cocking and Oakley describe that notion, is to have integration-integrity, and Cocking and Oakley's concerns about detachment echo those we have raised about integrity so understood.

Cocking and Oakley argue that Aristotelian psychic harmony does not preclude legitimate professional detachment. According to the Aristotelian or 'aretaic' virtue ethics they favour, acting well is determined by reference to what counts as excellence in performing various functions which are characteristic of a flourishing life, and 'so too what counts as acting well in the context of a professional role can be regarded as importantly determined by how well that role functions in serving the goals of the profession, and how those goals are connected with characteristic human activities'.²⁸ From here Cocking and Oakley offer an answer to the question 'When is detachment appropriate?' The moral status of a person's professional detachment from others in carrying out their role, they write:

> ... is importantly determined by whether their detachment serves the goal of their profession, and by the appropriateness of the professional goal itself. ... Professional detachment from others can be justified, and so need not be morally defective, if and only if: (1) a particular professional role can be shown to serve the goals of that profession; (2) psychological detachment in carrying out that role helps one meet its requirements and so uphold those goals; and (3) these goals, all things considered serve morally worthwhile ends.²⁹

Hence where the professional goals that detachment serves are morally questionable, (or where those goals are worthwhile but detachment does not help meet them), that detachment is itself morally questionable. The detachment maintained by a prostitute in order to preserve the possibility of an intimate life outside of their profession is not justified. While detachment helps proper performance of their role, 'it is not plausible at least in normal circumstances, to claim that the...proper performance of the role serves morally justified ends'.³⁰ By contrast, the detachment maintained by a palliative care nurse in order to avoid the professional burnout that would result if they felt the death of every patient

---

26   Aristotle, *Nichomachean Ethics*, in *The Basic Works of Aristotle* (ed.) and intro. Richard McKeon, trans. WD Ross, (New York, 1941) 1102b28.
27   Ibid., 1166b8-27.
28   Cocking and Oakley, *Virtue Ethics and Professional Roles*, p. 145.
29   Ibid., p. 139.
30   Ibid., p. 148.

as though it were the loss of a friend or loved one, is justified: the goals of their profession are morally justified, and detachment helps them fulfill a role necessary to the attainment of those goals.

I do not have much quarrel with this as an account of the *justification* of professional detachment, where the issue, we might suppose, is whether it is legitimate for a role to call upon occupants to seek detachment, though it does not seem especially distinctive of virtue ethics. As Cocking and Oakley's citation of David Luban, Gerald Postema and the current author in support of a legal example suggests, the broad structure of the model is likely to seem plausible to advocates of a range of theories and approaches. However, despite the authors' description of the approach as a way of showing how 'Aristotle's notion of psychic harmony can plausibly be applied to the problem of professional detachment', their statement of the model at least, omits what seems to be a crucial element in a bridge between detachment and psychic harmony. The justification of a given instance of role-detachment seems neither necessary nor sufficient to ensure psychic harmony. Psychic harmony, and integration-integrity, seems to stand or fall on the existence of a set of beliefs, attitudes, volitions, and the like, and the relations between them. It rests upon relations between 'internal' states of the agent, rather than upon relations between the agent and 'external' moral ends. When sketching four professional examples – an intensive care nurse, an insurance company lawyer, a prostitute and a criminal defence lawyer – Cocking and Oakley do speak in terms of the beliefs of the professionals they discuss: one can properly become reconciled to a level of professional detachment and render such detachment consistent with a level of professional integrity, they write, by 'seeing how' the maintenance of professional detachment helps one carry out one's role and how one's role is integral to serving the morally worthwhile goals of one's profession',[31] but their acknowledgement of the significance of an *appreciation* of the justification of some instance of detachment, rather than the justification itself, is sporadic. When they turn to two cases in which they find detachment to be unjustified, the prostitute and a lawyer helping an insurance company decline deserving claimants, their emphasis is on the absence of a justification for the practice, not upon the individual's failure to appreciate the availability of such a justification.

Such appreciation, however, is surely crucial to the attainment of psychic harmony or integration-integrity. Imagine a palliative care nurse who never manages to achieve sufficient psychological distance from her patients, though she desperately wants to do so, believing correctly that she would be a better professional and a happier person if she could. She feels the death of every patient as though it were the loss of a loved one, and is as a result miserable at home and a less than effective professional at work. Her plight is made even worse by her *acceptance* that she is failing to maintain appropriate detachment.[32] In Aristotelian

---

31 Ibid., p. 147.

32 Cocking and Oakley provide an example, drawn from a study by Mary Ramos, of an intensive-care nurse overcome by grief for a patient and his family: 'I just could not take

terms, we might suppose her 'beliefs, desires and emotions' are at war. She 'is at variance with herself, her soul rent by faction.'[33] Imagine, on the other hand, an executioner, serving an illegitimate and corrupt regime who is quite untroubled by the absence of moral justification for his role; his beliefs, desires, and emotions speaking in perfect harmony.[34] He might have perfect, albeit unjustified, psychic harmony. Of course we may regard his insouciance as yet another reason to condemn him, but subject to empirical doubts about whether he could really pull it off, it is not a reason to deny that he has attained psychic harmony.[35] If these cases are at all plausible, they suggest that we need to hold on to the 'internalism' of psychic harmony and integration-integrity, and so to face up to the formalism objection.

I turn, then, to the alternative response to that objection, that which accepts the force of the objection and rejects the integration view as an adequate account of integrity. The formalism objection protests that the integration view is committed to attributing integrity to someone with coherent but morally obnoxious views. I think the formalism objection tells us something important about integrity, but that it should not lead us to put aside the integration view too quickly. The objection is motivated by what we might call the 'content-independence' of integration-integrity. The integration view does not attribute *direct* significance to the content of the views to be integrated: that's why one might have integration-integrity even though the integrated views fall short of a moral ideal. I suggest in the rest of this

---

care of him,' the nurse is reported as saying, 'I felt so overwhelmed by all these losses, and I felt so bad for his wife, I cried every time I saw her… When you can't step back far enough not to feel so devastated yourself … you're one step too close to the patient' (Mary Carol Ramos, 'The Nurse-Patient Relationship: Themes and Variations', *Journal of Advanced Nursing*, vol. 17 (1992) 496–506, p. 501, reported in Cocking and Oakley, *Virtue Ethics and Professional Roles* at p. 141.

33   Aristotle, *Nichomachean Ethics*, 1166b8-27.

34   See Applbaum's *Ethics for Adversaries*; Chapter Two, 'Professional Detachment: The Executioner of Paris', pp. 14–42.

35   Cinematographic treatment of another executioner's story makes clear how reluctant we may be to grant this empirical point. Albert Pierrepoint, the United Kingdom's last 'chief executioner', hanged 433 men and 17 women between 1931 and 1956. By his own account, Albert never let his role as executioner intrude on his life outside the role. Happily married for 49 years, he dedicates his autobiography (*Executioner Pierrepoint*, 1974) to his wife Ann, who 'in forty years never asked a question'. A 2007 film of his life, (*Pierrepoint*, 2007: released in the United States as *The Last Hangman*) is an otherwise fairly accurate account of Albert's career, but which has as its central theme the almost certainly fictional claim that Albert could not maintain this detachment, portraying him ultimately breaking down, begging Ann for acknowledgement and forgiveness, flicking through a diary of his victims crying 'Of course it was me. It's always been me!!' In fact Albert, even when coming to express doubts about the justification of the death penalty, and whatever we may think of him, seems to have found psychic harmony or integration-integrity through something like the reconciliation strategy recommended in this book.

section, however, that the content of the desires and volitions an agent seeks to integrate is likely to have *indirect* significance for the project of integration, such that it is (almost always) more difficult to integrate morally obnoxious desires and volitions into a coherent pattern at a moment or across time, than more admirable alternatives. If this is right, the substantive threat of the formalism of the integration view will be significantly reduced. I think there are promising ways to develop this suggestion, and that what they bring to the fore, again, is the centrality of an agent's reflection upon and engagement with their moral position to assessments of integrity. The person of integrity will have an appropriate regard for integration-integrity. Such regard will lead them to just the process of reflection, of ordering, of weighting, described by Frankfurt. That process will almost always lead them towards a set of morally desirable goals and desires. For those of us who are not saints or angels, it will rarely deliver perfect integration-integrity: that is for the rest of us too demanding a target. Given its tendency toward the moral good, however, the pursuit of integration-integrity, and the reflection, weighing and ordering of desires, goals and volitions it involves, is a morally valuable and important part of the life of a person of integrity.

So how might we try to support this suggestion? Consider the method of 'reflective equilibrium'. We can regard the method as an elaboration of our everyday practice of testing our moral judgements about particular cases by seeing how they fit with our judgements about other cases, and our beliefs about a broader range of moral and factual matters. The method requires us to work back and forth between our considered judgements about cases, the principles and rules we think are relevant to them, and the wider theories, moral and empirical, that lead us to those rules and principles, revising and refining elements at all of these levels when we find challenges among and between them, seeking coherence among the widest set. According to the method of reflective equilibrium, a 'moral principle, or moral judgement about a particular case...would be justified if it cohered with the rest of our beliefs about right action...on due reflection and after appropriate revision throughout our system of beliefs.'[36] The method is more complex (and controversial) than this brief summary suggests, for our purposes, however, it will do to note that the method denies that we can justifiably hold a belief 'in isolation'. It requires us to reflect upon how particular beliefs and judgements fit into broader sets or systems of beliefs. And now we can ask whether the immoral person is likely to find it harder to satisfy this requirement than their moral counterpart. We might ask Sam, the car dealer who is prepared to blatantly lie to seal a deal, whether he would disapprove of a colleague who acted in just that way toward someone Sam cared about, and, if not, how his beliefs about his own conduct and that of his colleague could be accommodated in a coherent set of beliefs. The challenge to Sam, note, does not focus directly on the content of his view about the legitimacy of lying to customers. Instead, it appeals to an apparent tension

---

36 Norman Daniels, 'Reflective Equilibrium', *Stanford Encyclopedia of Philosophy* (online) Edward N. Zalta, (ed.) (2003).

between his beliefs about lying to strangers, on the one hand, and to his family and friends on the other: it is a challenge to the integration or integrity of his belief-set. And now the suggestion is that Sam is likely to find it harder to integrate his beliefs about honesty than some more moral colleague.

We might be disappointed: Sam might have an integrating story to tell. He might hold a sophisticated agent-relative theory of honesty, which leads him to draw a fairly coherent distinction between his obligations to strangers and to family and friends. Claudia Koonz suggests that just this sort of thing might be true of a far more troubling case. 'The Nazi conscience,' she writes, 'is not an oxymoron ... The popularisers of anti-Semitism and the planners of genocide followed a coherent set of severe ethical maxims derived from broad philosophical concepts.'[37] Suppose that Koonz is right; that at least some Nazis did hold coherent, integrated, belief-sets which would have allowed them to meet a formal challenge to the coherence of their beliefs, and so to claim integrity on the integration view. Would this show that we should reject the integration account of integrity? I do not think we should accept that conclusion too quickly. The method of reflective equilibrium calls upon agents to revise their beliefs as necessary to attain coherent sets of beliefs. Suppose Sam, the dodgy car dealer, holds a set of moral beliefs which is almost the same as that of some more moral colleague. When he is not fully engaged in selling cars, we might imagine, he is a fairly honest person, who values truth telling and fair dealing, he helps out at his children's school, thinks it important to obey the local fishing regulations, condemns those who drive while drunk, donates to various charities, and so on. He is, for the most part, we might suppose, rather like the rest of us. When confronted with the tensions between his view that it is alright to lie to prospective customers, his judgements about another dealer doing the same thing to someone he cares about, and the greater part of his broader moral views, Sam is likely to find it easier to achieve equilibrium by discarding his view about the moral status of his own lies, than to do so by revising the many other views with which that self-serving belief conflicts. Sam's nearest equilibrium point, that is to say – the one which requires the least radical belief revision – is one which is likely to bring him towards rather than away from a more morally palatable position. Things seem likely to be otherwise for the Nazi. His overall belief set, we might suppose, has little in common with those who condemn his conduct. The smallest belief revision required for him to obtain integrity might involve revising the few moral and empirical views he shares with his critics, shifting him to an integrated set of morally obnoxious views. Integration might take him away from, rather than towards, the moral light.

Perhaps this will seem of scant comfort to the defender of the integration view: they may be obliged, after all, to attribute integrity to the coherent Nazi. But the contrast between the dodgy car dealer and the Nazi is informative. If the analysis offered here is right, the Nazi is a very peculiar case indeed, and so may have less dramatic implications for the value of integration-integrity than seemed likely. If

---

37 Claudia Koonz, *The Nazi Conscience* (Cambridge, Mass., 2003) p. 1.

pursuit of integrity does not push the Nazi towards a more morally acceptable set of beliefs, it is only because his beliefs are thoroughly, more or less consistently, morally obnoxious to begin with. Most of us, however, and for the purposes of the current discussion, most lawyers, share very substantial moral ground with our fellows, even those with whom we disagree about particular cases and issues. The process of integration is likely to take us toward rather than away from common moral ground: we are much more like Sam than the Nazi, and hence for most of us, the pursuit of integrated views is likely to be a morally valuable exercise. When faced with common temptations to give undue weight to self-interest, or to the interests of those near to us, an attempt to integrate the compelling beliefs, desires and volitions often gives us grounds to resist those temptations. Of course, we may resist integration, preferring to ignore the niggling discomfort of inconsistency, and seek shelter in mild or gross self-deception, or more or less implausible special pleading. If so, however, we cast doubt not upon the normative potential of integration, but upon our willingness to accept its implications. We should not confuse our capacity to resist the implications of the integration project with a structural flaw in the approach itself. I think, then, that we should accept that the formalism objection states a genuine challenge to integration-integrity (and so we should reject the sort of move suggested by Cocking and Oakley), but that we need not accept the strongest implications of the objection: The formalism of integration-integrity, does not mean that its pursuit is not, for most of us, morally worthwhile.

The inconsistency objection   A quick sketch of another objection to integration-integrity will allow us to draw together the conclusions of this section and their implications for our broader project. In her classic treatment of integrity, Cheshire Calhoun offers a different objection to integration-integrity, arguing that integration can be *inconsistent* with integrity.[38] Calhoun presents Maria Lugones's description of a Hispanic Lesbian 'struggling against multiple oppressions',[39] concerned to affirm both her Latina identity, constituted within a strongly heterosexual Hispanic culture, and her lesbian identity, constituted within her lesbian community. But there is deep and irresolvable conflict between the value systems of these two communities. There is no integration point that accommodates both identities. For her, integration-integrity is not only unavailable, but would be undesirable: it would require denial of a conflict that is part of what she is. She is 'not a unitary but a multiplicitous being'.[40] We can imagine examples from the legal profession. Applicants to law school are often fired with enthusiasm for substantive issues. Youthful idealists enthused by Erin Brokovich set out to learn a trade which will allow them to fight for truth and justice (the current author began law school in order to become a trade union lawyer). Five years out from graduation, and many

---

38   Calhoun, 'Standing for Something', pp. 238–240.
39   Ibid., p. 239.
40   Ibid.

young lawyers will have fallen for the promises of a partnership and its material rewards or, perhaps less cynically, become genuinely engaged with the challenges of their profession (if not the rather different rewards of an academic life). They seek identity and affirmation from the dominant legal community. And yet, many still feel the call of a competing identity, built around altruistic concerns for others, and nurtured within an alternative community, outside the law. Imagine an extreme case, in which a lawyer, held in the warm embrace of a hyper-zealous professional community, taking great satisfaction from the challenges of her professional life, returns home each evening to her somewhat disapproving community of family and friends, occasionally imagining an especially disappointed glance from photographs of her earlier self, struggling to integrate the competing sets of desires and volitions generated by her competing identities and communities. Given sufficient psychological and emotional investment in her two communities, such a lawyer may well conclude that she is a multiplicitous rather than unitary being. Integration-integrity would come only at the cost of denying or downplaying the demands of one of these identities.

The force of Calhoun's objection is heightened when read in light of Frankfurt's suggestion that it is integration that creates 'a self out of the raw materials of inner life' where doing so requires 'wholeheartedly' endorsing a consistent set of desires, believes and volitions.[41] Now what is at stake is the very self of the divided agent. But, as Calhoun argues, the conflicted Latina lesbian is no 'mere wanton' giving in to whatever desire feels more pressing at a moment. She is not thoughtlessly suppressing things that matter to her. Instead, she is creating a self, a multiplicitous self, from the materials she has been dealt, ranking and arranging preferences, deciding what to act on at a moment, given her overview of who she is and what she wants. The Latina lesbian's lack of wholehearted commitment to either of her selves does not signal some personal failure to make up her mind about 'what she really wants'. The same might go for the conflicted lawyer. She too may have reflected upon the justification for her role, come to endorse some version of the argument for robust role-differentiated obligations, even while being unable or unwilling to abandon the 'at home' identity which does not easily accommodate all of the permissions and obligations of her professional role. Professional roles will at least occasionally make demands role-occupants would, in their private personas, rather avoid. Accepting those demands does not, of itself, show role-occupants to lack integrity. We need to know about their roles and their beliefs about them; about the process of reflection they have been through.

What these cases show, I think, is that what matters for integrity is not the *outcome* of the pursuit of integration-integrity – not the attainment of perfect integration – but instead the critical engagement with one's position, the acknowledgement of the tensions it contains, the participation in finding a way to live a satisfying life in the face of its competing demands. We should often be prepared to regard someone who has reflected upon their situation and decided

---

41   Frankfurt, 'Identification and Wholeheartedness', p. 170.

what weight to give to what preferences in what circumstances, who can describe their situation, who gives an account of why they have something other than unitary ordering of desires and volitions, as a person of integrity even if they do not attain perfect integration-integrity. Frankfurt, this is to say, is right about the need to reflect upon and order one's desires and volitions, but he is wrong about the required *outcome* of that process of reflection and ordering.

Integrity as identity

An important part of our everyday use of integrity as a moral term is the idea that the person of integrity 'holds together' at a moment or across time. We have seen this aspect of integrity in the integration view,[42] and it is also manifest in another familiar component of the everyday moral sense of integrity, namely the idea that the person of integrity holds fast to commitments or projects which are central to who they are, to the way they understand themselves and are understood by others. It is common to ground this notion of integrity on Bernard Williams's account of 'identity-conferring commitments'. Fidelity to such commitments, Williams argues, is 'the condition of my existence, in the sense that unless I am propelled forward' by those commitments and projects it is unclear that *I* go on at all.[43] When I abandon such commitments, I lose my identity and my integrity: I become a different person. To have integrity is to have identity, and to have identity is to maintain fidelity to identity-conferring commitments and ground projects.

It was this sense of integrity that was at stake, I claimed, in my interpretation of Atticus Finch as a tragic figure. Faced with the shooting of another mockingbird when called upon to decide whether Boo should be charged over the killing of Bob Ewell, Atticus put aside his commitment to the rule of law, to principles he had passionately defended, in terms of which others had understood him. If integrity does consist in holding fast to identity-conferring commitments, and I correctly identified the commitments which filled that role, then Atticus lacked integrity: The Atticus who went along with the sheriff, trying Boo in the secret courts of their own hearts, was not the same man who pleaded for the jury to avoid doing that very thing in Tom's case. The conclusion that Atticus lacked integrity will strike many as absurd, as reason to reject the identity view of integrity,[44] since Atticus is widely regarded as the exemplar of that virtue. I think there is something to this. Like autonomy and integration, fidelity to identity-conferring commitments is one of the things to which a person of integrity should have proper regard in a process of sincere and thorough reflection, but integrity does not consist in such fidelity.

---

42   Though, it may be at tension with some extreme views of the demands of the autonomy view.

43   Bernard Williams, 'Integrity' in J.J.C. Smart and Bernard Williams *Utilitarianism: For and Against* (1973) pp. 108–117, and *Moral Luck: Philosophical Papers 1973–1980* (Cambridge, 1981).

44   Or, of course, as a reason to reject my account of Atticus.

Integrity rests largely upon reflection, upon the disposition to engage in it and take it seriously, not upon its outcome. Even on this reading, emphasising the centrality of reflection to integrity, we will still have reason to question Atticus's integrity, I think, since there is little sign that Atticus does reflect upon his situation, upon what might have happened if Boo had appeared before a grand jury, upon the wisdom of covering up the circumstances of Bob Ewell's death,[45] but if he lacks integrity it is because of that failure and not because of his failure to maintain fidelity to his earlier identity-conferring commitments.

Calhoun's distinction between types of identity-conferring commitments, and her argument that not all of them secure integrity, takes us a long way toward the view of identity-integrity I have in mind. Calhoun is responding to a version of the formalism objection. Like integration-integrity, the identity view appears to offer only formal constraints on integrity. Provided a person maintains fidelity to identity-conferring commitments, they will have integrity, no matter what their commitments or ground projects, hence 'one might have [identity-]integrity even though one's identity-conferring projects are nonmoral or even morally despicable.'[46] Much of the discussion of the deployment of this objection against identity-integrity has focused on a case posed by Williams, a fictionalised account of the life of the great artist Gauguin who, on Williams's account, abandons his family to poverty in France in order to pursue his art in Tahiti. Williams's Gauguin 'turns away from definite and pressing human claims on him in order to live a life in which, as he supposes, he can pursue his art'.[47]

Does Williams's Gauguin have integrity? According to the identity view that will depend not upon whether he acts morally – on this account morality is not one of Gauguin's identity-conferring commitments or ground projects – but upon whether following his muse to Tahiti is for him such a project or commitment: is this the thing that he 'finds his life bound up with', that propels him forward, that is a condition of him going on as the same self? According to Calhoun, however, it is not enough simply to identity with such commitments. We also need to ask how Gauguin came to have them. Sometimes, she points out, people are merely the passive recipients of identity-conferring commitments or projects. I vote Labour (think Democrat), suppose, and always have done; I was raised that way. These days, I am hard pressed to explain my fidelity to the party on principled grounds. Policy differences between them and their opponents have steadily reduced as they have increasingly focused on the political middle ground. Still, we might suppose, being a Labour voter is an identity-conferring commitment for me: I would think of myself as a different person if I voted National (think Republican or Conservative); my family would be surprised, perhaps even shocked. On Calhoun's account

---

45 The sorts of factors discussed in the section 'Challenges to Atticus as Phronemos', in Chapter 6, are reasons to think Atticus a poor example of the *phronemos*, or expert practical reasoner.
46 Calhoun, 'Standing for Something', p. 242.
47 Williams, *Moral Luck*, p. 22.

such a commitment is merely a deep psychological identification, something, in Williams's phrase, I simply 'find my life bound up with', and she writes, ' ... insofar as we imagine that Gauguin, in pursuing "what he found his life bound up with", acted merely on a psychologically deep impulse without critically reflecting on the value of doing so, we may suspect him of not acting with integrity.'[48] The commitments or projects fidelity to which might plausibly ground identity-integrity, on Calhoun's account, are those an agent has subjected to a process of appropriate critical reflection and endorsed, not those he simply finds himself bound up with as a matter of psychological fact. 'In short,' Calhoun concludes, 'integrity involves fidelity to one's endorsements, not to merely psychologically deep identifications.'[49]

We can go further. As Calhoun points out, the appropriate outcome of this process of reflection may be a decision to abandon or revise one's fidelity to hitherto identity-conferring commitments or ground projects. If I come to realise that my fidelity to the Labour Party is grounded upon nothing more than tradition, I ought to be prepared to abandon it, to shift political allegiance to a party whose policies I endorse. Such decisions will often seem to enhance rather than threaten integrity. The person who realises that their identity is founded upon projects and commitments they do not endorse, which they have simply found their life bound up with because of history, and who decides to abandon them in favour of projects and commitments they do endorse, might act *with* rather than *against* integrity.

Given the discussion in this chapter so far, it will probably be clear what I want out of these remarks. Identity is relevant to integrity, but what matters is not simply fidelity to identity-conferring commitments or projects. Instead, what matters for integrity is that the agent has engaged in appropriate critical reflection upon the projects or commitments upon which they purport to ground their identity and that they are prepared to act upon that reflection. Fidelity to identity-conferring projects and commitments, like autonomy and integration, is something to which a person of integrity should have regard in a process of critical reflection, but integrity is not simply a matter of maintaining such fidelity.

We have focused on philosopher's examples appealing a fictionalised version of the life of a long dead French artist, and it may be worth bringing the discussion back to examples more closely linked to the life in the law. Now our questions might be: Does the lawyer who sees the law as an instrument for substantive justice abandon an identity-conferring commitment when they feel they simply have to advise a client seeking to avoid a just debt that a statute of limitations will see off at least an attempt to compel payment through the courts? Has the erstwhile youthful idealist who came to law in order to fight for truth and justice but who, five years after graduation, has fallen for the promise of a partnership or perhaps become genuinely engaged with the challenges of their profession, also become a different person? Have they abandoned an identity-conferring commitment or

---

48   Calhoun, 'Standing for Something', p. 244.
49   Ibid.

ground project? And, most importantly, what do the answers to these questions tell us about the integrity of these professionals? If they have abandoned or modified their stance to what were once for them identity-conferring commitments, do they have integrity? The arguments offered here suggest that the answer to these final questions about the significance of ongoing fidelity to identity-conferring commitments for integrity depends in large part upon whether those commitments are 'endorsements', upon whether the individuals have reflected carefully and sincerely, and been prepared to embrace the recommendations of such reflection. We might judge them to have integrity even if they have abandoned what were for them at one point identity-conferring commitments; indeed we may think a readiness to do so is a condition of integrity.

We could stop there: we have our main conclusion. But some will no doubt still be troubled by the formalism objection to identity-integrity. Does the conclusion that what really matters is identity founded upon commitments that have survived a process of critical reflection meet that objection? We might hope that such reflection will tend toward endorsement of morally palatable commitments and ground projects, but the link between reflection and such endorsements seems less direct when it is identity, rather than integration, which is at issue. I suggested that there was something about integration itself, characterised in terms of the method of reflective equilibrium, such that the pursuit of integration would lead most of us toward morally palatable beliefs, desires and volitions. The introduction of a similar requirement in the context of a discussion of identity-integrity does not seem to lead us quite so directly to morally palatable views. There is nothing about identity *itself* to prevent Williams's Gauguin resolving, after appropriate reflection, to endorse his decision to abandon his family to pursue his art in Tahiti. There is nothing about identity itself which rules out a lawyer who, on reflection, endorses hyper-zealous advocacy. While we might hope, and perhaps even expect, that such reflection will tend toward morally palatable commitments – since people will have non-identity related reasons to endorse such commitments – we are left, I think, with the more modest conclusion that the identity-conferring commitments and projects which might properly feature in a plausible account of integrity are those which have survived a process of critical reflection, hoping for a partial if not complete answer to the formalism objection to identity-integrity.

Conclusion

Some of the most important strands of the critique of the standard conception are motivated by concerns about 'detachment' or 'professional distance', and the threats these phenomena pose to personal integrity. I have tried to show that my version of the conception has a response to these concerns. The central idea has been that integrity depends crucially upon whether agents have engaged in a process of sincere and thorough critical reflection upon their situation and been prepared to embrace the recommendations of that reflection. I have argued that plausible accounts of integrity require, but do not always acknowledge, just this sort of reflection; that it is that reflective requirement which drives our intuitions about the importance of autonomy, integration and identity. These remarks about the concept of integrity are offered against the background of the model of legal ethics defended throughout this book. That model addresses the problems of distance, detachment and integrity on a number of fronts: it seeks to minimise the conflict between the demands of role-morality and those of ordinary or broad-based morality by limiting the excesses of advocacy; it offers a model of professional roles which, while insisting on a 'clean break' between role-morality and broad-based morality, nonetheless recognises the contribution of ordinary morality at the point of institutional design; it offers a moral argument for the particular role differentiated demands of the lawyer's role, suggesting that there are reasons of ordinary morality to take those demands seriously; and it shows that lawyers have a professional moral obligation to engage in a constant process of law reform, aimed at promoting fit between the lawyer's role-morality and broad-based morality. Now the suggestion is that these are the sorts of arguments, considerations and issues to which we should expect the lawyer of integrity to have proper regard in a process of sincere and thorough critical reflection. For such an agent, there is no essential conflict between role-obligation and personal integrity. An agent of integrity may (I think should) recognise the authority of such obligations, should want to do so, and should see doing so as an identity-conferring commitment or ground project.

Chapter 8
Conclusion: A Response to the Critique

We began, where almost all treatments of legal ethics begin, by noting the widespread perception that lawyers are grasping, callous, self-serving, devious and indifferent to justice, truth and the public good. The perception, I suggested, has less to do with lawyers who are simply crooks than with the demands of the standard conception of the lawyer's role, under which even good lawyers may be permitted or required to act in ways which might properly be condemned from the perspective of ordinary morality. The widespread suspicion of lawyers' ethics flows less from rare cases of misappropriation than from common perceptions of the day-to-day business of law. Many commentators have concluded that the standard conception should be put aside in favour of some alternative that gives ordinary morality a greater or more direct bearing on the conduct of lawyers. I have been concerned to resist this movement to reject the standard conception. In a modified form it is, I have argued, essentially the right way to conceive of the ethical obligations of lawyers. My overall strategy has been straightforward: I have argued that lawyers have *moral* grounds for regarding themselves as having duties to their clients which may allow or require them to act in ways which would be immoral were they acting outside of their professional roles. The fact that lawyers act within professional roles, I have claimed, makes a moral difference.

In Chapter 2 I sketched the various strands of the critique of the standard conception. According to the critique, I said, lawyers acting under the standard conception were alienated from ordinary morality; were invited to deny responsibility for the things they do (and thus to deny their status as moral agents, capable of choosing to do otherwise); were rendered morally insensitive in ways which impaired their ability both to live a satisfactory life outside of their professional roles and to perform their professional roles adequately; and were likely to find their work deeply unsatisfying because of the striking discord between the apparently obvious and public concern of law and lawyers with justice and morality, and the reality of practice under a conception which separates the moral obligations of the lawyer from those of the rest. I remarked that we would return to the critique armed with the approach to legal ethics defended in subsequent chapters, and that the success of the approach might at least in some degree be measured by its capacity to provide a response – if not a refutation – to the various strands of the critique. This final chapter brings us to that task.

The critique revisited

Morality and the standard conception

In its bluntest formulation, the first strand of the critique portrays the standard conception as claiming that 'standards of ordinary morality have no place in the evaluation of [the lawyer's] professional conduct.'[1] But, the objection insists, whether or not one acts morally is to be determined by a common moral standard. Lawyers acting in ways that would be judged immoral from the perspective of general morality are acting immorally *simpliciter*. They cannot properly avoid moral censure by appeal to a distinct institutional morality. According to David Luban, '[T]he lawyer's role carries no moral privileges and immunities. ... If a lawyer is permitted to puff, bluff, or threaten on certain occasions, this is not because of the [standard conception] ...but because in such circumstances, anyone would be permitted to do these things...'[2] The basic idea, then, is that no significant role-differentiated permissions or obligations attach to the lawyer's role. If Pakel's lawyer acted immorally by the lights of general morality, then he acted immorally and that assessment is not altered by the fact that he acted within a professional role.

The model of legal ethics offered in this book responds to this objection in a number of ways. Most generally, I argue that lawyers have *moral* grounds for regarding themselves as having duties to their clients which may allow or require them to act in ways which would be immoral were they acting outside of their professional roles. The standard conception recognises the vulnerability of clients within client/professional relationships, and that contemporary liberal communities rely to a considerable extent upon the practice of law as conceived by the standard conception. Law so practised allows people who are committed to a range of diverse but reasonable views about how we should live to form stable and just communities. If there are moral reasons for taking the standard conception seriously, we should not too readily accept the claim that the conception alienates lawyers from morality, or overdraw the conception's break between 'personal' or 'ordinary' morality on the one hand and professional morality on the other. An adequate personal or ordinary morality will entail a proper respect for the moral demands and permissions of professional roles.

Second I have attempted to mitigate the excesses of the standard conception, arguing that the conception does not require or allow lawyers to pursue every advantage available to clients through the law. Once the moral arguments for the standard conception are made explicit, those arguments themselves suggest limits to the things lawyers may justifiably do within their professional roles. The moral implications of the standard conception are often mischaracterised. Commentators suggest that the conception requires lawyers to secure any advantage the law can

---

1 Cocking and Oakley, 'Doing Justice to the Lawyer's Role', p. 84.
2 Luban, *Lawyers and Justice*, pp. 154–155.

be made to give. But I have argued that the standard conception, understood in light of its proper moral justification, requires no such thing. It justifies a more limited and moderate sphere of professional conduct than is commonly supposed.

In addition, I argued that the model I defend allows us to accommodate an important feature of ethical legal practice. I made use of John Rawls' distinction between constitutive and practice rules to explain how role-differentiated obligations were possible, and to show how an institution and the roles it supports might be designed with reference to the resources of broad-based morality and yet it be the case that the occupants of those institutional roles were not at liberty to appeal to broad-based morality from within their roles. Rawls's model, I argued, allowed us to maintain a 'clean break' between role-morality and broad-based morality without making it the case that standards of ordinary morality have no place in the evaluation of professional conduct, and so supports the suggestion that the break between role-morality and ordinary morality should not be overdrawn. It also has another function. According to the model, a lawyer noticing, for instance, that a statute of limitations or current rules or practices of cross examination have produced results regrettable from the perspective of ordinary morality cannot act, qua advocate, other than the existing rules of the practice recognise. The role is constituted by those rules and the actions available to them are settled by the role. I have argued, however, that the model allows us to see more clearly than we otherwise might, how role-occupants are able to move between roles. The relevant move here is between the roles of advocate and 'reformer'. The Rawlsian model makes very clear how and why we might conceive of lawyers as subject to an obligation to work to improve the fit between role and ordinary morality where, in some respect, the institution, built with reference to the resources of ordinary morality, has come apart from ordinary morality.[3] Qua advocate, the lawyer confronted with such a case will normally have to stick with his client, helping the client secure their rights under the law. When the client's case is complete, however, the lawyer may well bear a responsibility to take on the role of law reformer arguing for reform, the need for and nature of which their legal expertise and familiarity with the particular case may have made especially clear.[4] As George Eliot's Lydgate notices, professionals seeking moral engagement may positively value the opportunity to be engaged in the reform of their professions, pursuing

---

3 I appeal to the Rawlsian model in support of an argument that we *can* conceive of obligations and permissions as role-differentiated. The normative argument, that we should do so, is given in Chapter 5 above.

4 William Simon praises the New York Tax Bar for just this sort of practice: William H. Simon, 'After Confidentiality: Rethinking the Professional Responsibilities for the Business Lawyer', *Fordham Law Review*, vol. 75 (2006) pp. 1453–172, p. 1458.

their calling with an eye both to the day-to-day obligations generated by a complex practice designed by fallible humans[5] and to their profession 'as it might be'.[6]

In sum, the model addresses the first strand of the critique on a number of fronts: it seeks to minimise the conflict between the demands of role morality and those of ordinary or broad-based morality by limiting the excesses of advocacy; it offers a model of professional roles which, while insisting on a 'clean break' between role-morality and broad-based morality nonetheless recognises the contribution of ordinary morality at the point of institutional design; it offers a moral argument for the particular role-differentiated demands of the lawyer's role, suggesting that there are reasons of ordinary morality to take those demands seriously; and it shows that lawyers have a professional moral obligation to engage in a constant process of law reform, aimed at promoting fit between the lawyer's role morality and broad based morality.

Roles and responsibility

According to the second strand of the critique, the standard conception invites role-occupants to deny responsibility for who are they are and what they do. In Gerald Postema's words:

> [Role] identification is a strategy for evading one's freedom and, consequently, one's responsibility for who one is and what one does. By taking shelter in the role, the individual places the responsibility for all his acts at the door of the institutional author of the role.[7]

Postema's response to the problem is to propose what he calls the 'recourse role conception', under which lawyers are entitled or required to draw on the full resources of their broader moral experience in order to balance the legitimate demands of professional roles with the demands of personal integrity, and to cope

---

5 'It is a feature of the human predicament ... that we labour under two connected handicaps ... The first ... is our relative ignorance of fact; the second is our relative indeterminacy of aim. If the world in which we lived were characterised only by a finite number of features, and these together with all the modes in which they combine were known to us, then provision could be made in advance for every possibility. ... This would be a world fit for mechanical jurisprudence. Plainly this world is not our world...' H.L.A. Hart, *The Concept of Law*, p. 123.

6 'Lydgate ... carried to his studies ... the conviction that the medical profession as it might be was the finest in the world; ... offering the most direct alliance between intellectual conquest and the social good. Lydgate's nature demanded this combination: he was an emotional creature, with a flesh-and-blood sense of fellowship which withstood all the abstractions of special study. He cared not only for 'cases,' but for John and Elizabeth ... There was another attraction in his profession: it wanted reform ... ' George Eliot, *Middlemarch*.

7 Postema, 'Moral Responsibility in Professional Ethics', p. 74.

with the limitations of necessarily general statements of legal and professional obligation. I have argued for a more robust role-differentiated conception of professional roles. Postema's defence of his alternative has a number of strands. One strand, apparent in the passage just quoted, emphasises the conflict between the recognition of institutionally specified role-demands and the demands of personal integrity. 'The central issue I address,' Postema writes,

> ... is not whether there is sufficient justification for a distinct professional code for lawyers, but whether, given the need for such a code, it is possible to preserve one's sense of responsibility. ... I contend that a sense of responsibility and sound practical judgment depend not only on the quality of one's professional training, but also on one's ability to draw on the resources of a broader moral experience. This, in turn, requires that one seek to achieve a fully integrated moral personality. Because this is not possible under the [standard] conception of the lawyer's role ... that conception must be abandoned, to be replaced by a conception that better allows the lawyer to bring his full moral sensibilities to play in his professional role.[8]

I hope to have gone some way to responding to this strand of Postema's criticism of the standard conception. I have assumed from the outset that lawyers are not merely passive recipients of professional norms or instruments of client preferences. The aim from the beginning has been to provide lawyers themselves with moral reasons to take their roles seriously. Discussing integrity in Chapter 7 I suggested that the key to a response to a cluster of concerns about integrity lay in the moral engagement this approach assumes, and that given such engagement, there was no essential conflict between personal integrity and recognition of the authority of role-obligations. In particular, I argued that the version of the autonomy view of integrity that painted an essential conflict between autonomy and authority was implausible. Autonomy itself does not prevent a role-occupant acknowledging the force of reasons for action generated by the rules that constitute the roles they take on. Autonomous agents can and do acknowledge the authority of the role norms to which they are subject. Often, following the sort of reflection which I argue underpins integrity (and which I take to differ from the reasoning of Postema's recourse agent more in outcome than process), the autonomous agent will accept that prior autonomous decisions to promise, to commit, to accept systems of rules, have made direct recourse to the resources of ordinary morality illegitimate. The version of the autonomy view of integrity that I reject goes wrong when it fails to see that the kind of reflection it correctly emphasises as an element of autonomy need not issue in only one form of legitimate reasons for action. We can hold on to its appreciation of the need for such reflection for both autonomy and integrity, without accepting its narrow view of the range of reasons for action which might legitimately be endorsed by such reflection.

---

8   Ibid., p. 64.

Another strand of Postema's statement of the 'roles and responsibilities' objection focuses on the difficulty of stating in advance a set of principles of right action which we can be confident will deal adequately with the particular cases and concerns likely to confront role-occupants. There is, he writes, 'always likely to be a significant gap between general practical theory and actual decision and practice'.[9] Here Postema – anticipating the somewhat later rise of virtue theory in legal ethics – turns to Aristotle, in whose view, he writes:

> ... this gap is bridged by the faculty of practical judgment – what he called practical wisdom. Our ability to resolve conflicts on a rational basis often outstrips our ability to enunciate general principles. In doing so, we exercise judgment. Judgment is neither a matter of simply applying general rules to particular cases nor a matter of mere intuition. It is a complex faculty, difficult to characterise, in which general principles or values and the particularities of the case both play important roles. The principles or values provide a framework within which to work and a target at which to aim. But they do not determine decisions. Instead, we rely on our judgment to achieve a coherence among the conflicting values which is sensitive to the particular circumstances. Judgment thus involves the ability to take a comprehensive view of the values and concerns at stake, based on one's experience and knowledge of the world. And this involves awareness of the full range of shared experience, beliefs, relations, and expectations within which these values and concerns have significance.[10]

As with much else of Postema's position I accept much of his analysis of the problems we face in generating adequate practical principles of right action. For the reasons explored in Chapter 6, however, I am not convinced that encouraging lawyers to 'take a comprehensive view of the values and concerns at stake, based on [their] experience and knowledge of the world' is the answer. Not, at least, unless it is made clear that that the practically wise lawyer will only rarely legitimately give priority to their own wisdom over the demands of professional roles. Without that caveat, law and lawyers will too often fail to fill their essential roles serving vulnerable clients and enabling stable communities between reasonable persons who disagree in just the ways that drive the call for resort to practical wisdom at the outset.

This is not to suggest that lawyers should dumbly stand by while the institution they serve creates injustice. There is much the virtuous lawyer can do to improve the legal system. They are uniquely well placed to identify shortcomings in the system and to campaign for improvement. I have argued that they have a professional moral obligation to do so. I think an essentially deontological model, which structures the lawyer's roles under public principles, making these activities

---

9   Ibid., p. 67.
10 Ibid., p. 68.

as open as possible, is to be preferred to a model which licenses appeal to a facility which is, in Postema's terms, 'complex [and] difficult to characterize'.[11]

Moral insensitivity

Moral insensitivity: Significance outside the professional role   The 'moral insensitivity' objection claims that role-differentiation and the standard conception undermine the moral sensitivity of lawyers, requiring them to develop a moral callousness or indifference to the situations they confront. Even if we accept that lawyers should not be blamed for the wrongdoings of their clients, nevertheless the standard conception portrays them as playing a central role in projects in which wrongs are done. Occupying this role continually, even with the benefit of the institutional excuse, seems to require lawyers to develop an insensitivity to wrongs in which they are involved. These concerns are sometimes directed at the significance of this moral insensitivity for lawyers acting outside their professional roles and sometimes at its significance for lawyers acting within those roles. When directed at the effect on lawyers outside their professional roles, the concern may be motivated by concern for the communities lawyers serve as citizens or by concern for the wellbeing of lawyers as individuals.

We used Kazuo Ishiguro's butler, Mr Stevens, as an illustration. *The Remains of the Day* is the story of a man so steeped in his role, that he cannot respond other than through the norms of the role – norms which on Mr Stevens's reading demand crippling dignity and distance. We returned to Mr Stevens in our discussion of integrity. There is no question that his inability to relate to others other than through the norms of his role is pathological, the more so given the restraint and distance he takes the role to demand. But Mr Stevens's attitude towards his role-obligations *is* pathological. I suggested that we might see his failure as an illustration of the centrality of reflection to integrity. Mr Stevens lacks autonomy, and so integrity, not because he follows the norms of his role but because he does so with no genuine reflection or engagement upon their demands, their point, or their value. It is hard to believe that if he had reflected on the demands of the role he would not have seen that they did not require the self-denial he imposed upon himself. We can put the same point in the language of integration-integrity: we think Mr Stevens a tragic figure in part because we don't believe he wants to be the kind of person who cannot declare his love for Miss Kenton, or who takes pride in serving soup rather than going to his father's deathbed, or who really endorses the value of the bantering butler. He does not, we suspect, really have the higher-order desires to have the lower-order desires he has or claims to have.

But, I argued, there is little reason to generalise from Mr Stevens to role-occupants in general. I have suggested that there are moral reasons for role-occupants to take the obligations of their roles seriously; that the clash between the demands of ordinary morality and role-morality might be much less dramatic

---

11   Ibid., p. 68.

than is commonly supposed, especially if the duty of zeal is properly interpreted as a duty of mere- rather than hyper-zeal, that lawyers should take pride in their roles given the contribution of law as conceived under the revised standard conception to the viability of pluralist communities, and that role-occupants should be encouraged to both consider the need for and take active steps toward institutional reform to diminish the gap between role and ordinary morality. As I remarked, we do not need to suppose that any lawyer accepts all of these suggestions, or that the suggestions, even if accepted, eliminate all the tensions between role and ordinary morality. However, whatever one think of Mr Stevens it is easy to imagine role-occupants reasoning that there are higher-order reasons to respect the lower-order demands of roles.

Moral insensitivity: Significance inside the professional role   Other forms of the concern for moral sensitivity focus upon the need for such sensitivity within the lawyer's role. Ironically given the standard conception's claim to give priority to the interests of clients, the suggestion goes, effective promotion of the interests of clients requires access to the full resources of ordinary morality and personal moral experience – precisely the resources put aside under the standard conception. Hence the very structure of the standard reduces the ability of lawyers to promote client interests. Again, there seemed to be a number of strands to the objection, a number of ways in which limiting lawyers to the moral resources of the role seemed to threaten their professional competence.

One strand observed that clients often seek what is essentially moral advice. Their main concern in talking to a lawyer about estate-planning may be to obtain advice on which of various courses of action possible under the law is *fair*: should they take the relative wealth of surviving children into account, should they exclude one child, or give different shares to male and female children, should they leave a large portion of their estate to a favourite charity? Such questions may not be answered by a technical account of the requirements of family protection legislation and the like. An adequate response seems to require moral sensitivity and access to general morality apparently excluded by the standard conception and the idea of role-differentiation. This thread of the 'moral insensitivity' strand of the critique is most powerful when directed at versions of the standard conception that deny to individuals who are lawyers all access to the resources of the ordinary morality and their own moral experience; denies them access, that is to the sorts of resources and experience one might draw upon when giving the sort of moral advice such clients seek. The model defended here quite explicitly rejects this view. The perspective of ordinary morality always remains available to reflective role-occupants. The ethical lawyer should reflect upon the moral point of the role she fills, and she should do so from the perspective of 'ordinary' morality. What she should not do, is forget that morality favours robust role-differentiation. When appropriate, however, it may be that the moral lawyer will step into other roles in ways that do not compromise their professional obligations: they may take on the role of law reformer, friend, confidant or counsellor. I emphasised obvious dangers in these moves between roles. There is no particular reason to think that legal training gives people the kind of expertise which makes them good moral advisors or counsellors (in the non-legal sense), and great care is required to ensure that clients are clear about the nature of the advice that is being given. Nevertheless, the model of professional roles defended here, which attempts to make the limits of professional roles explicit and calls upon role-occupants to signal clearly what role they occupy at a moment, both recognises that clients do seek moral advice from lawyers and highlights an important element in the strategy of those concerned to guard against confusion when they do so.

We traced another strand of the moral insensitivity criticism to broader philosophical issues about law and its relation to morality. I noted in Chapter 2 that one strand of the critique of the standard conception of the lawyer's role rested on scepticism as to the plausibility of positivist accounts of law, and the model of legal ethics defended in this book is broadly positivist. Law is portrayed as mediating between the diverse range of views of what ought to be done which mark pluralist communities and particular decisions about what is to be done, and as doing so by providing procedural reasons for action which operate independently of the substantive reasons which bear upon the question of action at hand. Hence the account assumes that we can identify law and the reasons for action it provides in a particular case without settling our substantive moral disagreement about what we ought to do in that case; it assumes, that is to say, the separability of law and morality. I do not imagine my response to this strand of the critique of the standard conception will have far advanced the jurisprudential debate between and within the major theories of law. I do hope, however, to have suggested that familiar criticisms of legal positivism should not lead too quickly to rejection of the modified version of the conception I have defended. In addition to recommending full engagement with ordinary moral discourse at the level of institutional design and critique – something all positivists have recommended (which they have, indeed, seen as a strength of their position) – I have also argued that judges and lawyers have recourse to moral considerations within law, albeit to those considerations as they have been incorporated into law in the guise of content-independent application criteria for the ostensibly moral terms and considerations that occur throughout law. Such an account, I argue, comfortably describes the legal practice of both judges and lawyers, and better preserves the function of law as a device that mediates between inconsistent views of the good.

If some such account of law and legal reasoning is plausible, then we also seem to have a response to a related thread of this strand of the critique, which derived from the observation that systems of rules always require the support of background moral principles. No matter how carefully we construct our systems of rules and principles, cases inevitably arise in which we are unsure which rule applies, in which we want to make an exception to an applicable rule, or in which we think an apparently inapplicable rule should after all be applied in a particular case. In such cases, judgement or practical wisdom is required if we are to obtain the benefit of general rules and principles without paying the considerable costs threatened by their mindless application. It is true, I think, that the legal resources available to judges and lawyers, even when incorporated moral terms and considerations are available in the manner described, are narrower than the full resources of ordinary morality. That is a price we pay for the benefit of legal systems able to mediate between reasonable but inconsistent views of how we should resolve practical disputes. However, we should not underestimate the legal resources available to judges and lawyers: the legal well is deep. Nor should we forget that legal officials do have recourse to the full range of moral resources when engaged as legislators, commentators, law reformers, and so on. Armed with such resources, both within the law and outside the law, the legal system as a whole is not as morally handicapped as at least some criticisms of the standard conception and legal positivism suggest.

Law's crisis of morale

A further cluster of criticisms blames the standard conception and role-differentiation for a crisis of morale said to beset the legal profession. The conception, the various threads of this strand of the critique argue, threatens the morale of lawyers in a number of ways: by requiring individuals who may have chosen law seeking an opportunity to promote justice to zealously promote interests they find morally objectionable; by requiring them to live by two inconsistent sets of moral constraints; by lowering the public esteem in which lawyers are held; and by casting the good lawyer as a skilled technician, rather than someone of wisdom and judgement engaged in meaningful work.

Again, the model of legal ethics I have defended responds to this strand of the critique in a number of ways. First, I have attempted to cast doubt on the quick conclusion that the standard conception requires lawyers to act immorally. Everything said in response to the claim that the standard conception cannot be right since it allows or requires lawyers to act in ways which are immoral by the lights of ordinary morality seems to bear upon the first thread of this strand of the critique as well. In sum again, the model attempts to minimise the conflict between the demands of role-morality and those of ordinary or broad-based morality by limiting the excesses of advocacy; offers a model of professional roles which, while insisting on a 'clean break' between role-morality and broad-based morality, nonetheless recognises the contribution of ordinary morality at the point of institutional design; offers a moral argument for the particular role-differentiated demands of the lawyer's role, suggesting that there are reasons of ordinary morality to take those demands seriously; and argues that lawyers have a professional moral obligation to engage in a constant process of law reform, aimed at promoting fit between the lawyer's role-morality and broad-based morality. To the extent that these arguments succeed in casting doubt on the conclusion that the standard conception licenses immoral conduct, they should also address that version of that concern as it features in claims that the conception contributes to a crisis of morale. The crisis of morale is attributable, I suggest, more to a failure to appreciate the moral justification of the lawyer's role as conceived by the standard conception and the limits to legitimate advocacy which derive from that justification than to any general licensing of immoral professional conduct.

A further thread of this strand of the critique focuses on the effect of widespread condemnation of lawyers on professional morale. The model responds in two ways: first, the restriction of legitimate representation to merely-zealous advocacy might be expected to remove some of the motivation for such condemnation. While some will object even to lawyers pursuing their clients' entitlements zealously, much of the moral criticism of lawyers is directed at hyper-zealous advocacy. In addition, an account of the role of lawyers and its moral justification of the sort offered in this book might serve an educative role, explaining why the lawyers' role carries the role-differentiated obligations it does and targeting both lawyers and the members of communities they serve. Again, there seems to be little reason to think everybody will be convinced, but an approach which modifies and attempts to justify current practice seems more likely to assuage concern about the morality of lawyers than accounts which essentially share those concerns and suggest more radical solutions.[12]

The version of the standard conception I have defended also responds to the suggestion that law as conceived by the standard conception undercuts professional morale by portraying the lawyer's role as mechanical or mindless. The sorts of judgments involved in reasoning *within* law, I have argued, are subtle and complex. The domain of reasoning available to lawyers, qua role-occupants, may be limited, but still it is both large and rich, requiring reflection, engagement and judgment. The idea that the standard conception transforms lawyers into 'mere-technicians', wielding nothing more than 'learned understanding of the law's arcane requirements',[13] or that the 'web of rules becomes an 'iron cage' that restrains the exercise of will',[14] simply does not do justice to what lawyers and judges working with the rich resources of law actually do. The model also emphasises the responsibility upon good lawyers to reflect upon their roles from the perspective of ordinary morality, to seek to understand the ways in which particular demands are justified or not. Here too there is call for judgment and engaged critical reasoning. And, again, I have argued that the Rawlsian model allows us to see that individuals who are lawyers might also occupy other, more or less related roles. In addition to the rich resources available to lawyers qua lawyers, the individuals who are lawyers have access to the broader resources of ordinary morality in their capacity as the occupants of other roles. In sum, the

---

12 Of course this last point cannot be an argument in its own right. Those who reject the approach taken in this book and offer more pessimistic diagnoses and radical remedies will not be moved by an observation that their approaches are likely to be more alarming than that counselled here. The question, they will rightly think, is whether such reform and alarm is warranted. I hope to have said enough to suggest that we should think not.

13 Kronman, *The Lost Lawyer*, p. 16.

14 Simon *The Practice of Justice*, p. 113.

claim that lawyers may not appeal to ordinary morality from within their legal roles – when acting qua lawyer – does not imply that individuals who are lawyers, but who are much more besides, must reason on the basis of an implausible and demoralising set of normative resources.

The model also provides a response to the concern that the standard conception threatens the psychic harmony or integrity of lawyers. I have argued that integrity depends crucially upon sincere and thorough critical reflection and readiness to embrace the recommendations of such reflection. The lawyer of integrity should reflect upon the justifications of their role and its limits. I have argued that such reflection should lead to the conclusion that there is no essential conflict between role-obligation and personal integrity; lawyers should, I have argued, recognise the authority of their role-obligations. There is nothing in the concept of integrity itself, of course, which requires this conclusion in favour of the standard conception. Many will no doubt reflect carefully and disagree. The requirement of reflection is not enough to settle disagreements about the proper account of legal ethics. Perhaps it is enough, however, to substantially answer the worry about integrity and divided selves. Reflective role-occupants who appreciate why their roles are structured as they are and what they can do when those roles do come apart from their moral justifications – what they can do by way of *ex post facto* lobbying for reform for instance – are likely to be able to preserve integrity and morale even if occasionally called upon to act in ways which, as individuals rather than role-occupants, they consider improper.

In sum, concerns for professional morale are not, I think, good reasons to abandon the standard conception and its rule- and principle-based model of professional ethical obligation. Rather, lawyers should be brought to an appreciation of the significance of the social roles they serve, and to understand and take pride in fulfilling the duties that flow from those roles.

Concluding remarks

This chapter has revisited the various threads and strands of the critique of the standard conception in light of the modified version of the standard conception I have been concerned to defend. Despite its name, the standard conception and its role-differentiated obligations that occasionally allow or require lawyers to act in ways properly condemned from the perspective of ordinary morality are not widely accepted. According to critics, lawyers acting under the conception are alienated from ordinary morality, invited to deny responsibility for the things they do and their status as moral agents, rendered morally insensitive, and are likely to find themselves in the grip of a debilitating crisis of morale because of the striking discord between the concern of law and lawyers with justice, and the reality of practice under a conception which restricts access to the resources most directly relevant to those concerns. I have argued, however, that lawyers have moral grounds for taking their role-differentiated obligations seriously. If this is right, many of the criticisms of the standard conception can be answered. If there are moral reasons for taking the standard conception seriously then we should not exaggerate the distinction between 'ordinary' and professional morality. If the moral defence of the standard conception is successful an adequate ordinary morality will encourage respect for the demands and permissions of professional roles. I have suggested that the moral argument also provides a solution to the crisis of morale. Contemporary liberal communities, the argument goes, rely to a considerable extent upon the practice of law as conceived by the standard conception. The lawyer's role so conceived is one in which lawyers should take satisfaction.

A good deal of criticism of the standard conception is motivated by the perception that it demands excessive advocacy from lawyers. Lawyers acting under the conception, the argument goes, must zealously pursue every advantage that can be wrung from the law for their clients. I have argued that this is a misunderstanding of the conception. The moral argument for the conception itself specifies limits to the things lawyers may justifiably do within their professional roles. Understood in light of its proper moral justification, the standard conception demands what I have called mere-zeal, and forbids hyper-zeal. Lawyers must zealously pursue their clients' legal rights, but they are under no obligation to pursue every collateral advantage the law can be made to give: indeed in terms of the standard conception understood in light of its underlying moral obligation they act improperly when they do so. The standard conception, this is to say, endorses a more limited and moderate sphere of advocacy than critics commonly suppose.

I do not imagine the arguments offered in this book amount to a refutation of the careful and considered criticisms that have been offered by opponents of the standard conception. As the moral argument I have offered for the conception itself assumes, these are matters over which reasonable people might properly disagree. I remarked earlier, however, that the success of the approach offered in this book might to at least some degree be measured by its capacity to provide a response to the various strands of the critique of the standard conception. I hope in this concluding chapter to have shown that the modified version of the standard conception does provide such a response, and hence to have given reason to think that it is essentially the right way to conceive of the ethical obligations of lawyers.

Bibliography

American Bar Association, *Canons of Professional Ethics*, 1908.
American Bar Association, *Code of Professional Responsibility*, 1969.
Andre, Judith, 'Role Morality as a Complex Instance of Ordinary Morality' *American Philosophical Quarterly*, vol. 28 (1991) pp. 73–79.
Applbaum, Arthur, *Ethics for Adversaries: The Morality of Roles in Public and Professional Life* (Princeton: Princeton University Press, 1999).
Aquinas, St Thomas, 'Treatise on Law' (1265–1272) in *Basic Writings of St Thomas Aquinas* edited and annotated by Anton C. Pegis (New York: Random House, 1944).
Aristotle, 'Nichomachean Ethics', in *The Basic Works of Aristotle* edited and intro. Richard McKeon, trans. WD Ross, (New York: Random House, 1941).
Austin, John, *The Province of Jurisprudence Determined* (1832), H.L.A. Hart (ed.) (London: Weidenfelf and Nicolson, 1954).
Baier, Kurt, 'Justice and the Aims of Political Philosophy', *Ethics*, vol. 99 (1989) pp. 771–790.
Basten, John 'Control and the Lawyer-Client Relationship', *Journal of the Legal Profession*, vol. 6 (1981) pp. 7–38.
Bray v *Ford* [1896] AC 44.
Caboolture Park Shopping Centre Pty Ltd (In liquidation) v *White Industries (Qld) Pty Ltd* (1993) 45 FCR 224.
Calhoun, Cheshire, 'Standing for Something', *Journal of Philosophy*, vol. 42 (1995) pp. 235–260.
Carroll, Noël 'On Jokes', *Midwest Studies in Philosophy*, vol. 16 (1991) pp. 280–301.
Clarke, Stanley G. and Simpson, Evan, *Anti-Theory in Ethics and Moral Conservatism* (Albany: State University of New York Press, 1989).
Cocking, Dean and Oakley, Justin, *Virtue Ethics and Professional Roles* (Cambridge: Cambridge University Press, 2001).
Cocking, Dean and Oakley, Justin, 'Doing Justice to the Lawyer's Role', Proceedings of the Fourth Annual Conference of the Australasian Association for Professional and Applied Ethics (Melbourne, 1998) pp. 77–86.
Cohen Committee Report of the Committee on Company Law Amendment (1945) (Cmd 6659).
Cohen, Ted, 'Jokes', *Encyclopedia of Aesthetics*, vol. 3 (ed.) Michael Kelly (Oxford: Oxford University Press 1998) pp. 9–12.
*Coke Report*s (1738), 63, 65 (pt. 12, 4th edn 1738), reprinted in 77 Eng Rep 1342, 1343 (1907).

Cox, Damian, La Caze, Marguerite and Levine, Michael, 'Integrity', in the *Stanford Encyclopedia of Philosophy* (online) Edward N. Zalta, (ed.) 2008, available at http://plato.stanford.edu/entries/integrity/, pp. 1–17.

Curtis, Charles P., 'The Ethics of Advocacy', *Stanford Law Review*, vol. 4 (1951) pp. 3–23.

Daniels, Norman, 'Reflective Equilibrium', *Stanford Encyclopedia of Philosophy* (online) Edward N. Zalta, (ed.) (2003), available at http://plato.stanford.edu/entries/reflective-equilibrium/, pp. 1–17.

Dare, Tim, 'Lawyers, Ethics and *To Kill a Mockingbird*', *Philosophy and Literature*, vol. 25 (2001) pp. 127–141.

Dare, Tim, 'Mere-Zeal, Hyper-Zeal and the Ethical Obligations of Lawyers', *Legal Ethics*, vol. 7 (2004) pp. 24–38.

Dare, Tim, 'Legal Ethics, Virtue Ethics, and Harper Lee's *To Kill a Mockingbird*' in Kim Economides (ed.) *Ethical Challenges to Legal Education and Conduct* (Oxford: Hart Publishing, 1998) pp. 39–60.

Dolovich, Sharon, 'Ethical Lawyering and the Possibility of Integrity', *Fordham Law Review*, vol. 70 (1979) pp. 1629–1687.

Dreyfus, Hubert L. and Dreyfus Stuart E., 'What is Morality? A Phenomenological Account of the Development of Ethical Expertise', in Rasmussen (ed.) *Universalism and Communitarianism* (Cambridge, Mass.: MIT Press, 1990) pp. 237–264.

Dworkin, Ronald, *Taking Rights Seriously* (Cambridge, Mass.: Harvard University Press, 2 edn, 1978).

Eliot, George, *Middlemarch* (1874) (London: Penguin, 1965).

Esthete, Andreas, 'Does a Lawyer's Conscience Matter?' in David Luban, *The Good Lawyer: Lawyers' Roles and Lawyers' Ethics* (Totowa, NJ: Rowman and Allenheld, 1983) pp. 270–285.

Ewin, R.E., 'Personal Morality and Professional Ethics: The Lawyer's Duty of Zeal', *International Journal of Applied Philosophy*, vol. 6 (1991) pp. 35–45.

Ex Parte Lloyd (1822) *Mont* 70 (note).

Finnis, John, *Natural Law and Natural Rights* (Oxford: Clarendon Press, 1979).

Frankena, William K., *Ethics* (Englewood Cliffs, NJ: Prentice-Hall, 1973).

Frankfurt, Harry G., 'Freedom of the Will and the Concept of a Person', *Journal of Philosophy*, vol. 68 (1971) pp. 5–20.

Frankfurt, Harry G., 'Identification and Wholeheartedness' in Frankfurt *The Importance of What We Care About* (Cambridge: Cambridge University Press, 1988) pp. 150–176.

Frankfurt, Harry G., 'The Anarchism of Robert Paul Wolff', *Political Theory*, vol. 1 (1973) pp. 405–414.

Freedman, Monroe, 'Atticus Finch – Right and Wrong', *Alabama Law Review*, vol. 45 (1994) pp. 473–482.

Freedman, Monroe, 'Atticus Finch, Esq., R.I.P.', *Legal Times* (24 February 1992) p. 20.

Fried, Charles, 'The Lawyer as Friend: The Moral Foundations of the Lawyer-Client Relation', *Yale Law Journal*, vol. 85 (1976) pp. 1060–1089.

Gillers, Stephen, *Regulation of Lawyers: Problems of Law and Ethics* 6th edn (New York: Aspen Publishers, 2002).

Goldman, Alan, *The Moral Foundations of Professional Ethics* (Totowa, NJ; Rowman and Littlefield, 1980).

Goldstein, Laurie, (1991) '1911 N.Y. Factory Fire Bought Wave of Reform', The *Washington Post* Sept 5, v114, pA6.

Grainger v *Hill* (1838) 4 Bing. (NC) 212 [132 ER 769].

Granville, Augustus, *George Canning and His Times* (London: John W. Parker and Son, 1859).

Green and Clara Pty Ltd v *Bestobel Industries Pty Ltd* [1982] WAR 1.

Greenwood, E., 'Attributes of a Profession', *Social Work*, vol. 2 (1957), pp. 45–55.

Hall, Timothy, 'Moral Character, the Practice of Law and Legal Education', *Mississippi Law Review* (1990) pp. 511–525.

Hardimon, Michael, 'Role Obligations', *The Journal of Philosophy*, vol. 91 (1994) pp. 333–363.

Hart, H.L.A., 'Positivism and the Separation of Law and Morals', *Harvard Law Review*, vol. 71 (1958) pp. 593–629.

Hart, H.L.A., *The Concept of Law* (Oxford: Clarendon Press, 1961); 2nd edn, (eds) Penelope Bullock and Joseph Raz (Oxford: 1994).

Hursthouse, Rosalind, 'Normative Virtue Ethics' in *How Should One Live? Essays on the Virtues* (ed.) Roger Crisp (Oxford: Oxford University Press, 1996) pp. 19–36.

In Re Majory [1955] Ch 600.

International Code of Ethics, adopted Oslo July 1956, amended Mexico 1964.

Ishiguro, Kazuo, *The Remains of the Day* (London: Faber and Faber, 1989).

Johnson, Claudia, 'Without Tradition and Within Reason: Judge Horton and Atticus Finch in Court' *Alabama Law Review*, vol. 45 (1994) pp. 483–510.

Kagan, Shelly, *The Limits of Morality* (Oxford: Clarendon, 1989).

Kant, Immanuel, 'What is Enlightenment', 2nd edn, trans. LW Beck in *Foundations of the Metaphysics of Morals and 'What is Enlightenment?'* (Indianapolis, Bobbs-Merrill, 1959) pp. 83–90.

Kant, Immanuel, *Project for a Perpetual Peace: A Philosophical Essay* (London, Printed by S. Couchman for Vernor and Hood, 1796).

Koonz, Claudia, *The Nazi Conscience* (Cambridge, Mass.: Belknap Press, 2003).

Kornstein, Daniel J., 'Letter to Stephen Gillers', reprinted in Gillers, *Regulation of Lawyers: Problems of Law and Ethics*, p. 470.

Kornstein, Daniel J., 'A Tragic Fire – A Great Cross-Examination', *New York Law Journal*, 28 March 1986, p. 2; reprinted in Gillers, *Regulation of Lawyers: Problems of Law and Ethics*, pp. 466–469.

Kronman, Anthony, 'Practical Wisdom and Professional Character', *Social Philosophy and Policy*, vol. 4 (1986) pp. 203–234.

Kronman, Anthony, *The Lost Lawyer: Failing Ideals of the Legal Profession* (Cambridge, Mass.: Belknap Press, 1993).

Lee, Harper, *To Kill a Mockingbird* (London: Heinemann, 1960).

Leiter, Brian, 'Beyond the Hart/Dworkin Debate: The Methodological Problem in Jurisprudence' *American Journal of Jurisprudence*, vol. 48 (2003) pp. 17–51.

Luban, David, 'Smith Against the Ethicists', *Law and Philosophy*, vol. 9 (1990–1991) pp. 417–433.

Luban, David (ed.), *The Good Lawyer: Lawyer's Roles and Lawyers Ethics* (Totowa, NJ; Rowman and Allenheld, 1983).

Luban, David, 'Freedom and Constraint in Legal Ethics: Some Mid-Course Corrections to *Lawyers and Justice*', *Maryland Law Review*, vol. 49 (1990) pp. 424–459.

Luban, David, *Lawyers and Justice* (Princeton University Press; Princeton, 1988).

Macaulay, Thomas Babington, Lord Macaulay, 'Lord Bacon' (1837), in Macaulay, *Critical and Historical Essays contributed to the Edinburgh Review,* 5th edn in 3 vols. (London: Longman, Brown, Green, and Longmans, 1848), vol. 2, pp. 280–429.

Martin, Mike W., 'Reason and Utopianism in Wolff's Anarchism', *Southern Journal of Philosophy*, vol. 18 (1980), 323–334.

McDowell, John, 'Virtue and Reason' in Clarke and Simpson, *Anti-Theory in Ethics and Moral Conservatism* (Albany: State University of New York Press, 1989) pp. 87–109.

McFall, Lynne, 'Integrity' *Ethics*, vol. 98 (1987) pp. 5–20.

Mill, John Stuart, *Utilitarianism* (Indianapolis, Hackett, 1979).

Montaigne, Michel de, 'Of Husbanding Your Will' (1580) in *The Complete Works of Montaigne: Essays, Travel Journal, Letters*, (ed.) Donald M. Frame (London, 1958) pp. 766–784.

Mulgan, Tim, *The Demands of Consequentialism* (Oxford: Oxford University Press, 2001).

New Zealand Law Society, *Rules of Professional Conduct for Barristers and Solicitors*, (1990).

Nightingale, Joseph (ed.), *The Trial of Queen Caroline,* 3 Volumes (London: J Robins & Co. Albion Press, 1820–1821).

Nightingale, Joseph, *Memoirs of the Public and Private Life of Queen Caroline* (1820–21), ed. and intro. C. Hibbert, (London, Folio Society, 1978).

Nussbaum, Martha, 'Richly Aware and Finely Responsible: Literature and the Moral Imagination' in Clarke and Simpson (eds) *Anti-Theory in Ethics and Moral Conservatism* (Albany: State University of New York Press, 1989), pp. 122–134.

Nussbaum, Martha, *The Fragility of Goodness: Luck and Ethics in Greek Tragedy and Philosophy* (New York: Cambridge University Press, 1986).

O'Neill v *Phillips* [1999] 1 WLR 1092.

Orchard v *South Eastern Electricity Board* [1987] QB 565.

Pierrepoint, Albert, *Executioner Pierrepoint* (Hawkhurst: Eric Dobby 1974).
Pierson v *Post* [1805] 3 Cal. R. 175, 2 Am Dec. 264.
Postema, Gerald, 'Moral Responsibility in Professional Ethics', *New York University Law Review*, vol. 55 (1980) pp. 63–89.
Pritchard, Michael S., 'Wolff's Anarchism' *Journal of Value Inquiry*, vol. 7 (1973) pp. 297–302.
R v *Paine* (1792) 22 *State Trials* 357.
Ramos, Mary Carol, 'The Nurse-Patient Relationship: Themes and Variations' *Journal of Advanced Nursing*, vol. 17 (1992) pp. 496–506.
Rasmussen, David (ed.), *Universalism and Communitarianism* (Cambridge, Mass.: MIT Press, 1990).
Rawls, John, 'The Idea of an Overlapping Consensus', *Oxford Journal of Legal Studies*, vol. 7 (1981) pp. 1–25.
Rawls, John, 'Two Concepts of Rules', *Philosophical Review*, vol. 64 (1955) pp. 3–32.
Rawls, John, *Political Liberalism* (New York: Columbia University Press, 1993).
Raz, Joseph, 'Authority, Law, and Morality', *Monist*, vol. 68 (1985) pp. 295–324.
Raz, Joseph, *The Morality of Freedom* (Clarendon Press: Oxford, 1986).
Rochin v *California*, 342 U.S. 165 (1952).
Rondel v *Worsley* [1969] 1 AC 191.
Schwartz, Murray L, 'The Professionalism and Accountability of Lawyers', *California Law Review*, vol. 66 (1978) pp. 669–697.
Serrin, William, 'Labor Marks 75th Anniversary of Triangle Shirtwaist Fire', *The New York Times* March 25 1986, v135 p.13 (N) pB2 (L).
Shaffer, Thomas L., *Faith and the Professions* (Provo, Utah: Brigham Young University Press, 1987).
Shaffer, Thomas L., 'The Moral Theology of Atticus Finch', *University of Pittsburg Law Review*, vol. 42 (1981) pp. 181–224.
Shergold, Adrian, (director) *Pierrepoint* released by Lionsgate (2007) (released in the United States as *Pierrepoint: The Last Hangman* in 2007 by IFC Films).
Sidgwick, Henry, *The Methods of Ethics* (Indianapolis: Hackett, 1962).
Sim v *Graig Bell and Bond* [1991] NZLR 535, 543 per Richardson J.
Simon, William, *The Practice of Justice: A Theory of Lawyers' Ethics* (Cambridge, Mass.: Harvard University Press, 1998).
Smart, J.J.C. and Williams, Bernard, *Utilitarianism: For and Against* (New York: Cambridge University Press, 1973).
Smith, M.B.E., 'Wolff's Argument for Anarchism', *Journal of Value Inquiry*, vol. 7 (1973) pp. 291–306.
Spautz v *Williams* [1983] 2 NSWLR 506, 539.
Stapleton, Augustus Granville, *George Canning and His Times* (London: Parker and Sons, 1859).
Sterba, James P., 'The Decline of Wolff's Anarchism', *Journal of Value Inquiry*, vol. 11(1977) pp. 213–217.
Story, J., *Equity Jurisprudence* (1918) 14th edn, vol. 1, Section 433.

Taylor, Gabriele, 'Integrity', *Proc. Aristotelian Society* Supp. vol. 55 (1981) pp. 143–159.
Tremblay, Paul, 'Client-Centered Counseling and Moral Activism' contribution to Robert F. Cochrane, Jnr, Deborah L. Rhode, Paul R. Tremblay, Thomas L. Shaffer 'Symposium: Client Counseling and Moral Responsibility' 30 (2002–2003) *Pepperdine Law Review* pp. 591–639.
Waluchow, Wilfrid, *Inclusive Legal Positivism* (Oxford: Clarendon Press, 1993).
Wasserman, David, 'Should a Good Lawyer Do the Right Thing? David Luban on the Morality of Adversary Representation', *Maryland Law Review*, vol. 49 (1990) pp. 392–423.
Wasserstrom, Richard, 'Lawyers as Professionals: Some Moral Issues' *Human Rights*, vol. 5 (1975) pp. 1–24.
Wendel, W. Bradley, 'Professional Roles and Moral Agency', A review of *Ethics for Adversaries: The Morality of Roles in Public and Professional Life* by Arthur Isak Applbaum, *Georgetown Law Journal* (2001) 89 pp. 667–718.
Wendel, W. Bradley, 'Legal Ethics and the Separation of Law and Morals', *Cornell Law Review*, vol. 91 (2005–2006) pp. 67–128.
Westmoreland & Cambria Natural Gas Company v *DeWitt*, 130 Pa.235, 18 A.724, 725, 5 L.R.A. 73 (1889).
White Industries (Qld) Pty Ltd v *Flower & Hart (a firm)* [1998] 156 ALR 169.
William H. Simon, 'After Confidentiality: Rethinking the Professional Responsibilities for the Business Lawyer', *Fordham Law Review*, vol. 75 (2006) pp. 1453–172, p. 1458.
Williams & Ors v *Spautz* (1991–1992) 174 CLR 509.
Williams, Bernard, 'Integrity' in J.J.C. Smart and Bernard Williams *Utilitarianism: For and Against* (New York: Cambridge University Press, 1973) pp. 108–117.
Williams, Bernard, *Moral Luck: Philosophical Papers 1973–1980* (Cambridge: Cambridge University Press, 1981).
Williams, Bernard, *Morality: An Introduction to Ethics* (New York: Harper Torchbooks, 1972).
Wittgenstein, Ludwig, *Philosophical Investigations* trans. G.E.M. Anscombe (Oxford: Basil Blackwell, 1953).
Wolff, Robert Paul, 'Reply to Professors Pritchard and Smith',*Journal of Value Inquiry*, vol. 7 (1973) pp. 303–306.
Wolff, Robert Paul, *In Defense of Anarchism* (New York: Harper & Row, 1970).
Woo, Elaine, 'Last Survivor of 1911 Sweatshop Fire Dies: Rose Freedman was a Link to New York's Triangle Shirtwaist blaze, a Turning Point for U.S. Labor' (Obituary) *Los Angeles Times* Feb 17, 2001 p. A–1.
Wueste, Daniel, 'Taking Role Moralities Seriously', *Southern Journal of Philosophy*, vol. 24 (1991) pp. 407–417.
Zabella v *Pakel* 42 F2d 452 (7th Cir. 1957).

Index

abuse of process
    and mere- and hyper- zeal 81–6
    functional account of 82
    and collateral or ulterior advantages 82–83
    and the wishes of clients 84–85
    and the need for caution in the exercise of the jurisdiction 83
    and lawful goals 83–84
    and delaying or preventing proceedings 85
    and existing limitations on zealous advocacy 86
adversary system
    and the principle of partisanship 7, 18
    and David Luban's critique of the duty of zeal 36–39
American Bar Association 6
American Civil Liberties Union (ACLU) 11
Applbaum, Arthur
    and the argument from Rawl's 'Two Concepts of Rules' 47–57
    and the Executioner of Paris 137
Aristotle
    and *phonesis* (practical wisdom) 24, 101
    and Anthony Kronman 26–7, 118
    and virtue ethics 101–2, 111
    and integrity as integration (or psychic harmony) 134–7
    and Gerald Postema 152
Atticus Finch
    as a tragic figure 113–114
    as *phronemos* 113–117
    and integrity 142–143
    and see To Kill a Mockingbird
Austin, John 64
autonomy
    and the principle of neutrality 9
    Charles Fried on 98
    and practical reasoning 128–9, 130
    integrity as autonomy (*see* integrity)

Baier, Kurt 62
Basten, John
    ACLU and the Skokie march 11
Brougham, Lord Henry 5–6, 11, 78

cab-rank rule 9–10, 11
Calhoun, Cheshire. 124, 132, 140–141, 143–4
character-based ethics *see* virtue ethics
client–professional relationship
    the imbalance of power and expertise in 89–90, 93–4, 96
    the importance of the matters at issue in 90–1, 93–4, 96
    opacity of expertise and diligence in 91–2, 93–4, 96
    the limited nature of such relationships 92–3
    and its significance for ethical obligations 93–4
    and its significance for the standard conception of the lawyer's role 94–6
    trust and vulnerability in 94–99, 119–120
    and Charles Fried's 'special purpose friendship' analysis 96–99
Cocking, Dean and Oakley, Justin
    and the irrelevance of ordinary morality under the standard conception 46–7
    and Kant's conflicted pastor 56
    and Sarat's artists and the nasty landlord case 86–88
    and virtue ethics and rules 121

and professional detachment and
 Aristotelian psychic harmony
 134–137
constitutive *vs* practice rules 47–53, 57–8,
 149–50
Cox, Damian, La Caze, Marguerite and
 Levine, Michael
 and the formalism objection to integrity
  as integration 134, 138–140
critical reflection *see* integrity
critique of the standard conception
 morality and the standard conception
  15–19, 148–150
 roles and responsibility 19–20,
  150–153
 moral insensitivity 20–24, 153–156
 crisis of morale in legal profession 3,4,
  13, 24–7, 119, 123, 156–8
 response to critique 147–59

dependent rules *see* role-obligations
detachment, professional 123–124, 134–7
 and Albert Pierrepoint (*The Last
  Hangman*) 137
Dolovich, Sharon 126–7
Dreyfus, Hubert L. and Dreyfus, Stuart E.
 analysis of ethical expertise 103–6
duty of zeal *see* partisanship principle
Dworkin, Ronald 23, 70

Erskine, Thomas 10
Esthete, Andreas 18
Ewin, Robert E. 78, 99
exclusive positivism *see* legal positivism

fiduciary obligations 93–4
Frankena, William 122
Frankfurt, Harry
 and integrity as integration 132–4
 and the formalism objection to
  integrity as integration 138–142
Freedman, Monroe
 and Atticus Finch 107, 112, 121
Fried, Charles
 and the need for legal advisors 9
 objection to utilitarianism 35
 and the lawyer as the client's 'special
  purpose friend' 96–9

friendship *see* trust and vulnerability in
 client–professional relationships

Grainger v *Hill* 82, 83–4

Hardiman, Michael.
 and the nature of role-obligations 30,
  31, 32
Hart, H.L.A.
 and the minimum content of natural
  law 23
 and the legislative predicament 49, 51
 and the separation of law and morality
  64
 and judicial discretion 67
 and the rule of recognition 68, 70
 and inclusive legal positivism 70
Hursthouse, Rosalind
 virtue ethics and rules 121–2
hyper-zeal *see* mere zeal

identity *see* integrity as identity
inclusive legal positivism *see* legal
 positivism
institutional excuse
 compared with justifications 15
 and David Luban 37, 42
integrity
 threatened by the standard conception
  25, 123–125, 158
 as autonomy 125–131, 142, 151
 as integration 132–42
 formalism objection to integrity as
  integration 133–140, 143, 145
 inconsistency objection to integrity as
  integration 140–2
 as identity 142–5
 and Ishiguro's Mr Stevens 131, 133,
  151
 and Gerald Postema 150–151
 and critical reflection 144, 145,
  154–155, 158
 and reflective equilibrium 138–139
International Code of Ethics 6–7
Ishiguro, Kazuo *see The Remains of the
 Day*

Johnson, Claudia. 110–11

Kant, Immanuel
  and lawyers and injustice 1
  and the conflicted pastor 55–7
Koonz, Claudia
  and the Nazi conscience 139
Kornstein, Daniel
  and the Triangle Shirtwaist Fire case 16, 17
Kronman, Anthony.
  and law's crisis of morale 24–5, 26–7, 118–19
  and the lawyer-statesman 118–19
  and Aristotelian practical wisdom 102, 112
  and critical reflection 157

La Caze, Marguerite *see* Cox, Damian
Lake Pleasant Bodies case *see* Luban, David
Lee, Harper *see* To Kill a Mocking Bird (character of Atticus)
legal positivism
  legal ethics and legal positivism 63–73, 155–156
  inclusive legal positivism 23, 68–73
  exclusive legal positivism 69–73
  and Brad Wendel 71–73
Levine, Michael *see* Cox, Damian
Luban, David
  and excessive advocacy 8, 18–19
  and the derivation of role obligations by the direct route 36–44
  and the Lake Pleasant Bodies Case 39–40
  and the derivation of role obligations by the less direct route 40–44
  and act and rule utilitarianism 40–44
  and the derivation of role obligations by the indirect route 45–46
  and mere and hyper-zeal 75–80
  and the inadequacy of existing limitations of zealous advocacy 86

McDowell, John
  and the uncodifiability of morality 102
  and character-based ethics 121
mere-zeal and hyper zeal 7–8, 76–78, 81–6, 157, 159
  and abuse of process 81–6
  the derivation of mere-zeal 77–8
  the problem of hyper-zeal 78–81
  and Charles Fried 98–99
  David Luban and 36
Montaigne, Michel de
  and the separation of lay and professional personalities 13, 20, 25, 123,
  and integrity as integration 133
multiple roles *see* role differentiation 53–5

natural law 23, 70
neutrality, principle of *see* standard conception of the lawyer's role
New Zealand Law Society Rules of Professional Conduct 7, 93
non-accountability, principle of *see* standard conception of the lawyer's role
Nussbaum, Martha
  and moral rules and principles 102
  and character-based ethics 121

Oakley, Justin *see* Cocking, Dean and Oakley Justin
O'Neill v *Phillips* 65–6

Paine, Thomas
  and *The Rights of Man* case 10
partisanship, principle of *see* standard conception of the lawyer's role
phronesis/phronemos see Aristotle and *To Kill a Mockingbird*
pluralist communities
  law and reasonable pluralism 60–63
  liberal responses to pluralism 61–63
  legal positivism and pluralism 63, 65. 70
  and the principle of neutrality 74–75
  and the principle of non-accountability 75
  and the principle of partisanship 75–76
  and mere-zeal and hyper-zeal 77–81
  and abuse of process 86
  and character based ethics 117–18
  and law's crisis of morale 119

Postema, Gerald.
    roles and the denial of responsibility 19–20, 101, 150
    and the conflict between role morality and adequate advocacy 24
    and the need for *phronesis* (Aristotelian practical wisdom) 102, 152–153
    and integrity 123, 151
practice *vs* constitutive rules *see* constitutive rules *vs* practice rules
psychic harmony *see* Aristotle and Cocking, Dean and Oakley, Justin
public esteem of lawyers, 25–6, 156

Queen Caroline case 5–6

Rawls, John
    the Rawlsian model and the derivation of role obligations 44–7, 57–58, 149
    Applbaum's critique 47–53
    the Rawlsian model and the possibility of multiple role 53–55, 157
    and reasonable pluralism 60–63
Raz, Joseph
    rules and pluralist communities 61
    and exclusive legal positivism 69–70
The Remains of the Day (character of Mr Stevens)
    and the desensitizing effects of roles 21–2, 123, 153
    and the preconstruction of roles 30
    and integrity as autonomy 131
    and integrity as integration 133
    and critical engagement with roles 153–4
Riggs v *Palmer* 70
role of law
    and the lawyer's role 74–86
    and legal positivism 63–73
    in pluralist communities 60–3, 74, 75, 77, 117–18, 119
role-differentiated obligations
    the idea of 12–14, 30–1
    prima facie case for 31–3
    derivation of 33–47
    and multiple roles 53–5, 149
    and client–professional relationship 95–6
    consistency with integrity 126–146, 150–1
    relationship between role morality and ordinary morality 33–57
    reform and advocacy roles 53–5, 149–150, 154
role(s)
    definition of 30–1
    see also standard conception of lawyer's role, role-differentiated obligation
role-obligation/role morality *see* role-differentiated obligation
rules
    allowing pluralist communities 61–62
rule of recognition 68, 69, 71, 72–3

Sarat, Austin.
    The case of the artists and the nasty landlord 86–88
Sartre, Jean Paul 19
Simon, William
    and law's crisis of morale 25, 26, 27
    and the role of lawyers as law reformers 149
standard conception of the lawyer's role
    principle of:partisanship 5–8, 10, 11–12, 75–76 *see also* mere-zeal and hyper-zeal
    principle of:neutrality, 8–10, 11–12, 74–5
    principle of:non-accountability, 10–12, 75
    see also critique of the standard conception and role-differentiated obligation
Steuer, Max D. *see* Triangle Shirtwaist Fire Case
Story, Joseph 93–4

To Kill a Mockingbird (Harper Lee) 106–20
    Overview 106–108
    key episodes for legal ethics 108–110
    and virtue ethics 110–112
    and the role of law 117–118

and Anthony Kronman 118–119
and the client professional relationship 119–120
and see Atticus Finch
Triangle Shirtwaist Fire case 16–18

utilitarianism
and role morality 33–5
act-utilitarianism 40–1, 42, 43, 44–5
rule-utilitarianism 41–3, 44–5

virtue ethics 101–3
approach to professional detachment 134–5
and rules 120–2
and see To Kill a Mockingbird and Atticus Finch

Wasserstrom, Richard 8–9, 21, 43
Wendel, W. Bradley
and role differentiated obligations 32
and Arthur Applbaum 50–1
and legal positivism 71–3

White Industries (Qld) Pty Ltd v *Flower & Hart (a Firm)* 82, 84–5
Williams, Bernard
and act and rule utilitarianism 42
and integrity as identity 142, 143–4, 145
Williams v *Spautz* 82, 84
Wolff, Robert Paul
and integrity as autonomy 125–131
and practical reasoning 128–131
unanimous direct democracy 129–30

Zabella v *Pakel*
and the standard conception of the lawyer's role 2–3, 19, 149
and role-differentiated obligation 12, 25
and Arthur Applbaum 48–51

and legal positivism 64
Zealous advocacy
See the standard conception of the lawyer's role, the principle of partisanship and mere-zeal and hyper-zeal

If we accept that we have a choice of who to act for →
What arguments for not acting for someone we disagree with
— immorality